WINE DOGS

USA EDITION

the dogs of North American wineries

Craig McGill and Susan Elliott

A Giant Dog book

for Tarka, Stella and Tok

CONTENTS

FOREWORD

by Robert M. Parker Jr

I am honored *and pleased to write this introduction about wine dogs in the United States. In short, I believe dogs are one of God's greatest gifts to mankind. I have had dogs since I was born, and they have been an unending source of joy, pleasure, and companionship. Throughout my childhood and teenage years, our dogs were cocker spaniels, which my mother adored and treated like spoiled children. In all of my childhood memories, I recall them always at my side. My father, who was a serious hunter, also kept a pack of hound dogs, mostly blue tick hounds and ones he called red bone, as their hair, not bones, was red. Unlike the cocker spaniels, they were kept outside, but they were a great source of rough-housing and play. As an only child in a rural environment, they provided me with immense joy and companionship, and often served as the sibling pals I lacked while growing up.*

Going away to college and law school meant no live-in pets, but it was always fun to return home where the dogs greeted me as if I were their favorite person in the world. After my wife and I were married, we acquired a dog I had always wanted to have, a three-month-old basset hound named Watson. Something about their long, droopy ears, half-opened, bloodshot eyes, lethargic personalities, and expressive song (their whining and howling) has always appealed to me. Since 1969, we have had a succession of basset hounds in our lives, every one of them completely different in personality, but all sharing the breed's love of eating, sniffing, and chasing ... anything ... their owners, tennis balls, or some of the feral cats in the area. We are now on our fifth basset hound, Hoover, a beautiful, big-boned, short-legged investigator who is pictured in this book. Hoover is unusual in the sense that he is totally dedicated and loyal to the entire family, but seems to care little for anyone else, unlike his predecessors. Fifteen years ago we added an extraordinary English bulldog named

George, another breed we had always wanted to own because we thought they looked like little old men or canine versions of a Buddha. George became quite a celebrity as he was featured in many of the profiles written on me. An incredibly photogenic chap, he had two large black patches around his broad-set eyes, making visitors often call him "The Lone Ranger" or the "Masked Man". George won the top performance by a canine in a documentary movie at the Cannes Film Festival in 2004. Instead of the Palme d'Or, which is given to the year's top movie, he won the "Palme Dog". On the day he passed away at age 12, I tried to give him CPR, but he died instantly, which spared us the pain of having to have him euthanized. His successor, Buddy (named after my father), is almost an identical clone – relentless in his play, and obsessed with bumblebees or anything that makes him run around like a crazy man.

Of course, dogs are also an intricate part of vineyards. One of the most famous stories about my career involves a nasty schnauzer at Château Cheval Blanc in Bordeaux's famed St.-Emilion region. In 1983, while visiting Bordeaux and tasting the 1982 vintage, Cheval Blanc's owner, Jacques Hébrard, refused to let me taste his wine. One evening I called him and presented my arguments on why I should be permitted to taste. He told me to come on over, which I did. After knocking on the door, I was greeted by an eight-to ten-pound schnauzer who quickly attached his teeth to my ankle. Mr Hébrard didn't bat an eye, and after what seemed like a long period of time, the schnauzer let go, but not before ripping my pants and socks and tearing my skin. As I sat at a desk listening to Mr Hébrard berate me for not understanding his wines, not one word was mentioned about the schnauzer's sneak attack or, for that matter, my bloody ankle. I always thought that if I were to ever commit a crime against a dog (a cardinal sin the way I see it), it would be against that dog. However, he passed away several years later, and the story became embellished and exaggerated in wine circles both abroad and here in the States, with several French stories suggesting I was behind the dog's demise.

After twenty-eight years in this profession, it is wonderful to see how many times winery dogs are sitting at the top of a ridge line, watching their owners direct a vineyard's harvest, or sleeping next to the fermenter or beside their master's desk. I have always admonished friends that anyone who did not love a dog had to be approached with considerable suspicion, and would probably not be someone with whom I would want to spend much time. Dogs are indeed a special gift to all of us. They give us companionship, they act as full-time therapists, they amuse us, and they lift our spirits when we're down. It is often said that a vine is most content in the shadow of a man. If that is true, then a dog is also happiest when it is in the shadow of its owner.

I love the book that Craig and Sue put together for Wine Dogs of Australia, and hope this edition for the United States is a howling success ... as my basset hound Hoover would say.

ROBERT M. PARKER JR WAS BORN IN BALTIMORE, MARYLAND AND INITIALLY PURSUED A CAREER IN LAW. HIS INTEREST IN WINE BEGAN IN 1967 AND IT WASN'T LONG BEFORE ROBERT HAD STARTED TO CARVE OUT A SPECTACULAR CAREER IN WINE WRITING THAT NOW SPANS OVER 28 YEARS. HE IS THE FOUNDER OF *THE WINE ADVOCATE* AND IS THE CONTRIBUTING EDITOR FOR *FOOD AND WINE* MAGAZINE. HE ALSO PERIODICALLY CONTRIBUTES TO OTHER MAGAZINES INCLUDING *THE FIELD* AND FRANCE'S *L'EXPRESS*. HE IS THE AUTHOR OF MANY BEST-SELLING AND AWARDED WINE BOOKS INCLUDING *BORDEAUX, BURGUNDY, PARKER'S WINE BUYER'S GUIDE* AND *THE WINES OF THE RHONE VALLEY AND PROVENCE*. ROBERT'S BULLDOG GEORGE WON THE COVETED "PALME DOG" PRIZE AT THE CANNES FILM FESTIVAL FOR BEST CANINE PERFORMANCE IN A FILM FOR HIS CAMEO IN THE DOCUMENTARY *MONDOVINO*.

*" The average dog is a nicer person
than the average person."*

—————— ANDY ROONEY

FAVORITE TOY: ROBERT
FAVORITE PASTIME: EATING
FAVORITE FOOD: ROAST CHICKEN
NAUGHTIEST DEED: STEALING FOOD
PET PEEVE: HAVING HIS EARS CLEANED
KNOWN ACCOMPLICE: BUDDY THE BULLDOG

HOOVER

BUDDY

PET PEEVES: BEES AND WASPS
FAVORITE FOOD: CONFIT OF DUCK
FAVORITE TOY: TALKING TOY BULLDOG
NAUGHTIEST DEED: ATTACKING MISTY THE CAT
FAVORITE PASTIME: DEMOLISHING GARDEN HOSES
KNOWN ACCOMPLICE: HOOVER THE BASSET HOUND

Coming soon to your favorite TV channel...
..."Rex in the City"

Four beautiful New Yorkers gossip about their sex life (or lack of thereof) as they try to navigate the rocky terrain of being single, sexually active dogs in the new millennium. The show features the dogs walking the streets, parks and salons of New York while pushing the envelope of fashion and shattering sexual taboos.

Can't wait for that one ...

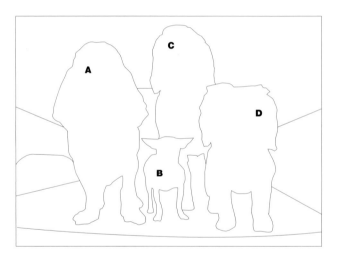

A *NORMAND: BASSET HOUND, 11*
FAVORITE PASTIME: STEALING FOOD
FAVORITE TOY: GOAT HOOF
NAUGHTIEST DEED: STEALING YURI'S DINNER
FAVORITE FOOD: EVERYTHING EXCEPT VEGETABLES
PET PEEVE: GETTING CLAWS CLIPPED

B *DAFFODIL: CHIHUAHUA, 3*
FAVORITE FOOD: STEAK
FAVORITE TOY: GOAT HOOF
KNOWN ACCOMPLICE: REMO
NAUGHTIEST DEED: TEARING UP TISSUES
PET PEEVE: GETTING HER CLAWS CLIPPED
FAVORITE PASTIME: A NAP ON SOMEONE'S LAP

C *JAKIE: GOLDENDOODLE, 1*
FAVORITE PASTIMES: GALLOPING
AND STEALING FOOD FROM THE COUNTER
NAUGHTIEST DEED: STEALING FOOD
FAVORITE FOOD: STEAK
FAVORITE TOY: BALL
PET PEEVE: BATH

D *REMO: COTON DE TULEAR, 5*
FAVORITE PASTIME: PLAYING BALL
NAUGHTIEST DEED: MAKING SURE
THE OTHER 3 DOGS KNOW WHO'S BOSS
PET PEEVE: GETTING CLAWS CLIPPED
FAVORITE FOOD: STEAK
FAVORITE TOY: BALL

SUGAR

FAVORITE TOY: A STICK
FAVORITE FOOD: CRACKERS
KNOWN ACCOMPLICE: OMAR
PET PEEVE: BEING LEFT ALONE
FAVORITE PASTIME: CHASING ANYTHING
NAUGHTIEST DEED: CHEWING THE DOOR

FAVORITE TOY: DUCKIE
FAVORITE FOOD: DONUTS
NAUGHTIEST DEED: THE GREAT ESCAPE
KNOWN ACCOMPLICE: SPARKY THE CAT
PET PEEVE: PUTTING ON HER WETSUIT
DURING DUCK HUNTING SEASON
FAVORITE PASTIME: RETRIEVING ANYTHING

DAISY

OWNERS: JIM AND JUDY BARRETT | LABRADOR, 8 | **CHATEAU MONTELENA** CALISTOGA, CA

COOPER

KNOWN ACCOMPLICES: BACCHUS AND CHABBA
FAVORITE PASTIME: BEING THE WINERY AMBASSADOR
FAVORITE FOOD: OYSTER CRACKERS FOR THE TASTING BAR
PET PEEVE: ANNOYING DOGS STUCK IN CUSTOMERS' CARS
FAVORITE TOYS: PURSES, GLOVES, LOOSE ENDS AND EMPTY BOXES IN THE TASTING ROOM

BOWERS HARBOR VINEYARDS TRAVERSE CITY, MI | BERNESE MOUNTAIN DOG 3 | OWNERS: SPENCER AND LINDA STEGENGA

FAVORITE TOY: TENNIS BALL
KNOWN ACCOMPLICE: FANNY
FAVORITE PASTIME: RUNNING FAST
FAVORITE FOODS: BRIE, ROQUEFORT, GOUDA
PET PEEVE: NOT BEING ALLOWED TO SLEEP ON THE BED
NAUGHTIEST DEED: EATING STEVEN'S SLIPPERS – TWICE

PIXIE

KNOWN ACCOMPLICE: JORGE
FAVORITE FOOD: EVERYTHING
NAUGHTIEST DEED: ATTEMPTING TO BITE
FAVORITE TOY: A STUFFED TOY DOG NAMED IVY
PET PEEVE: GETTING DRESSED UP IN DOLL'S CLOTHES
FAVORITE PASTIMES: RUNNING AND CHASING AFTER THE TRUCK

TITO

SNIFFY

PET PEEVE: BEING COLD
FAVORITE TOY: RAW HIDES
FAVORITE FOOD: ANYTHING NOT SPICY
KNOWN ACCOMPLICES: SUSAN AND SUNNY
NAUGHTIEST DEED: TOO NAUGHTY FOR PUBLICATION
FAVORITE PASTIME: SLEEPING BY THE FIRE IN THE EVENING

SUNNY

FAVORITE FOOD: PEOPLE FOOD
PET PEEVES: WIND AND GUNSHOTS
KNOWN ACCOMPLICES: SUSAN AND SNIFFY
NAUGHTIEST DEED: LICKING PEOPLE IN THE FACE
FAVORITE PASTIME: RUNNING UP THE MOUNTAIN

JACQUE

FAVORITE PASTIME: PLAYING WITH CHU CHU
FAVORITE FOODS: STEAK AND CHEERIOS
NAUGHTIEST DEED: TAKING EVERYTHING AWAY
FROM CHU CHU AND SHADOW
KNOWN ACCOMPLICES: STEVE AND CAROLE

PET PEEVE: USELESS DOGS
FAVORITE TOY: TENNIS BALL
KNOWN ACCOMPLICE: THE FEDEX MAN
FAVORITE FOOD: PEANUT BUTTER COOKIES
FAVORITE PASTIME: CHASING RABBITS IN THE VINEYARDS
NAUGHTIEST DEED: STEALING BOB'S CHEESE AND BOLOGNA SANDWICH

HERSHAL

AKAELA

PET PEEVE: SKUNKS
FAVORITE FOOD: PEDIGREE
KNOWN ACCOMPLICE: COOPER
FAVORITE TOY: OFFICIAL SIZED BASKETBALL
NAUGHTIEST DEED: NOT PLAYING NICE WITH OTHER DOGS
FAVORITE PASTIMES: CHASING RABBITS AND THE OCCASIONAL COYOTE

FAVORITE FOOD: PIG EARS
PET PEEVE: BACKSEAT DRIVERS
FAVORITE PASTIME: FLYING PLANES
KNOWN ACCOMPLICES: DOC, BABE, RANDY, ERIN AND KRISTINA
NAUGHTIEST DEED: TRYING TO TAKE OVER THE CONTROLS OF THE PLANE

TIMBER

CODY

FAVORITE TOY: A TENNIS BALL
KNOWN ACCOMPLICES: LUCKY AND LUNA
FAVORITE FOOD: GRANDMA BRYS' MEATBALLS
PET PEEVES: DOG FOOD AND GOING TO THE GROOMER
FAVORITE PASTIME: CHASING BIRDS AWAY FROM THE VINES
NAUGHTIEST DEEDS: BEGGING FOR FOOD AND ESCAPING UNDER THE FENCE

PET PEEVE: SQUIRRELS
FAVORITE FOOD: BREAD
FAVORITE TOY: THE FRISBEE
KNOWN ACCOMPLICE: GUY NOIR
FAVORITE PASTIME: HIKING THE TRAILS OF MT. HOOD
NAUGHTIEST DEED: FALLING OFF A CLIFF ON MT. HOOD AND
BEING RESCUED BY OREGON HUMANE SOCIETY RESCUE GROUP

STELLA

TRUFFLES

FAVORITE TOY: THE TV
FAVORITE FOOD: POPCORN
PET PEEVE: TALKING ANIMALS ON TV
FAVORITE PASTIMES: WATCHING ANIMAL PLANET AND CHASING WATER
NAUGHTIEST DEED: GETTING ANAPHYLAXIS FROM BEE STINGS DURING HARVEST

FAVORITE TOY: SQUEAKY TOYS
KNOWN ACCOMPLICE: AUNT MARSHA
FAVORITE PASTIME: TAKING DIPS IN THE POND
PET PEEVE: BEING LEFT ALONE WHEN HE COULD HAVE GONE FOR A RIDE
NAUGHTIEST DEED: TAKING ALL THE TOYS THAT WERE BOUGHT FOR A DOG BIRTHDAY PARTY

TYLER

BUKI

FAVORITE FOOD: TABLE SCRAPS
PET PEEVE: MIKE HENDRY'S CAT
FAVORITE TOY: WINE BOTTLE CORKS
FAVORITE PASTIME: WALKING AROUND
THE VINEYARD WITH GEORGE
KNOWN ACCOMPLICES: MANUEL AND NACHO
NAUGHTIEST DEED: TRYING TO EAT MIKE'S CAT

CHOW MEI MEI

FAVORITE FOOD: MEAT
FAVORITE PASTIME: SLEEPING
FAVORITE TOY: RUBBER SNAKE
PET PEEVE: LOVES EVERYTHING
KNOWN ACCOMPLICE: JOY LUCK
NAUGHTIEST DEED: MISSING THE PAPER

CHINA MOON

PET PEEVE: LOUD CATS
NAUGHTIEST DEED: HIDING
FAVORITE FOOD: ASPARAGUS
FAVORITE PASTIME: SLEEPING
FAVORITE TOY: STUFFED DUCKS
KNOWN ACCOMPLICE: FRANK FAT

FRANK FAT

PET PEEVE: BARKLEY
FAVORITE FOOD: TACOS
FAVORITE PASTIME: EATING
FAVORITE TOY: HORSE HOOF
NAUGHTIEST DEED: CENSORED

FAVORITE FOOD: PEANUTS
KNOWN ACCOMPLICE: CHINA MOON
FAVORITE TOY: STUFFED MUSICAL TOYS
FAVORITE PASTIME: PLAYING WITH CHOW FUN
PET PEEVE: SEEING OTHER ANIMALS ON TELEVISION
NAUGHTIEST DEED: BARKING AND LEAPING AT ANIMALS ON TELEVISION

JOY LUCK

MOJO MAXIMUS

PET PEEVE: BABY TALK
KNOWN ACCOMPLICE: GABBY
NAUGHTIEST DEED: NO SUCH THING
FAVORITE FOODS: SALAMI PIZZA AND FRENCH FRIES
FAVORITE TOY: THE SQUEAKER FROM INSIDE A TOY
FAVORITE PASTIME: SWIMMING AT HIS SECRET SPOT IN THE CREEK

PET PEEVE: BIRDS
FAVORITE TOY: LIFE-SIZED STUFFED CAT
FAVORITE PASTIME: SLEEPING ON SUZANNE'S PILLOW
FAVORITE FOOD: STOLEN HOT DOGS FROM A TODDLER'S PLATE
NAUGHTIEST DEED: STEALING HOT DOGS FROM A TODDLER'S PLATE
KNOWN ACCOMPLICES: CHINA MOON, FRANK FAT, JOY LUCK, CHOW MEI MEI

CHOW FUN

JOSIE

FAVORITE FOOD: LAMB
FAVORITE TOY: FRISBEE
KNOWN ACCOMPLICES: DAVID AND BARBARA
NAUGHTIEST DEED: DEMANDING TO PLAY 24 HOURS A DAY
FAVORITE PASTIME: PLAYING WITH STICKS, FRISBEE AND BALLS
PET PEEVES: THUNDER, RAIN AND STAYING IN THE HOUSE ALL DAY

FAVORITE TOYS: DUCK OR PONY
FAVORITE FOODS: STILTON BLUE, PIZZA AND BACON
PET PEEVES: SEAFOOD AND THINGS STUCK IN HIS FUR
FAVORITE PASTIMES: HUNTING AND SLEEPING ON THE COUCH
NAUGHTIEST DEEDS: STANDING ON A DINING ROOM TABLE AND
JUMPING IN A CUSTOMER'S MIATA CONVERTIBLE
KNOWN ACCOMPLICES: PATCH, WILLOW, REMINGTON, COWBOY, OBIE AND BABY

NICK

FAVORITE TOY: RUBBER DONUT
PET PEEVE: BEING LEFT BEHIND
FAVORITE PASTIME: CHASING BIRDS
FAVORITE FOOD: AUSTRALIAN LIVER SNACKS
NAUGHTIEST DEED: TANGLING WITH SKUNKS
KNOWN ACCOMPLICES: ONLY HUMANS AND BEARS

IRIS

FAVORITE FOOD: ELK
FAVORITE TOY: STUFFED SQUIRREL
PET PEEVES: FOXES AND BIG BLACK BIRDS
KNOWN ACCOMPLICES: STASHA AND RUBY
NAUGHTIEST DEEDS: EATING TISSUES OUT OF THE
TRASH CAN AND TOILET PAPER OFF THE ROLL
FAVORITE PASTIME: CROSS-COUNTRY SKIING WITH CHARLIE

OWNERS: ANDREA AND CHARLIE FOSS | ENGLISH SPRINGER SPANIEL, 13 | ELKHORN RIDGE, MONMOUTH, OR

PET PEEVE: *BEING LEFT ALONE*
FAVORITE TOY: *STUFFED REINDEER*
FAVORITE FOOD: *ICE CUBES ON A HOT DAY*
KNOWN ACCOMPLICE: *YANKEE THE APPALOOSA HORSE*
FAVORITE PASTIMES: *FETCHING TOYS AND GREETING GUESTS*
NAUGHTIEST DEED: *SNEAKING INTO THE FERMENTATION ROOM*

LILY

LONG MEADOW RANCH *RUTHERFORD, CA* | *GOLDEN RETRIEVER, 5* | *OWNER: LADDIE HALL*

NAUGHTIEST DEED: EATING A COUCH
FAVORITE TOY: SUN THE GOLDEN RETRIEVER
PET PEEVES: LITTLE FLUFFY DOGS, BALLOONS AND CATS
FAVORITE FOODS: CHOCOLATE, GRAPES AND STRAWBERRIES
FAVORITE PASTIMES: FOLLOWING THE GARDENER AND WATCHING TV

ROMEO

PET PEEVE: BATHS
FAVORITE FOOD: ITALIAN SALAMI
FAVORITE TOY: TOO BUSY TO PLAY
NAUGHTIEST DEED: STEALING
A RIB EYE OFF THE COUNTER
KNOWN ACCOMPLICES: OREO AND PEPPER
FAVORITE PASTIME: LAYING IN THE GRASS

SALSA

FAVORITE FOOD: FISH
FAVORITE PASTIME: CLIMBING TREES
KNOWN ACCOMPLICES: PERRY AND RYAN
FAVORITE TOY: A SOCK WITH A KNOT IN IT
PET PEEVES: RACCOONS AND THE VACUUM CLEANER
NAUGHTIEST DEED: CRAWLING INTO BED COVERED IN MUD

DEKKA

PATTY

FAVORITE TOY: RABBITS
FAVORITE FOOD: EVERYTHING
FAVORITE PASTIME: CHASING CATS AND BIRDS
NAUGHTIEST DEED: OPENING THE DOOR TO THE WINE CELLAR
PET PEEVE: WATCHING WHISKEY CHASE AND RETRIEVE THE BALL

WHISKEY

PET PEEVE: BATHS
FAVORITE FOOD: GRAPES
FAVORITE TOY: ANYTHING THROWN
FAVORITE PASTIME: CHASING SQUIRRELS
NAUGHTIEST DEED: CHASING AND EATING RABBITS

PET PEEVE: MICE
FAVORITE TOY: RED BALL
FAVORITE FOOD: CHICKEN
FAVORITE PASTIME: CHASING THE BALL
KNOWN ACCOMPLICES: MACKENZIE AND ANNIE
NAUGHTIEST DEED: DIGGING UP THE LAVENDER BUSHES

PORCINI

RUBEE

FAVORITE TOY: A BALL
KNOWN ACCOMPLICE: ROXEE
PET PEEVE: HAVING HER TEETH BRUSHED
NAUGHTIEST DEED: HIDING AT BATH TIME
FAVORITE FOOD: DRIED CHICKEN BREAST TREATS
FAVORITE PASTIME: RIDING THROUGH THE VINEYARD ON THE BACK OF THE FOUR WHEELER

PET PEEVE: SKUNKS
FAVORITE TOY: FRISBEE
FAVORITE FOOD: ANYTHING BEEF
NAUGHTIEST DEED: DRINKING ANTIFREEZE AS A PUPPY
KNOWN ACCOMPLICES: COI AND PRINCESS SUGAR PUSS
FAVORITE PASTIME: STAYING BY TIM'S KNEE WITH EACH STEP

IRIS

JETTA

FAVORITE TOY: RUBBER BONE
KNOWN ACCOMPLICE: PENNY
FAVORITE PASTIME: HERDING OTHER DOGS
FAVORITE FOODS: SUGAR AND PEANUT BUTTER
NAUGHTIEST DEED: HELPING CHEW OTHER DOGS' BEDS

FAVORITE FOOD: PEDIGREE
KNOWN ACCOMPLICE: SERGIO
FAVORITE TOY: SERGIO'S SHOES
FAVORITE PASTIME: PLAYING IN THE VINEYARD
NAUGHTIEST DEED: CHEWING SERGIO'S SHOES

PINTO

OWNER: SERGIO MELGOZA | AUSTRALIAN SHEPHERD X · 3 MONTHS | ROSSA FAMILY VINEYARDS, NAPA, CA 47

*"The good Lord in His ultimate wisdom
gave us three things to make life bearable:
hope, jokes and dogs, but the greatest
of these was dogs."*

———— ROBYN DAVIDSON

A WINEMAKER AND HIS DOG
by Harvey Posert

while famous wineries have semi-famous dogs, the most famous name in American wine was dogless until late in life. But that changed in 1990 with a dog appropriately named Fumé, and Robert Mondavi fell in love.

His wife Margrit Biever, a long-time dog owner and lover, brought the standard poodle named after the famous Sauvignon Blanc/Semillon blend into their home overlooking Napa Valley, and Robert and the dog bonded immediately.

"I never knew what having a dog could mean," Robert said, as he sneakily snuck a morsel under the table from the winery restaurant. "The warmth, the affection, the trust and the way he loves me show I missed a lot over the years."

Fumé lived with the Mondavis for twelve years before meeting his maker, but Robert no longer wanted to be without a dog. It wasn't long before Robert and Margrit were looking for a new companion. Now, at 94, he and Margrit have a Havanese, Luce, named after the joint venture the Mondavi family and Marchesi de' Frescobaldi created in Tuscany.

Napa Valley is another one of those American places that is not very dog friendly. A lot of wineries have no facilities for dogs and, like most places, they cannot run free in the county. At restaurants you can't bring your dog, as well behaved and leashed as they may be, even to outdoor areas. Margrit, a Swiss who has lived and traveled all over the globe, will have none of that. She has a large shopping bag lined with a comfortable cushion at the bottom, and Luce accompanies her shopping, lunching and visiting throughout the valley. Fortunately Luce is well behaved, like European dogs that relax under your restaurant table. "She's a member of our family, and she goes where I go," states Margrit.

MARGRIT, LUCE AND ROBERT

Robert is not able to travel as he did in his youth, and being confined doesn't suit him. But it is a lovely sight – an old man and his dog – together as the sun sets westward over the Mayacamas hills. Bob did marvelous things for Napa Valley wine, California wine, and wine everywhere in the world, and to see the joy that this wine dog brings to America's greatest winemaker gives joy to us all.

HARVEY POSERT IS AN AUTHOR AND PUBLIC RELATIONS CONSULTANT IN NAPA VALLEY. WITH OVER 40 YEARS PUBLIC RELATIONS EXPERIENCE IN THE WINE INDUSTRY. HE IS WIDELY KNOWN AS 'THE PR MAN'. WWW.HARVEYPOSERT.COM.

LUCE

FAVORITE FOOD: CHICKEN
FAVORITE TOY: A PLUSH MOLE
PET PEEVES: DARKNESS AND RAIN
FAVORITE PASTIME: PLAYING WITH MALBEC
KNOWN ACCOMPLICES: ROBERT AND MARGRIT
NAUGHTIEST DEED: DIGGING INTO SHEETS AND PILLOWS

ROBERT MONDAVI

FAVORITE TOY: LUCE
FAVORITE FOOD: PASTA
PET PEEVE: BEING LATE
FAVORITE PASTIMES: A NICE MEAL
WITH FRIENDS, GOOD WINE AND GOOD FOOD
NAUGHTIEST DEED: FLIRTING WITH PRETTY WOMEN
KNOWN ACCOMPLICES: MARGRIT, VINTNERS AND ARTISTS

GUINEA

FAVORITE FOOD:
RARE PRIME RIBS

PET PEEVE: BEING TOLD TO STAY

FAVORITE PASTIME: QUAIL HUNTING

NAUGHTIEST DEED: ROLLING IN FILTH
AND THEN JUMPING IN SCOTT'S TRUCK

PAYTON

FAVORITE FOOD: CEREAL
FAVORITE TOY: SOCCER BALL
PET PEEVE: RIDING IN THE BACK SEAT OF THE CAR
FAVORITE PASTIME: SLEEPING ON YOUR FEET OR SHOES
NAUGHTIEST DEED: EATING JEFF'S TRUCK CENTER CONSOLE

AGNES

FAVORITE FOOD: ROAST DUCK
PET PEEVE: BEING ON A LEASH
FAVORITE TOY: GIANT TEDDY BEAR
NAUGHTIEST DEED: BARKING AT ANIMALS ON TV
FAVORITE PASTIME: WATCHING DOG MOVIES ON TV
KNOWN ACCOMPLICES: BUGSY AND LOLA THE PUGS

TURNBULL WINE CELLARS OAKVILLE, CA | WEST HIGHLAND TERRIER, 1 | OWNERS: ZOÉ JOHNS AND MAX CATALANO

FAVORITE TOY: STUFFED SANTA
PET PEEVE: STRENUOUS EXERCISE
NAUGHTIEST DEED: CHASING THE CATS
KNOWN ACCOMPLICES: TESSA, ELVIS AND CARA
FAVORITE PASTIME: HANGING OUT WITH HIS FAMILY AND FRIENDS

CZOR

V. SATTUI ST. HELENA, CA   S: TOM AND CARA DAVIES

V. Sattui is located in the very heart *of Napa Valley and home to three beautiful Bernese mountain dogs – Czor, Tessa and Elvis. Ancestors of the Bernese mountain dogs were brought into Switzerland more than 2,000 years ago by forces of the invading Roman soldiers and can still be found on the farms of central Switzerland today. Although multi-purpose farm dogs capable of draft work as well as being kind, devoted family dogs, Czor, Tessa and Elvis have more modern, ambassadorial roles.*

These self-confident pups are good-natured, friendly and fearless but always have a wag of a tail for the next winery guest. Makes you think that those ancient Romans mustn't have been that bad to have kept such good company.

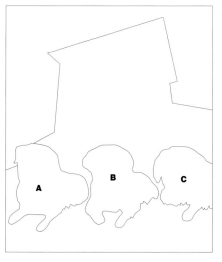

A *ELVIS:*
 FAVORITE PASTIME: RUNNING AROUND
 FAVORITE FOOD: DOG BISCUITS
 FAVORITE TOY: BLUE SUEDE SHOES
 NAUGHTIEST DEED: CHEWING A HOLE IN THE WALL
 PET PEEVE: BEING ON A LEASH

B *TESSA:*
 FAVORITE PASTIME: VISITING WITH CUSTOMERS
 FAVORITE FOODS: SALAMI AND CHEESE
 FAVORITE TOY: TENNIS BALL
 NAUGHTIEST DEED: STEALING SALAMI FROM THE DELI
 PET PEEVE: NOT GETTING ATTENTION

C *CZOR:*
 FAVORITE PASTIME: HANGING OUT WITH HIS FRIENDS
 FAVORITE FOOD: CHICKEN
 FAVORITE TOY: STUFFED SANTA
 NAUGHTIEST DEED: CHASING THE CATS
 PET PEEVE: STRENUOUS EXERCISE

PET PEEVE: COLD WEATHER
FAVORITE TOY: A TENNIS BALL
PARTNERS IN ACCOMPLICES: LUCY AND BODOG
NAUGHTIEST DEED: TINKLING ON PEOPLE WHEN HE MEETS THEM
FAVORITE PASTIME: TAKING THE BALL AWAY FROM LUCY AND BODOG

PET PEEVE: GOPHERS
FAVORITE TOY: TOY SQUIRREL
FAVORITE PASTIME: NAPPING
FAVORITE FOOD: PIZZA CRUST
KNOWN ACCOMPLICE: ISABELLA
NAUGHTIEST DEED: TRYING TO BITE
DIANE MILLER, THE OWNER OF THE WINERY

LULU

TOSCA

FAVORITE FOOD: ANYTHING AND EVERYTHING
NAUGHTIEST DEED: EATING VISITORS' LUNCHES
FAVORITE TOYS: TENNIS BALLS AND OLD BONES
FAVORITE PASTIME: HANGING OUT WITH VISITORS
PET PEEVE: BEING MOVED FROM HER SPOT IN THE TASTING ROOM

FAVORITE FOOD: PIG EARS
PET PEEVE: HARSH WORDS
FAVORITE TOY: ANY BIG STICK
FAVORITE PASTIME: HIKING WITH B&B GUESTS
NAUGHTIEST DEED: MARKING HIS TERRITORY IN THE WINERY

CHARLIE

PET PEEVE: BATHS
KNOWN ACCOMPLICE: DAISY
FAVORITE FOOD: LEFTOVER BONES
FAVORITE PASTIMES: SUNNING HIMSELF
AND PLAYING HIDE AND SEEK
NAUGHTIEST DEED: PLAYING WITH THE CHICKENS

SEVEN-UP

TIPPY

FAVORITE FOOD: TREVOR'S DINNER
KNOWN ACCOMPLICES: JEAN LAFITTE AND BIRDIE
FAVORITE TOYS: BED PILLOWS AND SOFA CUSHIONS
PET PEEVE: THE SOUND OF THE FRONT DOOR CLOSING
FAVORITE PASTIMES: CHASING SQUIRRELS AND CLIMBING TREES

FAVORITE TOY: BALL
FAVORITE FOOD: STEER PIZZLES
NAUGHTIEST DEED: EATING SHOES
PET PEEVE: THE CATS EATING HER FOOD
FAVORITE PASTIME: PLAYING WITH ABBEY, McCOVEY AND BOKI

EMMA

MAX

FAVORITE TOY: HIS OWNERS
FAVORITE FOODS: CANIDAE AND MEXICAN FOOD
NAUGHTIEST DEED: HAVING WET PAWS IN TASTING ROOM
KNOWN ACCOMPLICES: GUSTAVO, MARIA, MIKE AND ROBERT
FAVORITE PASTIME: CHASING TRACTORS AND BITING AT TIRES

FAVORITE TOY: FOOD
PET PEEVE: THE RAIN
FAVORITE PASTIME:
CHASING SQUIRRELS
FAVORITE FOOD: WHATEVER
KATHY'S EATING
NAUGHTIEST DEED: GOING POOH
POOH NEXT TO THE TOILET

EMMEBIRD

BEAR-B-Q

KNOWN ACCOMPLICE: BACCHUS
FAVORITE TOY: HIS GIRLFRIEND BACCHUS
FAVORITE PASTIME: HANGING WITH BACCHUS
FAVORITE FOOD: ANYTHING THAT IS CALLED DINNER
PET PEEVE: ANY FORM OF WATER THAT IS NOT FOR DRINKING
NAUGHTIEST DEED: BREAKING THROUGH A WINDOW AND TALKING HIS SISTER INTO FOLLOWING HIM

FAVORITE TOY: FRISBEE
FAVORITE FOOD: BREMNER WAFERS
KNOWN ACCOMPLICES: BRUNO AND MAGGIE
NAUGHTIEST DEED: RUMMAGING THROUGH TRASH
PET PEEVES: SLIPPERY FLOORS, ICE AND LOUD NOISES
FAVORITE PASTIME: GREETING GUESTS WITH A FIRM PAWSHAKE

SALLY

OWNERS: TONY FERNANDEZ, JR. AND DANA ESTENSEN | LABRADOR X 8 | **WILLIAM HILL ESTATE** NAPA, CA | 67

When you visit over 450 dogs across 10 states of the USA in 8 weeks, the really good ones seem to remain in your memory the longest. One handsome dog that I am most fond of is Shafer Vineyard's wine dog Tucker. This good-looking, suave canine has attitude – and I like it. Even owner, John Shafer, was artistically inspired by Tucker's grand stature and produced his first sculpture in Tucker's honour. A bust with an uncanny likeness of Tucker now greets visitors at the tasting room.

Every day Tucker comes out to the car park and admires himself. Yes, a quality wine dog if he has ever seen one.

KNOWN ACCOMPLICE: JOHN
FAVORITE FOOD: PEANUT BUTTER
PET PEEVE: JOHN'S TRAVEL SCHEDULE
NAUGHTIEST DEED: EATING A TRAY OF
CUPCAKES OFF A HIGH SHELF
FAVORITE PASTIME: DEFENDING THE
WINERY FROM DELIVERY TRUCKS

TUCKER

OWNER: JOHN SHAFER | LABRADOR, 7 | **SHAFER VINEYARDS** NAPA, CA

PACO

PET PEEVE: GOPHERS
FAVORITE FOOD: LAMB
FAVORITE TOY: STICKS
KNOWN ACCOMPLICE: MAYBEL
FAVORITE PASTIME: HERDING ANYTHING
NAUGHTIEST DEED: BITING PEOPLE'S HEELS

MONTINORE ESTATE · FOREST GROVE, OR · BLUE HEELER · 8 MONTHS · OWNER: RUDY MARCHESI

FAVORITE FOOD: CHICKEN
FAVORITE TOY: A GOOD BOOK
FAVORITE PASTIME: HANGING
WITH HER FAMILY
PET PEEVE: WENDY'S SUITCASE

DAPHNE

FAVORITE TOY: A BALL

NAUGHTIEST DEED:
EATING CHRIS'S SOCKS

PET PEEVE: THE WATER
AND AIR HOSE

FAVORITE FOOD:
ANYTHING YOU'RE EATING

KNOWN ACCOMPLICE: CHRIS

FAVORITE PASTIME: HUNTING
SQUIRRELS AND GOPHERS

DRU

FAVORITE TOY: SQUEAKY DUCK
PET PEEVE: THE VINEYARD'S CAT
SLEEPING IN HER DISH
FAVORITE FOODS: CHICKEN AND PASTA
FAVORITE PASTIME: WORKING THE WEEKEND
CROWDS IN THE TASTING ROOM

HANNAH

BEAN

FAVORITE TOY: STUFFED DOG
KNOWN ACCOMPLICES: PETER AND LINDA
NAUGHTIEST DEED: BRINGING HOME A BABY RABBIT
FAVORITE PASTIME: GOING ON WALKS IN THE VINEYARDS

FAVORITE TOY: PIXIE
PET PEEVE: SQUIRRELS
FAVORITE FOOD: WHAT THE
CAT LEAVES BEHIND
KNOWN ACCOMPLICE: PIXIE
FAVORITE PASTIME: CRUISING
VINEYARDS WITHOUT A LEASH
NAUGHTIEST DEED: DEVOURING SHOES

FANNY

smart dogs: *During our travels over the USA we came across many smart Wine Dogs. But I must admit that we were particularly impressed with the ones that could write. Two Mountain resident wordsmith, Bentley the scholar basset hound, is a prime example. This explains all of those university degrees hanging in his kennel.*

Dear Wine Dogs USA:

It's a hard job being a wine dog.

My brothers Rudy and Gus (the two yellow labs) and myself (the good-looking basset hound) took the job three years ago at Two Mountain Winery in Zillah, Washington. We were already part of the family and once we were asked to also be part of the family's winery, we immediately barked at the chance. After making it through our fourth harvest last year, things couldn't be better and we love our jobs.

The weekdays are when we work the hardest. Rudy has the job of riding in the back of our winemaker's pickup truck, Gus's job is to walk through the vineyards, taste testing the Merlot grapes to make sure they're growing okay. My job is to hold down the fort at the winery. I consider myself the watchdog of the trio, sniffing throughout the tasting room and greeting guests that stop by.

Last October, Gus put his life and his job on the line when he crossed the road in front of our winery, and forgot to look both ways. He was hit by a truck. His brother Rudy spent days standing by the side of the road, right where Gus was hit. After two broken hips, one broken femur and six weeks in the hospital, Gus has finally recovered and is now in top dog shape. Now the three of us are back together ... busy working that is.

We are very excited to be featured in the Wine Dogs USA book. Rudy, Gus and I believe that every dog has their day and we would be honored and of course feel it's our duty to represent Washington wineries.

Best regards,

Bentley (the good-looking basset hound).

LEFT – GUS: LABRADOR, 1

FAVORITE PASTIME: MILKING CUSTOMERS FOR ATTENTION

FAVORITE FOOD: MERLOT GRAPES

NAUGHTIEST DEED: CROSSING THE ROAD WITHOUT LOOKING

PET PEEVE: NOT GETTING ENOUGH ATTENTION

KNOWN ACCOMPLICE: ABBEY BAKER

CENTRE – BENTLEY: BASSET HOUND, 2

FAVORITE PASTIME: CHEWING ON GUS AND RUDY

FAVORITE FOOD: CHERRIES FROM THE ORCHARD

FAVORITE TOY: BUNGS FROM WINE BARRELS

NAUGHTIEST DEED: BARKING WHEN HE WANTS ATTENTION

PET PEEVE: BEING SO SHORT

RIGHT – RUDY: LABRADOR, 1

FAVORITE PASTIME: RIDING IN THE PICKUP TRUCK

FAVORITE FOOD: LEMBERGER GRAPES

FAVORITE TOY: BRANCHES LEFT FROM PRUNING

NAUGHTIEST DEED: EATING GRAPES OFF THE VINE

PET PEEVE: NOT BEING ALLOWED TO GO TO WORK

RUBY

FAVORITE FOOD: BACON
PET PEEVE: STAYING HOME
FAVORITE TOY: TOY'S CORGI WOODY
FAVORITE PASTIME: RIDING IN THE GATOR AND TRUCK
NAUGHTIEST DEED: EATING TOY'S BOYFRIEND'S SURFBOARD PATTERNS

FAVORITE TOY: SOCCER BALL
KNOWN ACCOMPLICE: JOJO MAXIMUS
PET PEEVE: WEDDINGS IN THE WINERY
FAVORITE FOOD: SOMETHING FROM A TOURIST
FAVORITE PASTIME: CHASING HER SOCCER BALL
NAUGHTIEST DEED: CHEWING $1,000 SKI GOGGLES

GABBY

JACQUE

PET PEEVES: BEING LEFT TOO LONG
IN HIS CRATE AND CHESTER THE CAT
FAVORITE TOYS: ALL OF CHU CHU'S TOYS
FAVORITE PASTIME: PLAYING TUG OF WAR
KNOWN ACCOMPLICES: STEVE AND CAROLE

ARE YOU CRAZY?

by Craig McGill

Prior to traveling *around the USA with our photographer, my mate Peter Herring and I traveled to Napa Valley for a ten-day pre-production trip, just to get a feel and taste for the area and hopefully meet some useful contacts for our return trip.*

As we sat in the To Kalon room of the Robert Mondavi Winery getting friendly with a dozen very generous tastings of their premium wines, two Japanese businessmen who spoke broken English joined us at the table. As you can imagine after a dose of jetlag and eight cabernet tastings, our Aussie accents were probably sounding like shorthand to the Japanese.

But all four of us struggled along with polite conversation and we eventually crossed the path of what brought us to Napa Valley. Peter and I explained to our new friends that our publishing company had released a best-selling book in Australia called Wine Dogs. They listened politely with confused looks on their faces but remained silent as we continued our rave. We explained that it was a photographic book on Wine Dogs that live in wineries and vineyards and we are about to embark on a USA edition of Wine Dogs. Every winery has a Wine Dog, we declared.

The Japanese reached into their bags and simultaneously brought out cameras and requested a photo. Initially we were flattered that they wanted to take our photos but after all, we were from the Wine Dogs book. However, flattery soon turned to embarrassment as they handed us their cameras and struck a pose.

They nodded to each other and, as they rose to leave, asked: "Blind Dogs! Who would buy a book of blind dogs?"

FAVORITE TOY: A BALL
PET PEEVE: BEING SCOLDED
FAVORITE FOOD: BEEF JERKY
NAUGHTIEST DEED: LOOKING FOR GIRLFRIENDS
KNOWN ACCOMPLICES: KRISTINA AND MICHAEL
FAVORITE PASTIME: RUNNING ABOUT LOOKING FOR BIRDS

MAGNUM

BADGE

PET PEEVE:
PEOPLE WHO
DON'T LIKE DOGS
KNOWN ACCOMPLICE: GINA
FAVORITE PASTIME: PILATES
FAVORITE FOOD: GRENACHE BLANC GRAPES
NAUGHTIEST DEEDS: TOO MANY TO COUNT

BREAKER MORANT

PET PEEVE: ROLAND
KNOWN ACCOMPLICE: GUNNER
FAVORITE PASTIME: GOING FOR WALKIES
FAVORITE TOYS: LARGE UNDERWATER ROCKS
FAVORITE FOOD: SCRAMBLED EGGS WITH WHITE TRUFFLES

CURRAN WINES LOMPOC, CA | GERMAN SHEPHERDS, 3 | OWNERS: KRIS CURRAN AND BRUNO D'ALFONSO

GUNNER

FAVORITE FOOD: PIG EARS
PET PEEVE: FLY SWATTERS
KNOWN ACCOMPLICE: TIGER
NAUGHTIEST DEED: STEALING A RIB
FROM A LADY'S PLATE AT A WEDDING
FAVORITE PASTIME: LOUNGING POOLSIDE

ROLAND

PET PEEVE: BEES
FAVORITE TOY: SOCCER BALLS
FAVORITE PASTIME: SWIMMING
FAVORITE FOOD: EXTRA SPICY BUFFALO WINGS
NAUGHTIEST DEED: JUMPING INTO A DITCH FULL OF MUD
KNOWN ACCOMPLICES: STEVE CLIFTON AND TOMMY "BAHAMA"

OWNERS: KRIS CURRAN AND BRUNO D'ALFONSO | GERMAN SHEPHERDS, 8 | **CURRAN WINES** LOMPOC, CA | 85

LULU

PET PEEVE: BATHS
FAVORITE FOOD: STEAK
FAVORITE TOY: SQUEAKY TOYS
KNOWN ACCOMPLICES: MISSY AND ACE
NAUGHTIEST DEED: DIGGING UP THE FLOWER BEDS
FAVORITE PASTIMES: SMELLING, HAT HUNTING AND RIDES WITH DAD

PHEASANT VALLEY VINEYARD AND WINERY HOOD RIVER, OR | BRITTANY, 4 | OWNERS: GAIL AND SCOTT HAGEE

FAVORITE TOY: BALLS
PET PEEVE: WAKING UP
FAVORITE FOOD: EDAMAME
FAVORITE PASTIME: PLAYING
WITH SOCCER BALLS
KNOWN ACCOMPLICES: SCOOP,
PUDGE AND PACO
NAUGHTIEST DEED: EATING CAT LITTER

MAYBEL

TANNER

PET PEEVE: DEER

FAVORITE FOOD:
KIBBLE CARBONARA

FAVORITE PASTIMES: HERDING
GRAPE VINES AND CHASING FRISBEES

FAVORITE TOY: FRISBEE
KNOWN ACCOMPLICE: WILL
NAUGHTIEST DEED: GETTING INTO THE TRASH
FAVORITE PASTIME: WALKING DOWN THE STREET
AND ACTING HUMAN

TANNER

MEGAN

FAVORITE TOY: TENNIS BALLS
PET PEEVE: BEING LEFT ALONE
KNOWN ACCOMPLICES: HER FAMILY
FAVORITE PASTIME: RUNNING WITH SONJA
FAVORITE FOOD: ANYTHING OFF THE KIDS' PLATES
NAUGHTIEST DEED: DIGGING THROUGH GARBAGE CANS

PET PEEVE: GOING HOME
FAVORITE TOY: AN OLD WHITE SOCK
KNOWN ACCOMPLICE: EMMA THE CAT
FAVORITE FOOD: WHOLE-WHEAT BREAD
FAVORITE PASTIME: RUNNING IN CIRCLES
NAUGHTIEST DEED: STEALING A LOAF OF BREAD FROM THE TABLE

XENA

LIBBY

PET PEEVE: BATHS
FAVORITE FOOD: ALPO
FAVORITE TOY: BASEBALL
FAVORITE PASTIME: ROUGH-HOUSING
NAUGHTIEST DEED: PEEING ON THE LAWN

FAVORITE FOODS: ALPO AND BACON
PET PEEVE: DRESS-UPS WITH MATTISEN
NAUGHTIEST DEED: CHEWING ALEXANDRIA'S FAVORITE SHOES
FAVORITE PASTIME: CHASING JARROD THROUGH THE VINEYARD

LEXY

PET PEEVE: BICYCLES
FAVORITE FOOD: STEAK
FAVORITE PASTIME: SLEEPING IN
THE CHAIR WITH DENNIS
FAVORITE TOY: ANYTHING SQUEAKY
KNOWN ACCOMPLICE: MUSCAT THE CAT
NAUGHTIEST DEED: HARASSING MUSCAT

KC

HERSHEY

PET PEEVE: FLIES
FAVORITE TOY:
SOMETHING SQUEAKY
FAVORITE FOOD: GARBAGE
FAVORITE PASTIME: SLEEPING
NAUGHTIEST DEED: STEALING BUNGS FROM FULL BARRELS

*FAVORITE PASTIME: PLAYING
WITH OPUS AND MIMIE
FAVORITE TOYS: BALLS AND BONES
PET PEEVE: NOT GETTING ATTENTION
NAUGHTIEST DEED: EATING EVERYTHING
KNOWN ACCOMPLICES: OPUS AND MIMIE*

CASPER

DALE

KNOWN ACCOMPLICE: CHIP
PET PEEVE: BEING LOCKED UP
FAVORITE PASTIME: CHASING DEER
FAVORITE FOOD: BREAKFAST FOOD
NAUGHTIEST DEED: CHEWING DOOR MATS
FAVORITE TOYS: SHOES AND HATS LEFT OUTSIDE

KNOWN ACCOMPLICE: DALE
FAVORITE FOOD: TABLE FOOD
PET PEEVE: BEING LOCKED UP
FAVORITE PASTIME: PLAYING WITH DALE
NAUGHTIEST DEED: CHEWING DOOR MATS
FAVORITE TOYS: SHOES AND HATS LEFT OUTSIDE

CHIP

YOUNGBERG HILL McMINNVILLE, OR | LABRADOR X, 2 AND 1 | OWNER: NICOLETTE BAILEY

PET PEEVE: *BEING IN THE BACKYARD ALONE*

KNOWN ACCOMPLICES: *CRYSTAL AND MIDNIGHT*

NAUGHTIEST DEED: *CHEWING THE FENCE DOWN AT GRANDMA'S HOUSE*

FAVORITE FOOD: *TILLAMOOK CHEDDAR CHEESE*

FAVORITE PASTIME: *WATCHING TV WITH THE FAMILY*

EDDIE

ETHYL

FAVORITE TOY: PEOPLE

KNOWN ACCOMPLICES:
MADELINE, LUCY AND FRED

NAUGHTIEST DEED: CHASING
TRUCKS, RVS AND LIMOS

FAVORITE PASTIME: DRINKING WINE

PET PEEVES: TEETOTALLERS, GROOMERS
AND LIVING ONE DAY AT A TIME

FAVORITE FOODS: MEATBALLS AND WINE

PET PEEVE: SQUIRRELS
FAVORITE FOOD: MEATBALLS
FAVORITE TOY: VINE CLIPPINGS
KNOWN ACCOMPLICES: ETHYL, FRED AND LUCY
NAUGHTIEST DEED: ROMPING IN PUBLIC FOUNTAINS
FAVORITE PASTIMES: FARTING AND CHASING SQUIRRELS

MADELINE

MIMIE

FAVORITE TOY: RABBITS
FAVORITE FOOD: DRIED MEAT CUBES
NAUGHTIEST DEED: DIGGING HOLES
KNOWN ACCOMPLICES: OPUS AND CASPER
FAVORITE PASTIMES: RUNNING AND CHASING RABBITS
PET PEEVES: GOING OUT IN THE RAIN AND BEING IGNORED

FAVORITE TOY: *STICKS*
FAVORITE FOOD: *STEAK*
PET PEEVES: *GROUND SQUIRRELS, SKUNKS AND CATS*
FAVORITE PASTIME: *EATING GRAPES ON THE CRUSH PAD*
NAUGHTIEST DEED: *DIGGING BIG HOLES IN THE VINEYARDS*

RASTUS

WIDGET

KNOWN ACCOMPLICE: GUSTAVO
NAUGHTIEST DEED: EATING A WALLET
FAVORITE TOY: ELMO, THE STUFFED ELEPHANT
FAVORITE PASTIMES: SWIMMING, HUNTING AND LOUNGING IN THE SUN
PET PEEVES: SQUIRRELS AND ANYONE GETTING TOO CLOSE TO HER TRUCK

FAVORITE FOOD: BACON
FAVORITE PASTIME: JUMPING
ON LITTLE OLD LADIES
NAUGHTIEST DEED: EATING THE SOFA
PET PEEVE: BEING LEFT OUT OF THE PARTY
KNOWN ACCOMPLICES: TRENT AND MARIO,
ADDISON AND MARSHALL
FAVORITE TOY: ANYTHING FUZZY OR SQUEAKY

JACKSON

MOLLY

NAUGHTIEST DEED: CHEWING
PET PEEVE: BEING BRUSHED
FAVORITE FOOD: WILSON WINERY TRI-TIP
FAVORITE TOYS: TUGGY TOY AND STUFFED FLAMINGO
KNOWN ACCOMPLICES: SADIE, DIXIE, MANDY AND ZEN
FAVORITE PASTIMES: RUNNING AND PLAYING TUG OF WAR

PET PEEVE: BEING SCOLDED
FAVORITE FOOD: MILK BONES
NAUGHTIEST DEED: CHEWING
UP THE DRIP SYSTEM
FAVORITE TOY: MOLLY'S FLAMINGO
KNOWN ACCOMPLICES: MANDY AND
MOLLY MALONE, CASEY AND MAGGI
FAVORITE PASTIME: GETTING ATTENTION

SADIE

RUDY

PET PEEVE: SWIMMING
FAVORITE FOOD: BULLY STICKS
FAVORITE TOY: SQUEAKY DUCK
KNOWN ACCOMPLICES: UMA AND SHASTA
FAVORITE PASTIME: CHASING OTHER DOGS
NAUGHTIEST DEED: JUMPING ON COUNTERS

COW DOG

by Adam Lechmere

– There he goes, Johnson said. See? The way he goes for the leg.

– He does, Splinter agreed. He really knows what he's doing, doesn't he?

The two men stood watching Johnson's dog, a big, handsome animal of indeterminate breed, as it wrestled with the Doberman. Both dogs concentrated hard on the fight, uttering low throaty growls. Every now and again one of them would scud off between the vines, then look around to see if it was chased.

Johnson spat into the red, dusty soil and pulled a pair of work gloves from his jeans pocket. He picked up the secateurs from where they hung on the endpost of the vines. It was hot even at 10 o'clock in the morning, the sage-smell of the ground cover rising from the baked earth.

The dogs staggered to the shade and flopped. For half an hour or so the men worked steadily down the row, expertly pruning the spurs of the vines. They took frequent drinks from a plastic bottle of water. Across the huge vineyard you could see groups of workers, most of them Hispanic, in hooded tops and baggy trousers, the women with their faces masked against the sun.

– He's got to be a cattle dog. And ridgeback, Splinter said at one point.

– He's ridgeback, Johnson answered. You can see it. And the way he goes for the leg. That's cattle dog for certain.

Johnson had come upon the dog six months before, trotting fixedly along the hard shoulder, looking up at every car that passed, and then staring straight ahead as he *went on, exhausted but with a strength born of certainty that what he was looking for he would find. Johnson had stopped his truck and waited for the dog to reach him, which it did and, with the briefest of looks, aimed to swerve past him with purpose. Johnson had said, Here boy, and held out a hand, but the dog had run on, making Johnson get back in the truck, overtake him again, and again try to intercept him. The third time it worked, and the dog sniffed his hand, then accepted a gush of water from Johnson's bottle.*

He was a big brindled brute standing as high as a man's hip, with a blunt muzzle and pricked ears, and a barrel chest. He looked strong, but his pads were bleeding and he was weak with thirst. Fur on his left front leg was matted with blood, which Johnson, running a hand along his flank, saw came from a vicious raw graze.

– I guess he'd been thrown from a truck. On purpose or not I don't know. Certain he was looking for something, Johnson would say. I watched him. Every time he heard a car, his head would come up and he'd look. If it was a truck then he'd really be interested.

At lunchtime Johnson and Splinter sat side by side in the shade of a scrubby oak and ate their lunch. Neither was talkative and the silence was broken only by the distant pounding of the highway, the steady rhythm of the men's jaws on their sandwiches, and the occasional loud glugging of the water bottle.

– What's ZZ saying about the test? Splinter asked.

– Seeing him tonight, Johnson answered. I tell you, I'd sooner get it done on the dog than on me. Prove a hell of a lot more.

ZZ Feathers was the proud proprietor of Feathers Ranch, seven hundred acres of prime Napa vineland. Short and cuban-heeled, the first African-American winemaker-owner in California, he was Chicago born and bred, had left home at 13 to sell computer parts, had migrated west with his first ten thousand, and had made his first million by the time he was 27. He retired at 55, bought the ranch, hired the best consultant winemaker north of LA, and was now producing a few thousand cases of ultra-expensive Napa cabernet sauvignon with his mugshot on the back label, jaw thrust out in a classic picture of American can-do.

Boxy, pugnacious, foul-mouthed, cunning, and wealthy even by Napa standards, he held his own with the local aristocracy, his wide and ready smile never quite reaching the wrinkles around his eyes.

– He's keen, I'll say that, Johnson muttered. Splinter nodded but said nothing.

When they had finished the day's work the two men packed their gear in the truck's topbox and headed out of the vineyard, the dogs in the back, standing up and steadying themselves against every pitch and yaw of the rolling metal floor.

Johnson dropped Splinter off at his house and headed into town, to the suburban two-bedroom he shared with his girlfriend. He was due at the Feathers house at seven.

Johnson was another anomaly in Napa. He'd come from South Africa, taking advantage of an exchange program run by the Black Economic Empowerment initiative. He'd worked vineyards all his life and his dream was to run a winery as chief winemaker. The chance to work in Napa seemed heaven-sent, but it meant a couple of years apprenticeship. It was fate that had landed him on the doorstep of a stunted megalomaniac like Feathers, who claimed kin with Johnson on account of skin colour, but demanded he put in two seasons on the vines before he got a sniff of responsibility in the winery.

Then one day Feathers had roared up in his truck as Johnson was pulling leaves with a crew he was supervising.

– Take a look at this, Feathers had said, waving a newspaper. They can find out what tribe you're from. From your DNA.

Johnson took the paper and read, 'Are you searching for your African DNA? This report reveals your maternal line's deep history and tribal heritage.'

The report went on to detail the black celebrities who had taken the test, and gave advice on who to contact.

Feathers was looking serious. – What do you reckon? Find out you're full-blood Zulu. I'll put spears and shields all around the tasting room. The tourists'll be all over here like flies on shit. The first Zulu winemaker in Napa. And see what it can do for you. Look what happened to Hernandez up at Stetson Braggart. The first Hispanic winemaker. He went to the White House.

– Zeeze. Jesus man. Get it done yourself. Find out you're Yoruba. Stick a bone in your nose.

Feathers liked that. – I'm a damn Chicago sewer rat. I have no idea who my dad was, let alone my grandfather. My DNA's no better than the dog's.

He wouldn't let it alone. For two weeks now he'd been offering Johnson his own parcels of grapes, old vine Zin to do what he liked with, if he'd find out he was Zulu, Xhosa, goddamn blue-blood Pygmy for all he cared.

Lydia was waiting for him with supper. As he ate, Johnson talked of the coming meeting with Feathers.

– He won't let it go, man. What's he so interested for?

– He rates you, Lydia said. He likes you as well, but he likes the idea of a real African better. You don't see many black faces in St. Helena. He thinks the two of you together are a double act. You get the test done and it reflects on him.

It was true. It was the chip on his shoulder. Look at me, he was saying. I may be a hustler made good but this boy here from Africa is the real thing, and he's mine.

– Damned test, Johnson said. Says he'll make me assistant winemaker. Get it done and he'll see me through to the top.

– Honey, do what you want, Lydia said.

– Tell you what I want, Johnson replied. Test the dog. He's got better blood than me, I can see that. Look at the lines on him.

The dog was sitting alert at his side, waiting for the scraps that he would catch with a delicate clop of his great jaws.

– He's pure. Whatever there is in the rest of him, he's a cattle dog. With Splint's bitch this morning, he was going for her leg. The back leg every time, bring her down. That's cattle dog instinct.

– He's a mongrel, Lydia said. Heinz 57.

– Maybe, but the cattle dog part's the best part. He knows what to do.

At half past six Johnson drove out to the Feathers Ranch, the dog in the back sticking his blunt muzzle into the evening air.

The man himself was taking a glass of chilled riesling in a vine-covered arbor, still in his riding gear, shiny black boots and jodhpurs, emerald pin in a white cravat.

– Johnson, he said, smiling. Sit. Have a glass. How was the day?

– Not bad. He took the glass a white-gloved maid poured for him.

Feathers came straight to the point. – Are you going to do it then?

– Jesus, Zeeze. I don't know. Don't know if I'm in the mood to start handing out blood samples.

– Do this for me and you're made, Feathers replied. What's the difference? You're proving you're aristocracy. Black aristocracy. What are you afraid of? Think I'm going to make you wear a loincloth and call you Kunta Kinte, for Christ's sake?

The next day Johnson drove into town and visited the pharmacist. He bought a syringe and a sample bottle, swabs and disinfectant wipes.

That evening, he called the dog over. Here boy, he said. The dog raised himself from the pallet and blanket in the corner of the kitchen and pushed his damp, cold nose into the vineman's hand. He stood massive and square, breathing softly.

– This isn't going to hurt, boy, Johnson said gently, rubbing the dog's muscled flank. Here.

He rubbed a section of skin above the shoulder with a sterile swab and took the syringe. The dog's breathing increased a fraction, but it submitted stoically to whatever Johnson saw fit to do.

Johnson drew a sample of blood into the syringe and squirted it into the plastic flask, then stoppered it with the screwtop lid. He held it to the light.

– Looks like the blood of a prince, he said. The dog ambled over to its bed and lay down.

Several days later, Johnson and Splinter were sitting eating their sandwiches when Feathers' truck drew up. The winemaker pulled himself out of the cab and came over, whacking his baseball cap against his jeans.

– Hower yer, he said to Splinter, who replied, Zeeze.

– Hear you've made a decision, Feathers said to Johnson.

Johnson grunted. I'll do it, Zeeze.

– I like to hear it, Feathers said. This is one we won't regret.

Saturday morning ten days later, Johnson and Lydia were making pancakes for breakfast when the mail arrived. A brown envelope sat amongst the junk circulars. Johnson set it beside his plate and took a long sip of coffee.

– Let's see then, he said. He ran a thumb along the top of the package and drew out the single sheet it contained. He read it carefully, and grunted.

– What is it, Lydia asked, pan in hand.

Johnson said, – Five parts ridgeback. Three parts German shepherd. One part Staffordshire bull terrier. One part labrador. Labrador. Jesus.

The dog sat on its pallet, its tail gently thumping.

– ZZ's going to love this, Johnson said, and reached for the maple syrup.

ADAM LECHMERE IS EDITOR AT LARGE OF *DECANTER* MAGAZINE. HE LIVES IN LONDON WITH HIS WIFE AND THREE DAUGHTERS, AND SPENDS A GOOD DEAL OF TIME IN WINE COUNTRY FROM BORDEAUX TO BAROSSA VIA CALIFORNIA AND BURGUNDY. HE HAS A TASTE FOR GREAT BORDEAUX AND GREAT PINOT, AND WILL GO MANY MILES FOR THE PERFECT BOTTLE OF GRUNER VELTLINER.

ROMEO

PET PEEVE: NEW OAK
FAVORITE FOOD: GOULASH
FAVORITE TOY: SCREWPULL
NAUGHTIEST DEED: SWITCHING ALL
THE BARREL CARDS IN THE CELLAR
FAVORITE PASTIMES: WHINING,
CAJOLING AND STALKING SQUIRRELS
KNOWN ACCOMPLICES: ROMAN AND DR. SEUSS

ANDREW RICH WINES CARLTON, OR | HUNGARIAN VIZSLA, 8 | OWNER: ANDREW RICH

FAVORITE TOY: FRISBEE
FAVORITE FOOD: ANYTHING DAVID IS EATING
PET PEEVES: LOUD NOISES AND YELLOW JACKETS
KNOWN ACCOMPLICES: DAVID AND CHLOE FELLMAN
FAVORITE PASTIMES: CHASING GOPHERS AND SWIMMING

WISH

CHARLIE

FAVORITE FOOD: CHEESE
KNOWN ACCOMPLICE: PHOEBE
FAVORITE TOY: PLASTIC BOTTLE
PET PEEVES: SUDDEN MOVEMENTS AND NOISES
FAVORITE PASTIME: SLEEPING UNDER BED COVERS
NAUGHTIEST DEED: DIGGING A HOLE IN THE MIDDLE OF A CROQUET COURT

FAVORITE TOY: FRISBEE
PET PEEVES: LIGHTNING STORMS AND GUNS
KNOWN ACCOMPLICES: AMY, JOE AND SARAH
NAUGHTIEST DEED: CHEWING SPRINKLER HEADS OFF
FAVORITE PASTIMES: GOING CAMPING AND CATCHING BALLS
FAVORITE FOODS: BISCUITS IN THE MORNING, ALPO IN THE EVENING

KATIE

SYDNEY

PET PEEVE: CLASSIFIED
FAVORITE TOY: RUBBER KONK
KNOWN ACCOMPLICE: CLAUDIA
NAUGHTIEST DEED: EATING TOWELS
FAVORITE PASTIMES: SLEEPING AND EATING

FAVORITE PASTIME: SLEEPING
PET PEEVE: BEING WOKEN UP
FAVORITE TOY: NONE, HE'S TOO BUSY SLEEPING
KNOWN ACCOMPLICES: ALICIA, TRIXIE, ANDY AND SCRAPPY
NAUGHTIEST DEED: NIBBLING PEOPLE'S LEGS TO MAKE THEM WALK FASTER

HAAS

ANDREW

*FAVORITE PASTIME: RETRIEVING
BALLS FROM THE POOL*
FAVORITE TOY: TENNIS BALLS
KNOWN ACCOMPLICES: MOSES, MINNIE

FAVORITE FOOD: CAT FOOD
PET PEEVE: BEING IGNORED
NAUGHTIEST DEED: DESTROYING
DOWN CUSHIONS

ANDREW

MINNIE

FAVORITE TOY: TENNIS BALL
FAVORITE PASTIME: RETRIEVING
PET PEEVE: HAVING A PEDICURE
NAUGHTIEST DEED: CHEWING OLD RUGS
FAVORITE FOOD: POACHED EGGS ON TOAST
KNOWN ACCOMPLICE: SYLVIE THE FRENCH CAT

PET PEEVE: SKUNKS
FAVORITE PASTIME:
SLEEPING IN BULRUSHES
FAVORITE TOY: A BONE
FAVORITE FOOD: CAT FOOD
KNOWN ACCOMPLICE: ANDREW
NAUGHTIEST DEED: CHASING CATS

MOSES

KASEY

PET PEEVE: BATHS
FAVORITE TOYS: BIRDS OR RABBITS
FAVORITE PASTIMES: CATCHING RAYS
FAVORITE FOODS: PHEASANT AND SYRAH
NAUGHTIEST DEED: CHEWING THE COMPUTER,
KEYBOARD, SCANNER, MOUSE AND PHONE
KNOWN ACCOMPLICES: KRISTIN, RACHEL AND MOLLY

KASEY

KNOWN ACCOMPLICE: KELLY
NAUGHTIEST DEED: EATING OUT
OF THE TRASH CAN
FAVORITE TOY: JON'S GOLF CART
PET PEEVES: CATS AND THE TRASH MAN
FAVORITE FOOD: WHATEVER JON IS EATING
FAVORITE PASTIME: CHASING TENNIS BALLS

JET

FAVORITE TOY: A BONE
FAVORITE FOOD: RIB EYE BONES
FAVORITE PASTIME: EATING BONES
NAUGHTIEST DEED: BURYING BONES
KNOWN ACCOMPLICES: BENNY "THE BONE", BAILEY,
BRIAN, CLAUDIA, KENDYL, CONNOR
PET PEEVE: LOSING HIS BONE TO HIS BROTHER BAILEY

RILEY

Some tough bitch! *Yo man! When you hear the story of neglected, mistreated Lucy, who was shot, run over and found staggering with bleeding feet at the side of the road you'd be excused for thinking Lucy was a character out of an Eminem song or Martin Scorsese movie. But no, this is the true story of the beagle that now resides at Cooper Vineyards in Virginia.*

The kind folk at Cooper Vineyards found the battered and bleeding Lucy at the side of the road and immediately took her to hospital. After successful surgery, lots of love and dog treats at her new home, she shows little effects of the torment of her previous life. Apart from the occasional limp, caused by the remaining bullets lodged in her leg, she remains an active, smart, happy and very lucky girl.

As the days go by, the distant memories of her past must seem more and more like a nightmare or a scene from a bad Hollywood movie. But at least this story has a happy ending.

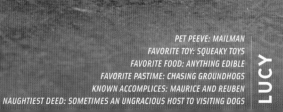

PET PEEVE: MAILMAN
FAVORITE TOY: SQUEAKY TOYS
FAVORITE FOOD: ANYTHING EDIBLE
FAVORITE PASTIME: CHASING GROUNDHOGS
KNOWN ACCOMPLICES: MAURICE AND REUBEN
NAUGHTIEST DEED: SOMETIMES AN UNGRACIOUS HOST TO VISITING DOGS

LUCY

MICKEY

FAVORITE FOOD: CHEESE

*PET PEEVE: OTHER DOGS
THAT STEAL HIS FOOD*

KNOWN ACCOMPLICE: KOALA

*NAUGHTIEST DEED: REFUSING
TO BE HOUSE BROKEN*

FAVORITE TOY: ANY SQUEAKY TOY

FAVORITE PASTIME: GOING ON WALKS

PET PEEVE: MOTORCYCLES
FAVORITE FOOD: LAMB BONES
KNOWN ACCOMPLICE: COOKIE
FAVORITE TOY: FIJI WATER BOTTLE
FAVORITE PASTIME: CHASING THE HORSES
NAUGHTIEST DEED: CHEWING THE CORNERS OF THE TEAK FURNITURE

COCO

ANNA BELLE

FAVORITE TOY: FRISBEE
KNOWN ACCOMPLICE: ZACH
PET PEEVE: AIR BEING BLOWN IN HER FACE
FAVORITE FOOD: ANYTHING YOU ARE EATING
NAUGHTIEST DEED: CHEWING THE STICK SHIFT IN THE CAR
FAVORITE PASTIMES: CATCHING FRISBEE AND SWIMMING IN THE BAY

PET PEEVE: GETTING A BATH
FAVORITE FOOD: FILET MIGNON
FAVORITE TOY: ANY KIND OF BONE
FAVORITE PASTIME: CATCHING CHEESE OFF HIS NOSE
NAUGHTIEST DEED: STEALING STEAKS FROM CATERERS

RODEO

BUBBA

FAVORITE FOOD: CHICKEN
KNOWN ACCOMPLICE: OTIS
FAVORITE TOY: AN OLD ROPE
FAVORITE PASTIME: SMELLING THE FLOWERS
PET PEEVE: NOT GETTING ALL THE ATTENTION
NAUGHTIEST DEED: RUINING A WOMAN'S
SUEDE PANTS WITH HIS MUDDY PAWS

PET PEEVE: WALKING STICKS
FAVORITE FOOD: RAW HAMBURGER
KNOWN ACCOMPLICES: SAMMY AND BUBBA
FAVORITE TOY: SPLOTCH – SQUEAKY GREEN TOY
NAUGHTIEST DEED: ATTACKING A SEEING EYE DOG

PINOT NOIR

OWNER: ELIZABETH GRUBEL | MINIATURE SCHNAUZER 3 | DEE VINE WINES SAN FRANCISCO CA | 125

JAN, HARRY POTTER AND DAVID

Champion Winelight Potter. *Rumor has it that people will go to great lengths to appear in our Wine Dogs book. But when we heard about David and Jan Bruce, we couldn't have hoped for better candidates for inclusion in the USA Edition.*

David Bruce is a bastion of the wine industry, with over 40 vintages under his belt and responsible for some of the country's most wonderful pinot noirs. He is widely regarded as one of Santa Cruz's top winemakers.

Jan's fame is also without peer within her field of dog breeding. Her skills and keen eye for dog talent led her to be named Spaniel Breeder of the Year in 2005 by the American Spaniel Club and the American Kennel Club. And it appears that Champion Winelight Potter, or Harry, as he is known to his friends, is just as highly awarded as David's wines.

So what do you get when you cross a legendary winemaker with a legendary dog breeder? Well – the perfect wine dog marriage of course.

PET PEEVE: BATHS
FAVORITE FOOD: COOKIES AND WINE
FAVORITE TOY: WINE CANES AFTER PRUNING
NAUGHTIEST DEED: LIFTING HIS LEG ON A JUDGE
FAVORITE PASTIMES: SHOWING OFF AND BEING AN AMERICAN CHAMPION

HARRY POTTER

MAYA

FAVORITE TOY: BUNGIE TOY
PET PEEVE: UNSOCIAL DOGS
FAVORITE FOOD: RAW CHICKEN
FAVORITE PASTIME: THE PURSUIT OF FOOD AND EATING
NAUGHTIEST DEED: EATING 3 LB OF DEFROSTING LAMB

KNOWN ACCOMPLICE: HUGO
FAVORITE TOY: TENNIS BALLS
PET PEEVE: BEING LEFT ALONE
FAVORITE FOOD: GERMAN SAUSAGE
FAVORITE PASTIME: ROLLING IN THE MUD
NAUGHTIEST DEED: CHASING CHRISTIAN'S HORSES

DIEGO

FAVORITE TOY: A BALL

NAUGHTIEST DEED: JUMPING UP
TO KISS PEOPLE AND DIRTYING THEIR SHIRTS

FAVORITE PASTIMES: PLAYING WITH BOCCE BALLS,
CHASING SQUIRRELS, TURKEYS AND OTHER BIRDS

BORDER COLLIE BOCCE

by Melodie Hilton

Posip is bilingual. *She speaks Croatian and English, which is exactly what you might expect from the dog of Mike Grgich – a man who has awfully high standards both in his wines, and his dogs. Miljenko "Mike" Grgich was born in Croatia and is winemaker of internationally known Grgich Hills Cellar in St. Helena.*

Posip takes her name from a dry white wine that is produced on the island of Korcula. This wine is considered one of the top Croatian wines, and is frequently served at state and diplomatic banquets. Mike's own 1997 Posip from his Croatian winery was served at the United Nations.

Not only does she carry such a distinguished – and bi-continental – wine pedigree, but Posip is also an astute judge of character. Greeting new visitors with a polite wag of the tail, once a connection is made she is free with her kisses. If the greeting is not returned, however, Posip moves on to someone more deserving of her attention.

In her free time, Posip loves afternoon bocce ball games with Mike and learned to play by nudging the heavy boccia around and eventually back to Mike. "We are partners now," he said. Her sport is not confined to small hard balls; she loves an enormous bouncing ball which she tries to corner and then attempt a hysterically funny balancing act. "She has something special," Mike says.

When she is not playing lazy afternoon games or assisting Mike on wine-related business, she enjoys the views from the deck of their Calistoga home looking up the slopes of Mt. St. Helena – a view, Mike says, that is amazingly similar to that of his Croatian homeland.

MELODIE HILTON IS EDITOR OF WINECOUNTRY.COM AND OVER THE YEARS HAS WRITTEN ON A NUMBER OF WINE-RELATED TOPICS. SHE LIVES IN NAPA, CA WITH HER LAZY BEAGLE, A TERRIER-MIX THAT GROWLS AT PEOPLE WHEN THEY LEAVE, TWO KIDS, AND A STRAY TURTLE.

PET PEEVE: CATS
KNOWN ACCOMPLICE: MIKE
FAVORITE FOODS: MEAT AND FISH

FAVORITE FOOD: APPLE CORES
FAVORITE TOY: SQUEAKY BEAR
PET PEEVES: BATHS AND CAR RIDES
KNOWN ACCOMPLICES: MANDY AND SMOKEY
NAUGHTIEST DEED: DIGGING UP MOM'S FLOWERS
FAVORITE PASTIMES: PLAYING BALL AND HANGING OUT WITH CHRIS

BAXTER

MAGGIE

FAVORITE TOY: CORKS
PET PEEVE: SQUIRRELS
FAVORITE FOOD: BONES
FAVORITE PASTIMES: LONG RUNS IN THE
VINEYARD AND NAPS ON THE COUCH
NAUGHTIEST DEED: ENJOYING THE THANKSGIVING
PUMPKIN PIE WHEN NO ONE WAS LOOKING
KNOWN ACCOMPLICES: McKENZIE, DAISY AND CALLIE

FAVORITE TOY: BUNG
FAVORITE FOOD: BACON BITS
KNOWN ACCOMPLICE: JANE ROGERS
PET PEEVE: MAILMEN WITH BLACK SHOES
FAVORITE PASTIME: RIDING IN THE GATOR
NAUGHTIEST DEED: HIDING CHEESE IN ALL THE UPHOLSTERY

SPANKY

OWNERS: MARY AND MIKE COLHOUN | JACK RUSSELL TERRIER, 14 | **LANDMARK VINEYARDS**, KENWOOD, CA | 145

MURRAY

FAVORITE FOOD: GOAT'S CHEESE
FAVORITE TOY: A DIRTY TENNIS BALL
KNOWN ACCOMPLICES: ARGUS AND RUBY
FAVORITE PASTIME: ENJOYING FINE CUISINE
PET PEEVE: PEOPLE NOT THROWING THE BALL BACK
NAUGHTIEST DEED: PULLING OUT THE FIRST VINE THAT WAS PLANTED

HIGHTOWER CELLARS BENTON CITY, WA | LABRADOR 4 | OWNERS: TIM AND KELLY HIGHTOWER

PET PEEVE: BEING LEFT ALONE
NAUGHTIEST DEED: GORGING HIMSELF
ON HIGH-PROTEIN CAT FOOD
KNOWN ACCOMPLICES: KUJO AND MAGGIE
FAVORITE FOOD: BEEF BONES AND CAT'S FOOD
FAVORITE PASTIME: CHASING RABBITS IN VINEYARDS
FAVORITE TOY: LAVATORY RUBBISH AND FINE FURNITURE

SIMBA

HUNTER

PET PEEVE: BATHS
FAVORITE TOY: BALL
FAVORITE FOOD: EVERYTHING
FAVORITE PASTIMES: HUNTING AND FETCHING
NAUGHTIEST DEED: CHEWING UP A CELL PHONE
KNOWN ACCOMPLICE: WENDY THE BLUETICK HOUND

FAVORITE TOY: OCTOPUS
FAVORITE FOOD: GREENIES
PET PEEVE: BEING TOLD NO
FAVORITE PASTIME: HUNTING GOPHERS
NAUGHTIEST DEED: DROPPING GAS BOMBS
KNOWN ACCOMPLICES: UMA, RUDY, JAKE AND MARLEY THE CAT

SHASTA

KNOWN ACCOMPLICE: OWEN

PET PEEVE: WINERY VISITORS
THAT DON'T THINK SHE'S CUTE

FAVORITE PASTIME: WALKING TO
BOUCHON BAKERY IN THE MORNING

FAVORITE FOODS: BRIE AND CAVIAR

NAUGHTIEST DEED: THROWING "PARTIES"
ON THE COUCH WHEN ALONE

MADDIE

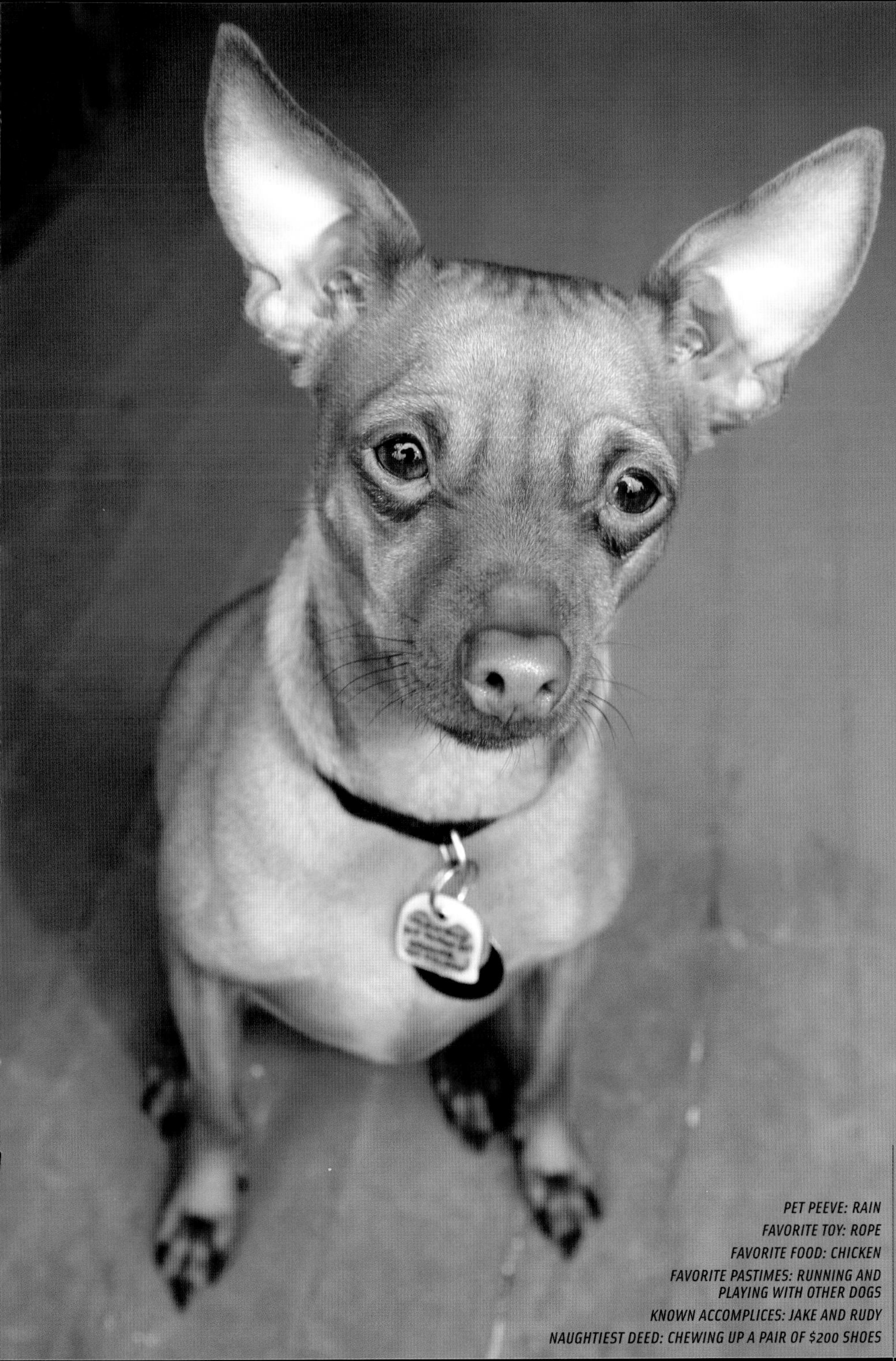

VALENTINO

PET PEEVE: RAIN
FAVORITE TOY: ROPE
FAVORITE FOOD: CHICKEN
FAVORITE PASTIMES: RUNNING AND PLAYING WITH OTHER DOGS
KNOWN ACCOMPLICES: JAKE AND RUDY
NAUGHTIEST DEED: CHEWING UP A PAIR OF $200 SHOES

OWNER: SUSAN L. SCARBROUGH | CHIHUAHUA X, 3 | **CASTLE VINEYARDS AND WINERY** SONOMA, CA

FAVORITE FOOD: GRAPES
FAVORITE TOY: BARREL BUNG
KNOWN ACCOMPLICES: RUBY AND V-MACK
NAUGHTIEST DEED: EATING A SACK OF FLOUR
FAVORITE PASTIME: SWIMMING IN THE RUSSIAN RIVER

CAMELLIA CELLARS HEALDSBURG, CA | GOLDEN RETRIEVER, 7 | OWNERS: CHRIS LEWAND AND BRUCE SNYDER

FAVORITE FOOD: TUNA FISH
KNOWN ACCOMPLICE: STARKIE
FAVORITE TOY: STUFFED RABBIT TOY
PET PEEVES: WATER, BATHS AND BEACHES
FAVORITE PASTIME: CHASING DEER AND LAYING UNDER THE COVERS
NAUGHTIEST DEED: DOING NUMBER TWOS ON THE BATHROOM FLOOR

MANGO

PET PEEVE: YOUNG PUPPIES
FAVORITE FOOD: RAW STEAK
FAVORITE TOY: A TENNIS BALL
KNOWN ACCOMPLICES: ZSA-ZSA, APOLLO AND WHITNEY
FAVORITE PASTIME: SAVING RABBITS FROM THE TRACTOR
NAUGHTIEST DEED: EATING THE CONTENTS OF A BURST PIÑATA

BOE

FAVORITE TOY: KONG
FAVORITE PASTIME: HIKING
PET PEEVE: BEING LEFT ALONE
NAUGHTIEST DEED:
UNRAVELING MARY'S KNITTING
KNOWN ACCOMPLICES: LUCIANO
AND KATIE SCARLETT
FAVORITE FOOD: MORNING MILK BONES

RALPH

PET PEEVE: ERIC GOING ON VACATION
FAVORITE PASTIMES: EATING HAMBURGERS
AND DIGGING WITH HIS ONLY FRONT LEG
FAVORITE TOY: CORKS FROM WINE BOTTLES
KNOWN ACCOMPLICES: MAZIE AND KONNIE
FAVORITE FOODS: HAMBURGERS AND SALMON
NAUGHTIEST DEED: USING HIS HANDICAP TO INVOKE PITY

PORT

PET PEEVE: *RABBITS*
NAUGHTIEST DEED: *PLAYING 'KEEP AWAY' WITH HER TOYS*
KNOWN ACCOMPLICE: *KONNIE*
FAVORITE FOOD: *DOGGIE BONES*
FAVORITE PASTIMES: *CHASING TENNIS BALLS AND TRAVELING WITH MIKE*

MAZIE

SABINE

PET PEEVE: THE CATS
FAVORITE TOY: HUGE BONE
KNOWN ACCOMPLICES: COYOTES
FAVORITE PASTIME: PLAYING CHESS
NAUGHTIEST DEED: CHASING
DEER THROUGH THE WOODS
FAVORITE FOOD: CABERNET SAUVIGNON
GRAPES, PREFERABLY AT 25 DEGREES BRIX

VOLKER EISELE FAMILY ESTATE ST. HELENA, CA | DOBERMAN ♂ | OWNER: LIESEL EISELE

PET PEEVE: *RAINY DAYS*
FAVORITE FOOD: *HOT DOGS*
FAVORITE TOY: *A TENNIS BALL*
KNOWN ACCOMPLICES: *BETSEY AND ROSIE*
NAUGHTIEST DEED: *RUNNING AWAY TO THE
STATE PARK TO STEAL CAMPERS' FOOD*
FAVORITE PASTIME: *WORKING IN THE VINEYARDS*

SCOOBY

ROSIE

PET PEEVE: BATHING
FAVORITE FOOD: CHEDDAR CHEESE
NAUGHTIEST DEED: EATING THE GARBAGE
KNOWN ACCOMPLICES: SCOOBY AND BETSEY
FAVORITE PASTIME: RUNNING THROUGH THE VINEYARDS
FAVORITE TOY: STUFFED ENGLISH SPRINGER SPANIEL TOY

PET PEEVE: BATHS
FAVORITE FOOD: ROASTED CHICKEN
KNOWN ACCOMPLICES: ROSIE AND SCOOBY
NAUGHTIEST DEED: STEALING THE BALL MID-GAME
FAVORITE TOYS: STUFFED TOY BEAR AND SOCCER BALL
FAVORITE PASTIME: CHEWING ON THE ALL-TERRAIN VEHICLE

BETSEY

JEAN LAFITTE

FAVORITE FOOD: CHEETOS
FAVORITE TOY: A TINY CHIHUAHUA
PET PEEVES: PERFUME AND HIGH HEELS
KNOWN ACCOMPLICES: HARVEY, TIPPY AND RUFUS
NAUGHTIEST DEED: RELIEVING HIMSELF ON THE SHOES OF OTHERS
FAVORITE PASTIMES: SUNBATHING AND LOUNGING UNDER THE COVERS

KNOWN ACCOMPLICE: MAX
FAVORITE PASTIME: WATCHING
NAUGHTIEST DEED: CHASING COWS
FAVORITE TOYS: RAWHIDE AND BONES
PET PEEVE: CRAIG AND VICKI LEAVING TOWN
FAVORITE FOOD: TREATS FROM WINERY GUESTS

POTTER

ZEPPLI

FAVORITE TOY: LIZARDS
PET PEEVE: GETTING A BATH
FAVORITE FOODS: COFFEE AND STEAK
FAVORITE PASTIME: CHASING WILD TURKEYS IN VINEYARDS
NAUGHTIEST DEEDS: STEALING WORKERS' LUNCHES AND PLAYING WITH RATTLESNAKES

EHLERS LANE

PET PEEVE: DIETS
FAVORITE FOOD: TACOS
FAVORITE TOY: A BARREL BUNG
NAUGHTIEST DEED: ROLLING IN THE COMPOST
FAVORITE PASTIMES: EATING TACOS AND KISSING
KNOWN ACCOMPLICES: EVERYONE IN THE TASTING ROOM

RIPLEY

PUCK

PET PEEVE: THE CAT
FAVORITE TOY: THE CAT
FAVOURITE PASTIME: BALANCING BISCUITS
FAVORITE FOODS: BIG MACS AND QUARTER POUNDERS
NAUGHTIEST DEED: GETTING TOO MUDDY IN THE VINEYARD

FAVORITE TOY: BALL
PET PEEVE: PEOPLE IN UNIFORM
FAVORITE FOOD: ZINFANDEL GRAPES
FAVORITE PASTIME: RIDING ON THE 4-WHEELER ATV
KNOWN ACCOMPLICES: LUCAS, SOPHIA AND MATTHEW
NAUGHTIEST DEED: BITING A FEDERAL EXPRESS MAN IN THE BUTT

"*I loathe people who keep dogs.
They are cowards who haven't got the guts
to bite people themselves.*"

─────── **AUGUST STRINDBERG**

HAROLD'S DOG
by Cole Danehower

Harold did not like dogs; *he hadn't liked them – so he said – since one bit him when he was an infant. If the subject came up, he'd show you a barely perceptible scratch (he called it a scar) just above his right elbow. "Damn cur took out two inches of skin," he'd say.*

In fact, animals in general didn't appeal to Harold, and some in particular caused him real trouble. He attributed the breakup of his marriage to his allergy to cats, he fought incessant battles against "those vile moles" in the vineyard, "cursed pesky" birds at harvest time, and in recent years, a few "vicious black bear brutes" that ravaged the vines at the edges of what he considered to be "his" vineyard.

Of course, Harold didn't much like people, either. He lived alone in a small old house at the far end of a 35-acre vineyard, hard up against the stony foothills of a boundary mountain in Southern Oregon. It was about as distant from the tasting room of the winery that employed him as it was possible to get and still be on the owner's land. Unfortunately, though, it was also closer to the bears, moles, and birds.

What Harold did like was grapevines, and he had a way with them. He'd fallen into the vineyard business seventeen years ago when a local farmer hired him to tend a newly planted vineyard. They both figured that fruit was fruit, and since Harold already knew all about peach orchards he could figure out how to grow good grapes. Implausibly, they were right.

As the vintages went by, Harold grew closer and closer to his grapes. He somehow seemed in touch with the rhythms of the vines and the earth, and the winemakers who purchased the fruit complimented him and the owner, and told the owner that he could never let Harold go because nobody else could grow grapes as good as he could.

For Harold, it had been a satisfying career. He got paid to work among the vines he loved, and he could live his solitary life comfortably insulated from the people he loathed. Even when the old farmer sold the vineyard to an absentee couple from Northern California, who built a small but fancy winery and what they called a "visitor facility", Harold's life continued as before: they enthusiastically maintained Harold's employment, only asking that he also be caretaker of the new building.

Of course, there were still the moles and birds and bears to plague him, but at least the new owners had hired a bright young woman to run the sales side of the winery so Harold didn't have to deal with the people that increasingly were visiting the new winery.

One early spring morning, when Harold was walking through the vineyard to go and unlock the tasting room before business hours began, he was unpleasantly brought to a sudden stop. Standing there in front of him between the vine rows was a dog.

"Shoo!" he shouted. "Get on. Go! Get away."

He didn't know what kind of dog it was. It had a long butterscotch-colored coat and a gangly pink tongue that dangled off the side of his mouth, pulsing with the dog's breath and threatening to get caught up in the jangle of sharp white teeth that showed so clearly.

The more Harold shouted at the dog, the faster it seemed the dog's tail wagged. When Harold tried lunging toward it threateningly, the dog just jumped back and wagged more fiercely.

By the time Harold got up to the winery, he had realized he wouldn't be able to shake the dog – it just followed behind him, at a safe distance. Harold thought about throwing a rock at it, but decided if he ended up hurting the dog it would just lie there yelping, and then he'd have to do something about it, so he decided to just ignore it.

When the tasting room woman came in that day, she went right over to the dog and petted it, got it a dish of fresh water, and found some old crackers to feed it. The next day, things pretty much repeated itself. And the next. And many more following that.

Weeks went by; vine leaves unfolded, grape flowers bloomed, and clusters began to swell. A shiny water bowl and painted dog dish appeared on the tasting room patio, a couple of old straw bales were made into a makeshift dog house on the building's side, and visitors billed and cooed around the dog as they sat and sipped their wine samples.

This was all fine with Harold. Except for meeting up with the dog in the vine rows each morning, he had no interaction with it. He never saw it during the daytime or at night, he knew it had acquired a name, but he refused to remember it, it never asked him for attention or affection, and Harold ignored the dog when he saw it in the vineyard – it had become a background feature of the landscape to Harold.

That all changed late one evening about three weeks after veraison.

The cool air from the top of the mountain behind the vineyard had begun slumping down across the grape rows, lightly chilling the warmth of the day. The sun was well behind more distant hills and the sky was turning a vibrant cobalt blue.

Harold was finishing an inspection of the vines when he heard what sounded like the noise of crashing underbrush coming from the near end of the vineyard, over toward his house. It was not a noise he had heard before, and curious, he began walking toward it. And then running.

There was suddenly the sound of barking and growling all at once, and thrashing noises of violence. Harold thought about ducking into the house to get his gun, but realized it was back in the closet, unloaded, and would be of little help in the immediacy of the ruckus.

Running, he turned the end of a vine row and suddenly stopped. Three rows down, just at the end, were two black bears being held at bay by the yelping, howling, barking dog. The dog's tail was sharp in the air, the fur stood up on its back, its feet were widely planted, and it was barking in a machine-gun rhythm.

Harold was transfixed. The slow and eager vineyard dog that so loved being petted by tasting room patrons was now a banshee virtually attacking two bears who were intent on getting nearly ripe grapes from Harold's vines.

The mangy thing was saving his grapes!

Suddenly one of the bears took a fast step toward the dog, testing its defense of the vines. The dog launched itself at the bear, rising off the ground and sinking its teeth into the furry flesh just above its right leg. The bear let out a scream and whirled around with its other leg, firmly smacking the dog dead on its side, sending it flying some feet before it crashed into the dirt while Harold stared on.

But the dog's attack had been enough for the bears. With a lumbering gait and a reluctant growl, they each turned back toward the underbrush and retreated to the rocky face of the foothills.

Harold rushed to the dog's side. It lay still. He could see no marks, but it was lifeless. Yet it couldn't be dead. It couldn't be ... not after having saved Harold's grapes ...

Suddenly Harold remembered playing football as a kid. He recalled being hit by a big linebacker. He remembered lying dazed on the ground, puzzled and panicked at having the breath knocked out of him.

That was it! The dog's breath had been knocked out of it by the bear's punch. The dog had to get it back. Without thinking, Harold kicked the dog in the chest – not too hard. That was it! That was the shock the dog needed. Suddenly its mouth shot open and its tongue started pulsing and it grunted and gasped for breath. It was back. It was breathing.

Some years later, Harold fell ill and died. There was a small funeral, and a few older winemakers came out to pay their respects.

There had been a problem, though, after Harold died. When people came up to Harold's house, they were confronted by his dog – that old stray he had picked up some years back. He'd even built that odd-looking house for the dog, right there on the front porch.

The dog wouldn't let anyone up the stairs when they approached. It just stood there on the front porch, tail sharp in the air, the fur standing up on its back, its feet widely planted, and it wailed in a low lamenting rhythm.

COLE DANEHOWER IS A JAMES BEARD FOUNDATION JOURNALISM AWARD-WINNING WINE AND FOOD WRITER, FOUNDER OF THE *OREGON WINE REPORT*, CO-PUBLISHER OF *NORTHWEST PALATE* MAGAZINE, AND IS OWNED BY MONTY, AN EXCEPTIONALLY INTELLIGENT AND RAMBUNCTIOUS CHOW/GOLDEN RETRIEVER MIX.

SHU-SHU

PET PEEVE: RABBITS
FAVORITE TOY: STUFFED RABBIT
NAUGHTIEST DEED: BEING STUBBORN
FAVORITE PASTIME: SLEEPING IN A LAP
KNOWN ACCOMPLICES: LIBERTY AND SADIE
FAVORITE FOODS: DOGGY BISCUITS AND BACON

FAVORITE TOY: BOBBI
PET PEEVE: STAYING HOME
NAUGHTIEST DEED: HIDING
BRAS IN THE GARDEN
FAVORITE PASTIME: CHASING
LINO'S TRUCK TO WORK
KNOWN ACCOMPLICES: LASSIE AND COBY

RIVA

FAVORITE TOY: PINK PIG
KNOWN ACCOMPLICE: CODY
FAVORITE FOOD: CHOCOLATE
NAUGHTIEST DEED: EATING MARK'S CHOCOLATE
PET PEEVES: HAVING A BATH AND HIS NAILS CLIPPED
FAVORITE PASTIME: RUNNING, RUNNING AND RUNNING

NAUGHTIEST DEED: THIEVING
FAVORITE FOOD: RAWHIDE BONES
PET PEEVE: HAVING HER PAWS TOUCHED
FAVORITE TOY: A SILICON WINE BARREL BUNG
FAVORITE PASTIME: RIDING IN THE PICKUP TRUCK

HALLIE

FIGEAC

FAVORITE TOY: A TENNIS BALL
KNOWN ACCOMPLICE: SHADOW
FAVORITE FOOD: TAYLOR'S BURGERS
PET PEEVE: HAVING HIS NAILS TRIMMED
FAVORITE PASTIME: HIDING BONES IN THE GARDEN
NAUGHTIEST DEED: CHEWING ON SHOES AND SUNGLASSES

FAVORITE FOOD: BEEF BONES
KNOWN ACCOMPLICES: RAE AND CLAY
NAUGHTIEST DEED: PEEING ON THE BED
FAVORITE TOYS: CHEW TOY, OLD VINE CLIPPINGS AND THE CAT
FAVORITE PASTIMES: PLAYING WITH CLAY AND SLEEPING ON BEDS

BRICK

DILLON

FAVORITE TOY: TUG OF WAR
NAUGHTIEST DEED: STEALING THE
BABY BOTTLE FROM THE BOSS'S BABY
FAVORITE FOOD: ANYTHING EXCEPT OLIVES
FAVORITE PASTIMES: SLEEPING IN THE
TASTING ROOM AND GREETING CUSTOMERS

ELK COVE VINEYARDS GASTON, OR | GOLDEN RETRIEVER, 12 | OWNER: KATHY KENNEDY

CODY

FAVORITE FOOD: TREATS
FAVORITE TOY: MAGGIE
PET PEEVE: LOUD NOISES
FAVORITE PASTIME: SLEEPING
KNOWN ACCOMPLICE: MAGGIE
NAUGHTIEST DEED: TAKING FOOD FROM THE TABLE

MAGGIE

FAVORITE TOY: CODY
FAVORITE FOOD: TREATS
KNOWN ACCOMPLICE: CODY
PET PEEVE: VACUUM CLEANER
FAVORITE PASTIME: RUNNING WILD
NAUGHTIEST DEED: TEARING UP EVERYTHING IN SIGHT

TRIXIE

FAVORITE FOOD: GRAPES
PET PEEVE: PRINCESS THE CAT
NAUGHTIEST DEED: GIVING ATTITUDE
KNOWN ACCOMPLICES: DIANA, SCRAPPY, HAAS AND ANDY
FAVORITE TOYS: A ROCK OR ANOTHER SMALL OBJECT TO YODEL WITH
FAVORITE PASTIME: WAITING FOR WINERY CUSTOMERS TO PET HER BELLY

FAVORITE TOY: STUFFED BEAR
PET PEEVE: SUDDEN LOUD NOISES
FAVORITE FOOD: DRIED CHICKEN STRIPS
KNOWN ACCOMPLICES: THE NEIGHBOR'S CATS
FAVORITE PASTIME: SAYING HELLO TO CHILDREN
NAUGHTIEST DEED: HUMPING THE STUFFED BEAR

GYPSY RAIN

JACKIE BROWN

FAVORITE FOOD: APPLES
FAVORITE TOY: ROPE TOY
KNOWN ACCOMPLICES: SHE WORKS SOLO
PET PEEVE: ANYTHING OR ANYONE THAT MOVES FAST
NAUGHTIEST DEED: HIDING HER BONES INSIDE THE HOUSE
FAVORITE PASTIMES: EATING GREENIES AND CHASING BIRDS

FAVORITE TOY: ANY STICK
PET PEEVE: EAR CLEANING
FAVORITE FOOD: BEEF JERKY
NAUGHTIEST DEED: BRINGING
DUCKS INTO THE WINERY OFFICE
FAVORITE PASTIME: DIGGING OUT GOPHERS

RILEY

SCOOBY

FAVORITE FOOD: FIGS
KNOWN ACCOMPLICE: SCRAPPY
FAVORITE TOYS: STICKS AND TENNIS BALLS
PET PEEVE: OTHER CRITTERS ON THE PROPERTY
FAVORITE PASTIMES: HANGING AROUND PARKING LOTS AND GREETING CARS

FAVORITE TOY: JULIO'S HAND
FAVORITE FOOD: CHICKEN BREAST
PET PEEVE: THE COLD WINTER DAYS IN NAPA
FAVORITE PASTIME: HELPING JULIO INSPECT THE VINEYARDS
NAUGHTIEST DEED: PEEING ON THE PHOTOGRAPHER'S CAMERA BAG

GINA

LADY SHADY GROVE

PET PEEVE: COWS
FAVORITE FOOD: BROCCOLI
FAVORITE PASTIME: SLEEPING
KNOWN ACCOMPLICE: BEAR-B-Q
FAVORITE TOY: LIVE GOPHERS OR LIZARDS
NAUGHTIEST DEEDS: FOLLOWING HER BROTHER
THROUGH A BROKEN WINDOW, CAUSING 28 STITCHES

FAVORITE FOOD: STEAK
FAVORITE TOY: MAKENA
PET PEEVE: GETTING
PEDICURES AT THE GROOMERS
NAUGHTIEST DEED: CHEWING UP
JACKIE'S DESIGNER JEANS
KNOWN ACCOMPLICES: ROBERT,
JACKIE, JESSICA AND MAKENA
FAVORITE PASTIME: WAITING FOR
ROBERT TO COME HOME

ANDRE

TICK

FAVORITE TOY: ANY BONE
KNOWN ACCOMPLICE: TATE
FAVORITE FOODS: BONES AND SOCKS
FAVORITE PASTIME: HERDING ANYONE AND ANYTHING
PET PEEVE: MOST ANYTHING THAT WASN'T HIS IDEA
NAUGHTIEST DEED: HERDING TRAVIS'S YEAR-OLD DAUGHTER

MONGA ZIN

FAVORITE TOY: STUFFED SNAKE
FAVORITE PASTIME: BEING CUDDLED
NAUGHTIEST DEED: HELPING ROCKY ESCAPE
KNOWN ACCOMPLICES: ROCKY, WILEY AND TROI
PET PEEVES: BEING LEFT ALONE AND BEING LOCKED UP

ROCKY RESERVE

FAVORITE TOY: SQUEAKY BALL
PET PEEVE: HIS BROTHER WILEY
FAVORITE FOOD: CHICKEN JERKY
KNOWN ACCOMPLICES: MONGA AND TROI
FAVORITE PASTIME: GOING FOR WALKS IN THE PARK
NAUGHTIEST DEED: DIGGING UNDER THE FENCE AND ESCAPING

SHADOW

FAVORITE TOY: JOLLY BALL
FAVORITE FOOD: LIVERWURST
PET PEEVE: ANY OTHER ANIMAL
FAVORITE PASTIME: CHASING CATS
KNOWN ACCOMPLICES: KELLY AND JACKIE
NAUGHTIEST DEED: STEALING THE NEIGHBOR'S DOG'S TOYS

KNOWN ACCOMPLICE: MICHAELE
FAVORITE TOY: CABERNET OLD VINE
FAVORITE FOOD: PROSCIUTTO DI PARMA
NAUGHTIEST DEED: MOOCHING FROM VISITORS
PET PEEVE: WHEN TAREQ AND MICHAELE GO ON HOLIDAYS
FAVORITE PASTIME: GETTING BACK RUBS FROM WINERY GUESTS

RIO

SADIE

PET PEEVE: FLYING BIRDS
FAVORITE PASTIME: SINGING
NAUGHTIEST DEED: JUMPING ON CARS
FAVORITE TOYS: THE CATS, PINK AND FLOYD
KNOWN ACCOMPLICES: HENRY, SISSY, BUGGSY AND GRIFFIN

FAVORITE FOOD: PINOT NOIR GRAPES
KNOWN ACCOMPLICES: DANIEL AND JONI
FAVORITE TOYS: KONG BALL AND TENNIS BALLS
FAVORITE PASTIMES: GETTING MASSAGED AND HUNK WATCHING
PET PEEVE: PEOPLE WATCHING HER WHILE SHE DOES HER BUSINESS
NAUGHTIEST DEED: DUMPING HER WATER BOWL OVER WHEN SHE'S MAD

POWDER

OWNERS: DANIEL KROLCZYK AND JONI SMOKER | LABRADOR, 8 | **L MAWBY** SUTTONS BAY, MI   195

FAVORITE FOOD: SCRAPS
FAVORITE TOY: TENNIS BALL
KNOWN ACCOMPLICES: JAMES, HAAS, TRIXIE AND ANDY
FAVORITE PASTIME: RIDING IN GOLF CARTS WITH JAMES
NAUGHTIEST DEED: TAKING THE MOST COMFORTABLE CHAIR
PET PEEVE: BEING MOVED OFF THE MOST COMFORTABLE CHAIR

REGUSCI WINERY, NAPA, CA | LABRADOR, 5 | OWNERS: JIM AND DIANA REGUSCI

FAVORITE TOY: THE CAT
FAVORITE FOOD: HAMBURGER
FAVORITE PASTIME: SLEEPING
PET PEEVE: SHARING THE COUCH
KNOWN ACCOMPLICES: POLLY AND IVAN
NAUGHTIEST DEED: SLEEPING ON THE BED

PATCH

LOGAN

PET PEEVE: BATHS
FAVORITE FOOD: STEAK
FAVORITE TOY: RAWHIDE
KNOWN ACCOMPLICE: ROXIE
FAVORITE PASTIME: SNACKING ON MILK BONES
NAUGHTIEST DEED: ACCIDENTALLY KILLING A PET PARAKEET

CARMIE

FAVORITE FOOD: FRENCH FRIES
FAVORITE TOY: LOGAN'S RAWHIDE
PET PEEVE: SPRINKLERS IN THE YARD
NAUGHTIEST DEED: TIPPING OVER THE GARBAGE
IN THE KITCHEN AND DRAGGING IT AROUND
FAVORITE PASTIME: SNUGGLING UNDER COZY BLANKETS

KNOWN ACCOMPLICE: TIMBER
NAUGHTIEST DEED: EATING A WHOLE
STACK OF BILLS AND TONY'S IPOD
FAVORITE FOOD: BANANAS AND EGGS
FAVORITE TOY: TONY'S SHOES AND IPOD
PET PEEVE: NOT HANGING OUT WITH TONY
FAVORITE PASTIME: PLAYING WITH THE CELLAR CREW

TRIGGER

OWNER: TONY LEONARDINI | LABRADOR, 6 MONTHS | **WHITEHALL LANE WINERY** ST. HELENA, CA

KATIE SCARLETT

FAVORITE TOY: SQUEAKY TOYS
PET PEEVE: WILLINDA LEAVING
FAVORITE PASTIME: CHASING BIRDS
FAVORITE FOOD: RIPE CHARDONNAY GRAPES
KNOWN ACCOMPLICES: RALPH AND LUCIANO
NAUGHTIEST DEED: GETTING COVERED IN BURRS

STONY HILL VINEYARD ST. HELENA, CA | BRITTANY, 7 | OWNERS: PETER AND WILLINDA McCREA

JACK

KNOWN ACCOMPLICES: LARRY AND SADIE
NAUGHTIEST DEED: HUMPING HIS BLANKIE
PET PEEVE: BIG DOGS THAT SURPRISE ATTACK
FAVORITE TOY: PIGGIE THE SMALL STUFFED PIG
FAVORITE FOOD: TRADER JOE'S BEEF LIVER TREATS
FAVORITE PASTIMES: WRESTLING WITH LARRY THE CAT AND RUNNING IN CIRCLES

KNOWN ACCOMPLICE: VITA
FAVORITE FOOD: DUCK CONFIT
PET PEEVE: CATS THAT DON'T RUN
NAUGHTIEST DEED: BURYING MARY'S
NIGHTGOWN IN A FLOWER POT
FAVORITE PASTIME: A MOUNT VEEDER HIKE
FAVORITE TOY: WHATEVER IS THROWN TO CHASE

PERCY

JACK

FAVORITE TOY: KONG
KNOWN ACCOMPLICE: PETE THE WINERY CAT
PET PEEVE: NOT GOING TO THE WINERY EVERY DAY
FAVORITE PASTIME: ROAMING AROUND THE VINEYARDS
FAVORITE FOOD: CAT FOOD THAT HE IS NOT SUPPOSED TO EAT
NAUGHTIEST DEED: CHECKING OUT THE CAT'S BOWL EACH MORNING

FAVORITE TOY: ANY TOY THAT SQUEAKS
PET PEEVE: NOT GETTING HIS DINNER FIRST
FAVORITE FOOD: ANYTHING IN A PICNIC BASKET
FAVORITE PASTIME: HANGING OUT IN THE WINERY OFFICE
NAUGHTIEST DEED: CHASING GOLF CARTS AND THE PEOPLE IN THEM
KNOWN ACCOMPLICES: CINDY IN THE OFFICE, HAAS, SCRAPPY AND TRIXIE

ANDY

KONA

PET PEEVE: BATH
FAVORITE TOY: KONG
KNOWN ACCOMPLICE: RUBY
FAVORITE PASTIME: CHASING RABBITS
NAUGHTIEST DEED: EATING PIE OFF THE COUNTER

ETUDE WINES NAPA, CA | LABRADOR, 6 | OWNER: FRANCI ASHTON

FAVORITE TOY: A SOCK
KNOWN ACCOMPLICE: MASON
FAVORITE FOOD: EXPENSIVE CHEESE
FAVORITE PASTIME: SNUGGLING UNDER
THE COVERS WITH EMILY AND MASON
PET PEEVES: BEING WET AND BEING EYEBALLED
NAUGHTIEST DEED: EATING BARBARA'S CELL PHONE

SASHA

JACK

FAVORITE FOOD: GRAPES
FAVORITE TOY: RUBBER KONG
KNOWN ACCOMPLICE: RUBBER KONG
PET PEEVE: SPENDING THE NIGHT IN HIS KENNEL
NAUGHTIEST DEED: GETTING IN CUSTOMERS' CARS
FAVORITE PASTIMES: DESTROYING HIS TOYS AND CHASING BIRDS

FAVORITE TOY: RED FELT BONE
PET PEEVE: GETTING BRUSHED
NAUGHTIEST DEED: STEALING FOOD
OFF THE KITCHEN COUNTER
FAVORITE FOOD: MACARONI AND CHEESE
FAVORITE PASTIME: SITTING ON STEPHANIE
KNOWN ACCOMPLICES: SOPHIE AND STEPHANIE

SPENCER

BUCKETT

FAVORITE FOOD: BANANAS
PET PEEVE: BEING BRUSHED
FAVORITE TOY: STUFFED MOUSE
NAUGHTIEST DEED: STEALING COTTON
BALLS FROM THE COFFEE TABLE
KNOWN ACCOMPLICE: THE STUFFED MOUSE
FAVORITE PASTIME: SPENDING TIME IN JUSTIN'S LAP

FAVORITE FOOD: BIG CRUNCHIES
PET PEEVE: OYSTER CATCHERS
NESTING ON THE ROCKS OFFSHORE
KNOWN ACCOMPLICES: TOBY AND OATY
FAVORITE PASTIME: BEING A WINERY TOUR GUIDE

SPOT

PEARL

FAVORITE FOOD: PEOPLE FOOD
FAVORITE TOY: THE NEIGHBOR'S CAT
FAVORITE PASTIME: GREETING CUSTOMERS
KNOWN ACCOMPLICE: SIR FRANCIS DRAKE THE CAT
NAUGHTIEST DEED: BEING TOO ROUGH WITH NEWBORN KITTENS

PET PEEVE: BIRD CANNONS
FAVORITE TOYS: DOUG AND MELISSA
FAVORITE PASTIME: MOOCHING TREATS
KNOWN ACCOMPLICES: GAMAY ROUGE,
GUY NOIR, STELLA AND BONNIE
FAVORITE FOOD: TILLAMOOK WHITE CHEDDAR
NAUGHTIEST DEED: TRYING TO HELP DRIVE THE
FORD EXPLORER THROUGH A SNOWSTORM

TRUE BLEU

"*The noblest dog of all is the hot dog:
it feeds the hand that bites it.*"

——— **LAURENCE J. PETER**

WHINE DOGS

by Darryl Roberts

First, are we talking real dogs here? *The furry, shedding, barking kind? Or are we talkin' really bad wine that we wouldn't feed to our dogs? If it's the former, I don't know so much about real dogs (except the barking thing). But if it's the latter ... now that I know a lot about. Trust me. Some of the swill (trying to pass as wine) that we taste here at* Wine X Magazine *isn't fit for human consumption. A dog's consumption. Any consumption. I wouldn't even make vinegar out of it. Some of it is vinegar. Really bad vinegar. Some of it makes you think, "What the heck could a winemaker possibly do to grapes to make them taste this bad?" Honestly. It boggles the mind. It's as if a winery dog took a swim in the tank and left behind its calling card. It's terroir! No. It's really bad wine that tastes like dog crap! Sorry!*

Dogs? No, I'm a cat person. Got two. They eat. They sleep. They shred the furniture. But they're mine. And they're low maintenance. I leave for two weeks, come home ... they don't care. Dogs? Can't do that with dogs. You leave for two weeks and come home to a dog ... you'll see how much they care ... all over your floor. Cats? Mine are pissed that I woke 'em up. Give me that cat look: "Can't you see that I'm sleeping stupid?" Lucky they're cute or I'd eat 'em.

Dogs on the other hand ... what do I know about dogs? Well, I know they bark all frickin' night. At least the ones next door do. They smell ... they smell kinda like cheap French wine. Okay, I know. That's unfair. To dogs, of course. They drink beer. Not wine, though. At least I haven't seen any dogs drink wine. Do cats drink wine? Mine don't. Probably because I keep a bottle of New Zealand sauvignon blanc on the counter at all times. One whiff of that bottled cat piss and mine are out the door faster than fleas off a dead dog. Oops, sorry.

Dogs make great movies. Lassie Come Home. The Adventures of Rin Tin Tin. Men in Black II (the dog had all of the best lines, didn't he?) And Mondovino. Now there's a great dog movie. Wine dogs everywhere. In the vineyard. In the winery. In Michel Rolland's wallet. "Oxygenate those dogs!" Now that would've been worth watching! Parker's dogs fart. (Like to see that on a 100-point scale.) They're definitely oxygenated. The other dogs? They just obey their handlers: Aime Guibert and his dog Vanille; Antonio Cabezas and his dog Luther King; Robert Mondavi and his dog Luce. All loyal. Trustworthy. Roll over on command.

Come to think of it, I do have wine dogs. My feet are wine dogs. On wine press trips. Poor, tortured, tired dogs dragged through winery after winery, vineyard after vineyard. Another winery. Another vineyard. Why? They gotta show me their winemaking toys! Those tanks. Those barrels. That dirt, err, sorry, terroir! It's as if the winemaker thinks it's my first time to a winery. "Gee, really? That's a stainless steel tank? Wow. Thanks for pointing that out, Bill!"

Tortured, tired wine dogs.

Rappers. Some of them are wine dogs. Well, wine dawgs. "Yo. Pass dat bottle, dawg." Wait. Now that has a ring to it. I can see a national advertising campaign for wine around that: "Pass dat bottle, dawg." Honestly. Who's gonna forget that tag line. We hire Snoop Dogg, coupla good-lookin' hos and... Too much?

Well, the wine industry's been talking about reaching out to different demographics, right? Here's their chance. Let's face it. Anything's better than those Garanimal labels. You know the ones. Cute little fuzzy animal labels. Puppies. Kitties. Freakishly large roosters. Yeah, like a 20-something's gonna buy a product that's been purposely dumbed down for them. Might as well state on the label: "Wine's too complicated for you. Therefore, we fashion our bottles with cute animals, one-syllable names, then fill them with overly bland crap that we can't sell under our regular label 'cause you won't know the difference." Good thinkin', dawgs.

And what about that enigma the Wine Market Council created a coupla years ago? You know the wine dog, "Wine: Since 6,ooo BC." (Insert finger down throat.) Yeah, yeah that'll get people runnin' for the wine isles. Nice job, morons. The least you could've done is gotten the tag line right. It should've been, "Wine: It's really old, just like the people that drink it." Now if that ain't the doggoned truth.

I Googled "dogs" 'cause I wanted to see where "wine dogs" came up on the list. I got: Dogs & Puppies; Reservoir Dogs; About Dogs; Guide Dogs; Sound Dogs (Sound Dogs?); Dirt Dogs; Therapy Dogs; Dogs for the Deaf; Shop with the Big Dogs; Leader Dogs; Must Love Dogs; Working Dogs; Street Dogs; Vegetarian Dogs (really?); Zombie Dogs; Dancing with Dogs ... but no "wine dogs". But that's cool, 'cause I didn't get "... the dogs of war" or "Mad Dogs and Englishmen" or "Let us bang those dogs of Seville", so I guess "wine dogs" is in good company. Very good company.

Speaking of company, dogs make good company, don't they? No matter what your situation. Happy. Sad. Trying to eat dinner. They're always there. With those big, sad eyes. Cold nose. Drooling jowls. They don't care. They're just there for you. For your love. Your company. Any scrap that may fall on the floor. Well, not necessarily in that order. But that's not what's important. What's important is that they're always there. Like a red wine stain on your new white carpet, your dog is a constant reminder that you should've gone with the tile floor – makes it a lot easier to deal with the messes of life.

I guess, in the end, we all have our favorite wine dogs. Mine? A Chicago Red Hot with the works, and a nice glass of syrah. Now that's a wine dog!

DARRYL ROBERTS IS FOUNDER/PUBLISHER OF *WINE X MAGAZINE*. HE RESIDES IN SANTA ROSA, CA WITH HIS TWO CATS (AND THE NEIGHBOR'S BARKING DOGS).

LUCE

FAVORITE FOOD: CHICKEN
FAVORITE TOY: A PLUSH MOLE
PET PEEVES: DARKNESS AND RAIN
FAVORITE PASTIME: PLAYING WITH MALBEC
KNOWN ACCOMPLICES: ROBERT AND MARGRIT
NAUGHTIEST DEED: DIGGING INTO SHEETS AND PILLOWS

ROBERT MONDAVI WINERY OAKVILLE, CA │ HAVANESE, 5 │ OWNERS: ROBERT AND MARGRIT MONDAVI

FAVORITE FOOD: CHEESE
FAVORITE TOY: HIS CHUCKIT
PET PEEVE: BEING IGNORED
NAUGHTIEST DEED: EATING RACHEL'S SKI GOGGLES
KNOWN ACCOMPLICES: HAOLE, TERRA, MICK, LOLA AND GUS
FAVORITE PASTIMES: BALLS, SWIMMING AND CHASING STICKS

FRIDAY

FAVORITE FOOD: CHEESE
KNOWN ACCOMPLICES: MAX AND AMOS
FAVORITE TOY: STUFFED QUACKING DUCK
NAUGHTIEST DEEDS: BEGGING AND BEING CURIOUS
PET PEEVES: BAD HAIR DAYS AND BEING BRUSHED
FAVORITE PASTIMES: BALL RETRIEVING AND GETTING TREATS

ALFIE

FAVORITE FOOD: STEAK
FAVORITE TOY: TENNIS BALL
FAVORITE PASTIME: CHASING HIS TAIL
KNOWN ACCOMPLICES: ROARK AND ALFIE
PET PEEVE: OTHER DOGS COMING INTO HIS OFFICE
NAUGHTIEST DEED: TAKING THE STUFFING OUT OF STUFFED OBJECTS

MAX

OWNER: IRMA MUÑIZ | AUSTRALIAN SHEPHERD X, 7 | **CLOS DU VAL** NAPA, CA

MURPHY

PET PEEVE: SWIMMING
FAVORITE TOY: OTHER DOGS' COLLARS
FAVORITE FOODS: GRAPES AND PERSIMMONS
FAVORITE PASTIME: LEANING AGAINST PEOPLE
NAUGHTIEST DEED: REFUSING TO GET INTO THE CAR

SPOTTSWOODE ESTATE VINEYARD AND WINERY ST. HELENA, CA | LABRADOR, 2 | OWNER: MARY NOVAK

FAVORITE TOY: CHLOÉ THE CAT
FAVORITE FOOD: CHEESECAKE
PET PEEVE: TRACI LEAVING HIS SIGHT
KNOWN ACCOMPLICES: PAYTON AND RILEY
NAUGHTIEST DEED: EATING AN ENTIRE CHEESECAKE
FAVORITE PASTIME: SWIMMING IN THE WINERY POND

ROARK

QUEENIE

FAVORITE TOY: BED
KNOWN ACCOMPLICE: BILLY
PET PEEVE: ALL OTHER DOGS
NAUGHTIEST DEED: VOMITING
FAVORITE FOOD: CANNED FOOD
FAVORITE PASTIMES:
RUNNING AND WORKING CATTLE

KNOWN ACCOMPLICES: STEVE AND JIM
FAVORITE FOOD: ANYTHING YOU'VE GOT
PET PEEVE: OTHER DOGS AT HIS WINERY
FAVORITE TOYS: TENNIS BALLS AND STEVE
FAVORITE PASTIME: LOOKING FOR HIDDEN TREATS
NAUGHTIEST DEED: SCOOTING DOWN HILLS ON HIS BUTT

GUS

CALLISTO

FAVORITE TOY: KIDS
FAVORITE FOOD: CHEESE
KNOWN ACCOMPLICES: IO
PET PEEVE: MEN WITH BEARDS,
DARK GLASSES AND HATS
NAUGHTIEST DEED: STRIPPING SPENCER'S
BED AND CHEWING UP ALL THE BEDDING
FAVORITE PASTIME: CHASING THE KIDS IN THE VINEYARD

FAVORITE TOY: SQUIRRELS
PET PEEVES: CATS AND CATS
KNOWN ACCOMPLICE: RUBY
NAUGHTIEST DEED: STEALING STEAKS
FAVORITE PASTIME: CHASING SQUIRRELS
FAVORITE FOOD: ANYTHING LISA IS EATING

PET PEEVE: GETTING WET
KNOWN ACCOMPLICE: ZACK
FAVORITE FOOD: ANYTHING EDIBLE
FAVORITE PASTIME: CHASING LIONS
FAVORITE TOY: WHATEVER ZACK HAS
NAUGHTIEST DEED: COUNTER SURFING A WHEEL OF BRIE

OWNER: LISA ENRIGHT | RHODESIAN RIDGEBACKS X 5 AND 2 | **RUBICON ESTATE** RUTHERFORD, CA

THE FESS PARKER THEME

Fess Parker was a man,
Yes, a big man!
Sitting with his two poodles
And as tall as a mountain was he!

Fess Parker was a man,
Yes, a big man!
And with his poodles on guard
Was as tough as a mighty oak tree!

But a peaceable, pioneer fella was Fess
And so his poodles would only offer a paw!
The singin'est, laughin'est, happiest dogs
Los Olivos ever saw!

(With apologies to Vera Matson)

FESS PARKER
BREED: TEXAN
FAVORITE PASTIME: ADMIRING ATTRACTIVE LADIES
FAVORITE FOOD: THE PARKER BURGER
FAVORITE TOY: 99 HUMMER
NAUGHTIEST DEED: KISSING PATRICIA BRADBURY
WHEN HE WAS THREE
PET PEEVE: TRANSPARENT POLITICIANS
KNOWN ACCOMPLICE: MARCELLA

JAKE

LUCY

PET PEEVE: STRANGERS
FAVORITE FOODS: TURKEY AND KIBBLE
KNOWN ACCOMPLICES: LUCY AND MARCELLA
NAUGHTIEST DEED: RAIDING THE WASTE BASKET

PET PEEVE: STRANGERS
KNOWN ACCOMPLICES:
JAKE AND FESS
FAVORITE PASTIME: SLEEPING
FAVORITE FOOD: COTTAGE CHEESE

FAVORITE FOOD: CHICKEN STRIPS
FAVORITE TOY: FUZZY TEDDY BEAR
FAVORITE PASTIME: GUARDING BONES
NAUGHTIEST DEED: POOPING IN THE HOUSE
KNOWN ACCOMPLICES: LUCY AND MAURICE
PET PEEVE: BEING SEPARATED FROM HIS MOMMA

COOPER VINEYARDS LOUISA, VA | POODLE, 10 | OWNER: JACQUE HOGGE

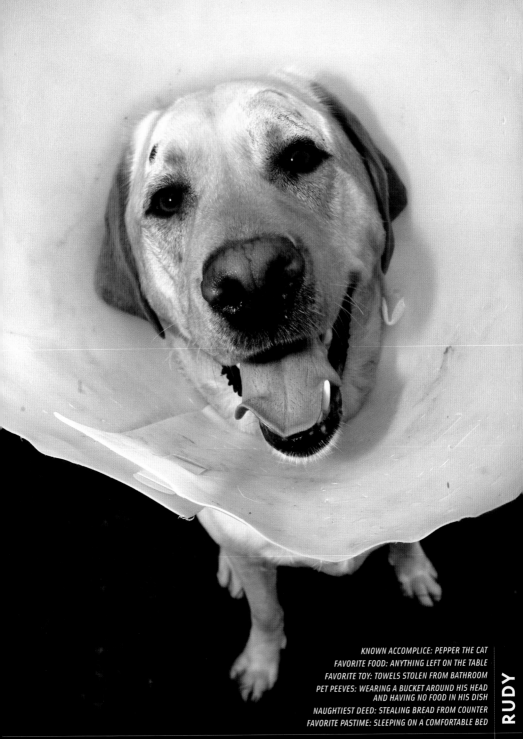

KNOWN ACCOMPLICE: PEPPER THE CAT
FAVORITE FOOD: ANYTHING LEFT ON THE TABLE
FAVORITE TOY: TOWELS STOLEN FROM BATHROOM
PET PEEVES: WEARING A BUCKET AROUND HIS HEAD
AND HAVING NO FOOD IN HIS DISH
NAUGHTIEST DEED: STEALING BREAD FROM COUNTER
FAVORITE PASTIME: SLEEPING ON A COMFORTABLE BED

RUDY

BUDDY

FAVORITE TOY: SHEEPSKIN SQUEAKY TOY
FAVORITE FOODS: JERKY TREATS AND CHICKEN GIBLETS
KNOWN ACCOMPLICES: REBEL THE HORSE AND TUX THE CAT
FAVORITE PASTIME: HANGING OUT WITH ANYONE WHO'S HUMAN
NAUGHTIEST DEED: EATING A CHOCOLATE CAKE FOUND IN THE TRASH
PET PEEVE: BEING CALLED TO COME HOME WHEN HE'S OUT EXPLORING

CARHARTT VINEYARD AND WINERY SOLVANG, CA | TOY RAT TERRIER 8 | OWNERS: MIKE AND BROOKE CARHARTT

PET PEEVE: SQUIRT BOTTLES
KNOWN ACCOMPLICE: CHARLIE
FAVORITE FOOD: CHICKEN BACKS
FAVORITE TOY: GIANT POOH BEAR
NAUGHTIEST DEED: IMPERSONATING A CHUPACABRA
FAVORITE PASTIME: GNAWING ON STUFFED POOH BEAR'S HEAD

PHOEBE

SAMMY

KNOWN ACCOMPLICE: PINOT
PET PEEVE: HAVING HIS PHOTO TAKEN
FAVORITE PASTIME: SWIMMING IN THE LAKE
FAVORITE TOYS: PHOTOGRAPHERS AND CHEESE
FAVORITE FOOD: BACON CHEESE BURGER FROM TAYLOR'S
NAUGHTIEST DEED: STEALING A GIANT WHEEL OF CHEESE AT A BLACK-TIE WINERY AFFAIR

QUINTESSA RUTHERFORD, CA | DALMATIAN / LABRADOR X, 9 | OWNER: AARON POTT

TUCKER

PET PEEVE: BATH TIME
KNOWN ACCOMPLICE: SUNNY THE CAT
FAVORITE PASTIME: RIDING IN THE TRUCK
FAVORITE TOY: ANYTHING YOU THROW AT HIM
NAUGHTIEST DEED: TEARING UP THE LAWN WHEN BORED

PET PEEVE: TAKING A BATH
FAVORITE TOY: THROW FLOATS
FAVORITE FOOD: DOG COOKIES
KNOWN ACCOMPLICE: SUNNY THE CAT
FAVORITE PASTIMES: SWIMMING AND FETCHING
NAUGHTIEST DEED: TEARING CAR COVERS OFF THE CAR

SUTTER

ELVIS

FAVORITE FOOD: BACON
FAVORITE TOY: BARREL BUNGS
PET PEEVE: CATS IN THE WINERY
KNOWN ACCOMPLICES: RUBY AND LULUBELLE
FAVORITE PASTIME: CHASING BUNGS IN THE CELLAR
NAUGHTIEST DEED: STEALING BUNGS OUT OF THE BARRELS

PET PEEVE: THE LAWNMOWER
KNOWN ACCOMPLICES:
MARGAUX AND JACQUI FALLON
NAUGHTIEST DEED: DESTROYING
A GREEN FEATHER BOA
FAVORITE PASTIMES: WALKING IN
THE PEAR ORCHARD AND CHEWING
FAVORITE TOY: OLD WORK GLOVES

OLIVE

MOLLY

FAVORITE TOY: BIRDS
PET PEEVE: RAINY DAYS
KNOWN ACCOMPLICE: OLIVE
FAVORITE PASTIME: A NAP AFTER A LONG RUN
NAUGHTIEST DEED: DIGGING IN THE GARDEN IN SEARCH OF PREY

PET PEEVE: CAMERAS
KNOWN ACCOMPLICE: MOLLY
FAVORITE PASTIME: PATROLLING FOR
RABBITS AND GOPHERS
FAVORITE TOY: HER SMALLER MOTHER MOLLY
NAUGHTIEST DEED: BADGERING MOLLY NONSTOP

OLIVE

FAVORITE FOOD: CHEESE
FAVORITE TOY: TENNIS BALLS
PET PEEVE: TAKING MEDICINE
KNOWN ACCOMPLICE: MIDNIGHT
NAUGHTIEST DEED: RUNNING AWAY
FAVORITE PASTIMES: CHASING LIZARDS AND SWIMMING

SUNSHINE

DONNA

PET PEEVE: RAIN
FAVORITE FOOD: CHICKEN
NAUGHTIEST DEED: EATING SHOES
FAVORITE PASTIME: EATING SHOES
FAVORITE TOY: CHEWY VUITON PILLOW
KNOWN ACCOMPLICES: SOOTS AND JOSH

PET PEEVE: BEING ALONE
FAVORITE FOOD: RIB EYE FILLET
FAVORITE PASTIMES: SWIMMING
AND SNOW PLAY
NAUGHTIEST DEED: CHASING CHICKENS
AND THEN EATING THEM

BAXTER

OTIS

FAVORITE FOOD: CRUNCHIES
KNOWN ACCOMPLICE: BUBBA
PET PEEVE: NON WINE DRINKERS
FAVORITE TOY: STUFFED TOY DUCK
NAUGHTIEST DEED: HIDING THINGS IN THE SOFA CUSHIONS
FAVORITE PASTIMES: EATING RED GRAPES AND BUMBLEBEES

FAVORITE TOY: BOOTS
KNOWN ACCOMPLICE: BRUCE
FAVORITE PASTIME: HUNTING
FAVORITE FOOD: MILK BONES
NAUGHTIEST DEED: CHEWING
BRUCE'S FAVORITE BOOTS
PET PEEVE: BEING ON A LEASH

SCRUT

ALLY

FAVORITE FOOD: *BABY GOOSE*
FAVORITE TOY: *FRESH GOPHER*
PET PEEVE: *NOT BEING TAKEN TO WORK*
FAVORITE PASTIME: *CHASING DEER AND GEESE*
NAUGHTIEST DEED: *BRINGING ROADKILL TO THE DINNER TABLE*

DOMAINE CHANDON YOUNTVILLE, CA | GERMAN SHORT HAIRED POINTER 4 | OWNER: RICK ALPINE

PET PEEVE: BIRDS CHIRPING
FAVORITE FOOD: WINE GRAPES
KNOWN ACCOMPLICES: TALON AND GUS
NAUGHTIEST DEED: MOVING OBJECTS UNDER THE BED
FAVORITE TOY: HIS SQUEAKY TOY THAT SAYS "THE VET"
FAVORITE PASTIME: RIDING ON GREG'S LAP ON THE FORKLIFT

BAILEY

SADIE

FAVORITE TOY: JAN

PET PEEVE: TOMATOES

KNOWN ACCOMPLICE: JAN

NAUGHTIEST DEED: RUNNING HOME FROM GRANDMA DOROTHY AND GRANDPA JOHN'S HOUSE

FAVORITE PASTIMES: RUNNING AND GOING ANYWHERE

FAVORITE FOOD: BEEF WELLINGTON

BACCHUS

KNOWN ACCOMPLICE: EROS
FAVORITE TOY: A STUFFED ANIMAL
FAVORITE PASTIME: HUNTING SQUIRRELS
PET PEEVE: SEEING THE SUITCASES COME OUT
NAUGHTIEST DEED: HIDING THE DIRTY CLOTHES OUTSIDE

FAVORITE TOY: OAK STICKS
FAVORITE FOOD: OAK STICKS
KNOWN ACCOMPLICE: BACCHUS
PET PEEVE: BEING CHASED BY A DUCK
FAVORITE PASTIME: AVOIDING DUCKS
NAUGHTIEST DEED: MARKING HIS TERRITORY INSIDE THE HOUSE

EROS

OWNERS: REBECCA AND PETER WORK | LABRADORS, 7 AND 4 | **AMPELOS CELLARS** LOMPOC, CA | 247

FAVORITE FOOD: BULLY STICKS
PET PEEVE: HAVING HER TAIL PULLED
FAVORITE PASTIMES: GOING TO WORK
WITH WARREN AND CATCHING GOPHERS
FAVORITE TOY: PLUSH SQUEAKY SOCCER BALL
NAUGHTIEST DEED: STEALING THE BABY'S SNACKS

DJANGO

FAVORITE FOOD: EVERYTHING
FAVORITE PASTIME: SLEEPING
NAUGHTIEST DEED: EATING SOCKS
FAVORITE TOY: SQUARE SQUEAKY TOY
PET PEEVE: GOING OUTSIDE IN THE RAIN
KNOWN ACCOMPLICES: BELLA, THE PROFESSOR AND CALLIE

BELLA

PET PEEVE: STRANGERS
FAVORITE FOOD: CHOCOLATE CHIP COOKIES
FAVORITE TOYS: THE PROFESSOR AND CALLIE
FAVORITE PASTIME: CHASING CARS DOWN DRIVEWAYS
KNOWN ACCOMPLICES: DJANGO, THE PROFESSOR AND CALLIE
NAUGHTIEST DEED: EATING 2 DOZEN CHOCOLATE CHIP COOKIES

OWNERS: TOM AND LAURIE SHELTON | STANDARD POODLES, 8 AND 3 | **JOSEPH PHELPS** ST. HELENA, CA

FAVORITE TOY:
OLD REINDEER
PET PEEVE: TAKING MEDICINE
KNOWN ACCOMPLICE: SCOOTY
FAVORITE PASTIME: FOLLOWING JEANNE AROUND
NAUGHTIEST DEED: TEARING UP THE LIVING ROOM CARPET

PET PEEVE: BATHS
FAVORITE TOY: BUNNIES
FAVORITE FOOD: CAT FOOD
NAUGHTIEST DEED: LICKING HIS PRIVATES
KNOWN ACCOMPLICES: ISABEL, VERDOT AND CHENIN
FAVORITE PASTIMES: BEING ADORED AND BARKING AT CRITTERS

MILO

BELLA

FAVORITE TOY: STUFFED SQUIRREL
NAUGHTIEST DEED: STEALING CORKS
KNOWN ACCOMPLICES: HAILEY AND LOREN
FAVORITE FOOD: AUSTRALIAN LIVER STRIPS
PET PEEVE: SQUIRRELS THAT SIT IN TREES AND TEASE HER
FAVORITE PASTIMES: PICKING GRAPES AND STEALING CORKS

PET PEEVE: *BEING ALONE*
FAVORITE FOOD: *RAWHIDES*
FAVORITE TOY: *PURPLE STUFFED ANIMAL*
KNOWN ACCOMPLICES: *LESLIE AND TOM WATSON*
NAUGHTIEST DEED: *EATING HALF A BAG OF DOG FOOD*
FAVORITE PASTIMES: *HIKING AND WATCHING ANIMAL PLANET ON TV*

MAMBO

PENNY

FAVORITE TOY: ROPE TOY
FAVORITE FOOD: PEANUT BUTTER
FAVORITE PASTIME: DIGGING UP ROCKS
NAUGHTIEST DEED: CHEWING UP SHOES
KNOWN ACCOMPLICES: COCOA AND JETTA

ZEAUX

BONNES MARES

FAVORITE FOODS: KIBBLE
AND JULIE'S ROAST CHICKEN
FAVORITE TOY: HER SQUEAKY STAR
KNOWN ACCOMPLICE: VIOLET THE CAT
NAUGHTIEST DEED: CHEWING HOLES IN UNDERWEAR
FAVORITE PASTIME: PLAYING WITH LAVERNE THE SHEEP
PET PEEVE: THE NASTY BITING DOG FROM DOWN THE ROAD

PET PEEVE: BEING ON A LEASH
KNOWN ACCOMPLICES: THE GOATS;
LEO, LARRY AND LITTLE LOUIS
NAUGHTIEST DEED: WANDERING TOO
FAR TO MAKE IT BACK HOME
FAVORITE PASTIME: CHASING RABBITS OR
THINKING ABOUT CHASING RABBITS
FAVORITE TOY: A FOOT TO RUB HER MUZZLE ON

CHU CHU

NAUGHTIEST DEED: PULLING ON JACK'S EARS
KNOWN ACCOMPLICES: STEVE AND CAROLE
PET PEEVE: HAVING HIS EYES CLEANED
FAVORITE PASTIME:
PLAYING WITH JACK
FAVORITE FOODS:
CHEESE AND CHEERIOS

LORD WENSLEYDALE WIGGLESWORTH

FAVORITE TOY: MISS LOUISA-BELLE
FAVORITE FOODS: WINE AND COTTAGE CHEESE
NAUGHTIEST DEED: HELPING HIMSELF TO CHEESE
FAVORITE PASTIMES: DRINKING WINE AND TAKING A BATH
PET PEEVE: BEING BUGGED BY TRUFFLES AND MISS LOUISA-BELLE

FANNIE MAE

FAVORITE FOOD: TRI TIP
FAVORITE PASTIME: PROTECTING BORDERS
NAUGHTIEST DEED: MANIPULATING PEOPLE
PET PEEVE: GETTING HER EARS CLEANED BY FLASH
FAVORITE TOY: EMPTY MILK CARTONS FROM RECYCLE BIN
KNOWN ACCOMPLICES: CHEETO AND THE NEIGHBOR'S JACKASS

FLASH

PET PEEVE: BATHS
FAVORITE FOOD: ANY KITCHEN SCRAPS
NAUGHTIEST DEED: SNIFFING CROTCHES
FAVORITE TOY: WATER HOSE WITH NOZZLE
FAVORITE PASTIME: CHASING THE
4-WHEELERS AND BITING THEIR TIRES
KNOWN ACCOMPLICES: LINDA,
GERHARD AND JULIA

FAVORITE TOY: TENNIS BALL
PET PEEVE: BEING SEPARATED
FROM HIS SISTER
NAUGHTIEST DEED: RUNNING
THROUGH THE GARDEN
KNOWN ACCOMPLICE: CALAFIA
FAVORITE FOOD: MEAT STRAPS
FAVORITE PASTIME: HUNTING LIZARDS

DIEGO

"*If your dog doesn't like someone,*
you probably shouldn't either."

——————— **JOHN WAYNE**

THE GHOST WINERIES

by Jack Burton

When you visit Northern California, *keep your eyes peeled – you might find a Ghost Winery.*

The term "Ghost Winery" refers to the many wineries established in the gold rush days before 1890, and then for reasons of vine disease or economics were left derelict.

Ghost Wineries are scattered here and there all around the wine country that lies north of the Golden Gate. Sometimes you see only the skeleton of an old estate, the falling down fruit trees and rows of ancient vines laid out like bleached bones around the footprint of an old stone structure. More often, nowadays, you might find a Ghost Winery fully restored and welcoming you to sample their delicious wines.

After the gold boom was over, and phylloxera had wasted the vines, the disaster of the Volstead Act doomed most of California's wineries in the early 1920s. A handful of vintners managed to survive Prohibition by one means or another, but the majority of family wineries simply failed. All the effort, the vines and the grand or simple structures were simply abandoned to the bats and the barn owls.

THE SPIRIT DOG OF GHOST WINERY COMMUNE

Uncle Buck says The Dog was "embrujado" (bewitched). Or perhaps he was a disembodied ancestor doing time back in our world. No one knew for sure, but Buck did know that the locals give him plenty of respect. Buck swears that The Dog was the same jimson weed-chewing, telepathic spirit being that had been in residence at the Ghost Winery since the early 1950s.

The Dog had come up from Texas with Ruby in an old green pickup. Ruby, The Dog and the truck had come part and parcel with the ruined old Northern California winery when Uncle Buck had purchased the place back in 1971.

Uncle Buck is a wildly bohemian fellow who had made a ton of money back in the 1960s by promoting free trade and entrepreneurship in Latin America. When Uncle Buck signed the papers for the Ghost Winery, he also became the Jolly Benefactor to a very spirited community that was developing around Ruby and The Dog. In its hippie heyday, over 30 people were calling the Ghost Winery home. They had all come by one connection or another to share a love of food and wine on Buck's old property. The place, the times, and the people of the commune were all ripe for new beginnings!

Ruby and The Dog provided practical and spiritual guidance as the new folks at Ghost Winery enthusiastically expanded Ruby's gardens and tended to the old vines, some of which had been planted in the days of the California Gold Rush. Ruby was locally famous for her winemaking, and was also a Medicine Woman held in high regard by her neighbors. She had developed a unique spiritual philosophy by borrowing freely from a bewildering number of cultural sources and combining them with her own Native American traditions. She had a detailed knowledge of plant medicine, and an ability to divine a clear course of action in times of trouble or confusion. It was also rumored that The Dog was her intermediary to the spirit realms. It was assumed The Dog had the ear of Coyote and was able to intervene at any gate or crossroad. Buck was convinced that The Dog could see over the horizon of our everyday, moment-to-moment existence. The Dog seemed always one step ahead, and Ruby consulted him regularly for all manner of advice.

One time back in the mid-1970s, on a visit to the commune at Ghost Winery, Buck found The Dog in his usual spot, sitting in the shotgun seat of Ruby's old truck.

His ears were up and he looked like he was ready to travel. Buck gave him a nice pat on the head and a good morning back scratch and asked:

"So, where do you think you're off to?"

The Dog looked him straight in the eye and crystal clear, this popped into his head: "It's time to gather the dreaming tea."... Now, that's a line to roll around in your brainpan a few times while the breakfast is cooking! Uncle Buck was only mildly surprised when Ruby announced at the table that she and The Dog were leaving for a few weeks on the road to gather the plants and herbs essential to her craft.

Ruby, The Dog and the truck are long gone now from Ghost Winery. The winery itself has a new name and new owners who are careful to preserve the good vibes the place had acquired. People say that the Spirit Dog's presence can still be perceived in the many generations of puppies descended from his years of carrying on with the neighbor dogs.

Just last week Uncle Buck was out to picnic in the vineyards when a winery dog ambled over to the table. He gave him a nice pat on the head and a scratch behind the ears. Buck was just thinking how this dog reminded him of Ruby's old Spirit Dog when the crazy thing looked him straight in the eye and, clear as a bell, this pops into his head: "Why that cabernet?"

Buck was only mildly surprised when he opened his picnic wine to find the bottle was hopelessly corked.

JACK BURTON IS A WELL-TRAVELED CHEF/AUTHOR WHO LIVES AND WORKS WITH HIS PICNIC PARTNER JANETTE IN HEALDSBURG, SONOMA COUNTY, CALIFORNIA. HIS AMUSING GUIDEBOOKS TO CALIFORNIA WINE COUNTRY AS WELL AS MANY STORIES, RECIPES AND PHOTOS CAN BE FOUND ONLINE AT WWW.SONOMAPICNIC.COM

PET PEEVE: BEING ALONE
KNOWN ACCOMPLICE: LUCE
FAVORITE TOYS: WINE CORKS
NAUGHTIEST DEED: CHASING TRACTORS
FAVORITE FOOD: SUMMERTIME FAMILY BBQS
FAVORITE PASTIMES: EATING LOW-HANGING FRUIT DURING HARVEST AND SNORING

PET PEEVE: BEING ALONE
FAVORITE TOY: CLOTH BONE
FAVORITE FOODS: ALPO AND EGGS
FAVORITE PASTIME: RIDING SHOTGUN IN THE TRUCK
NAUGHTIEST DEED: PEEING ON WELL-MANICURED LAWNS

HENRY

FRED

FAVORITE FOOD: CAT FOOD
FAVORITE TOY: A TENNIS BALL
PET PEEVE: BEING LEFT BEHIND
KNOWN ACCOMPLICES: AMBER AND BEAU-BO
NAUGHTIEST DEED: STEALING OTHER DOGS' TOYS
FAVORITE PASTIMES: SWIMMING AND GETTING PETTED

PET PEEVE: BATHS
FAVORITE PASTIME: WALKS
FAVORITE TOY: SQUEAKY BALL
KNOWN ACCOMPLICE: SHASTA
FAVORITE FOOD: CHICKEN TREATS
NAUGHTIEST DEED: STEALING UNDERWEAR FROM THE
LAUNDRY AND DISPLAYING IT ALL OVER THE LIVING ROOM

UMA

ROBO

FAVORITE TOY: ROCKS
FAVORITE FOOD: TACOS
PET PEEVES: BEING INSIDE AND RUNNING
KNOWN ACCOMPLICES: DANNY AND GUSTAVO
NAUGHTIEST DEED: PEEING ON TIRES AND LUNCHBOXES
FAVORITE PASTIME: SWIMMING IN THE POND DURING A RAINSTORM

FAVORITE PASTIME: EATING
FAVORITE TOY: A TENNIS BALL
KNOWN ACCOMPLICE: MARGE
FAVORITE FOODS: APPLES AND GRAPES
NAUGHTIEST DEED: TAKING ALL THE TRASH OUT OF THE TRASH CANS

FRITZ

PET PEEVE: BEING BAD.
NAUGHTIEST DEED: CROSSING THE RAILROAD
TRACKS AND BARKING IN DEFIANCE
FAVORITE FOOD: BITES OF KAY'S BREAKFAST BAGEL
FAVORITE PASTIMES: SLEEPING AND RABBIT CHASING
KNOWN ACCOMPLICES: COPPER AND SMOKEY THE CAT

FAVORITE TOY: KITTYMAN
KNOWN ACCOMPLICE: AUTUMN
PET PEEVE: BEING TOLD HE'S BAD.
NAUGHTIEST DEED: WALKING TO THE
NEIGHBOR'S FARM TO EAT CAT FOOD
FAVORITE PASTIME: GOING ON PICNICS
FAVORITE FOOD: FRESHLY BAKED BREAD

CHINOOK WINES PROSSER WA | GOLDEN RETRIEVERS 10 AND 5 | OWNERS: KAY SIMON AND CLAY MACKEY

FAVORITE FOOD: TREATS
FAVORITE TOY: CHEW BONE
PET PEEVE: HOT AIR BALLOONS
KNOWN ACCOMPLICES: WINSTON AND NIGEL
NAUGHTIEST DEED: TANGLING WITH A SKUNK
FAVORITE PASTIME: CHASING WILD TURKEYS, RABBITS AND SQUIRRELS

PUMPKIN

ROSÉ

FAVORITE FOOD: CHEESE
FAVORITE TOY: STUFFED TEDDY
NAUGHTIEST DEED: TAKING CHAP STICKS OUT OF PURSES
FAVORITE PASTIME: GREETING WINERY CUSTOMERS
KNOWN ACCOMPLICES: WINSTON, SCOOTER, OLIVER AND TOBY

PET PEEVE: BEES
FAVORITE FOOD: PIG EARS
FAVORITE TOY: DEER ANTLER
FAVORITE PASTIME: RUNNING NEXT
TO THE TRACTOR IN THE VINEYARD
NAUGHTIEST DEED: WHIZZING ON CUSTOMERS' TIRES
KNOWN ACCOMPLICES: CONNOR, ADAM AND CLAUDIA THE CAT

NEWMAN

PET PEEVE: THE LEAD
FAVORITE TOY: BIRDS
FAVORITE FOOD: LAMB CHOPS
KNOWN ACCOMPLICE: HIS MOTHER
NAUGHTIEST DEED: CATCHING BIRDS
FAVORITE PASTIME: WATCHING THE SHEEP IN THE VINEYARDS

KOON

PET PEEVE: FIREWORKS
KNOWN ACCOMPLICE: TEDDY
FAVORITE TOY: PINK FLAMINGO
NAUGHTIEST DEED: CHASING CATS
FAVORITE FOODS: PÂTE AND CHEESE
FAVORITE PASTIME: SOCIALIZING WITH THE WINERY PATRONS

BEAU D.

I AM A THERAPY DOG

COOPER

FAVORITE FOOD: CAT FOOD
PET PEEVE: BEING BRUSHED
KNOWN ACCOMPLICE: THOR
FAVORITE TOY: ANY STUFFED ANIMAL
FAVORITE PASTIMES: HANGING OUT
AND GREETING CUSTOMERS
NAUGHTIEST DEED: BRINGING DIRTY
PAWS IN THE WINERY OR HOUSE

FAVORITE FOOD: CHEESE
PET PEEVE: LARGE BIRDS
FAVORITE TOYS: CARS AND STICKS
FAVORITE PASTIME: CHASING WILD TURKEYS
KNOWN ACCOMPLICES: FRANK AND GIANCARLO

WOODY

MAX

PET PEEVE: *SHARING HIS FOOD*
FAVORITE PASTIME: *LOOKING FOR FOOD*
FAVORITE TOY: *BARBIE'S SQUEAKY DOG*
FAVORITE FOODS: *PEANUT BUTTER AND POPCORN*
KNOWN ACCOMPLICES: *KERRE AND ANNALISA*
NAUGHTIEST DEED: *EATING ANNALISA'S SURPRISE BIRTHDAY CAKE*

LUKE SKYWALKER (JEDI KNIGHT)

KNOWN ACCOMPLICE: REMINGTON
FAVORITE TOY: SHEEPSKIN BLANKET
FAVORITE FOODS: TURKEY NECKS AND LAMB BONES
NAUGHTIEST DEED: GETTING ON THE SOFA WHEN ALONE
PET PEEVES: BEING LOCKED OUTSIDE AND "THE DARK SIDE OF THE FORCE"
FAVORITE PASTIMES: VINEYARD WALKS AND FIGHTING FOR THE REBEL ALLIANCE

OLIVER

PET PEEVE: BEING ALONE
KNOWN ACCOMPLICE: TELLULAH
FAVORITE PASTIME: DIGGING HOLES
FAVORITE TOY: STUFFED SCHNAUZER DOLL
NAUGHTIEST DEED: RUNNING THROUGH THE HOUSE
WITH THE END OF THE TOILET PAPER IN HIS MOUTH

KNOWN ACCOMPLICE: LOBO

PET PEEVE: ALL OTHER DOGS

FAVORITE PASTIME: GETTING
MASSAGES FROM THE WINERY GUESTS

NAUGHTIEST DEED: BRINGING A BABY
JACK RABBIT TO THE FRONT DOOR

FAVORITE FOOD: GRILLED CHICKEN
BREAST, MARINATED IN LIME JUICE,
OLIVE OIL, GARLIC AND SAFFRON

BRUJA

TIYO

FAVORITE TOY: STUFFED HEDGEHOG
PET PEEVES: FIRECRACKERS AND DARTS
NAUGHTIEST DEED: EATING FORTUNE COOKIES
KNOWN ACCOMPLICES: POSSUM, EDDIE AND OTIS
FAVORITE PASTIMES: RUNNING IN THE VINEYARDS AND WRESTLING

PET PEEVE: RABBITS
FAVORITE FOOD: ICE-CREAM
KNOWN ACCOMPLICES: SAMMY AND ABE THE CAT
FAVORITE PASTIME: RUNNING AROUND THE VINEYARD
FAVORITE TOY: "BABY", A SMALL STUFFED BLACK AND WHITE DOG
NAUGHTIEST DEED: SLEEPING IN THE BED WITH BREE ANN AND CAMERON

SADIE

PET PEEVE: THE SUN
KNOWN ACCOMPLICE: PORT
FAVORITE FOOD: PORK RINDS
FAVORITE TOY: OLD SOCCER BALL
NAUGHTIEST DEED: DIGGING UP FLOWERS
FAVORITE PASTIME: FOLLOWING THE VINEYARD FOREMAN

TESS

EASTON VERANGELO

FAVORITE PASTIME: GREETING THE
TASTING ROOM CUSTOMERS
NAUGHTIEST DEED: ATTACKING PANTS LEGS
FAVORITE TOYS: STUFFED BALL AND ANKLES
PET PEEVE: NOT BEING THE CENTER OF ATTENTION
FAVORITE FOODS: CHEESE, STEAK AND LIMA BEANS

PET PEEVE: MEAN DOGS
FAVORITE FOOD: TREATS
FAVORITE TOYS: STUFFED ANIMALS
KNOWN ACCOMPLICE: MOMMA DOG
FAVORITE PASTIME: CHASING RABBITS
NAUGHTIEST DEED: STEALING
BONES FROM THE TRUCK

VERITAS VINEYARD AND WINERY AFTON, VA | BEAGLE, 8 | OWNERS: ANDREW AND PATRICIA HODSON

FAVORITE FOOD: CHEESE
FAVORITE TOY: TENNIS BALL
NAUGHTIEST DEED: ESCAPING
FAVORITE PASTIME: WALKS ON THE BEACH
KNOWN ACCOMPLICES: PAUL, LYNN AND LADY

MAJOR

CASEY

PET PEEVE: SHARP NOISES
KNOWN ACCOMPLICE: MAURICE
FAVORITE TOY: SQUEAKY MONKEY
FAVORITE FOODS: PIZZA AND FC SIENNA
FAVORITE PASTIME: CHASING CATS AND FLIES
NAUGHTIEST DEED: STEALING MAURICE'S TOYS

FAVORITE FOOD: GRAPES
KNOWN ACCOMPLICE: TAZ
PET PEEVE: DOING WHAT HE IS ASKED
FAVORITE PASTIME: GUARDING THE WINERY
NAUGHTIEST DEEDS: BEING STUBBORN AND TAKING HIS JOB TOO SERIOUSLY

KOBE

PET PEEVE: MEN
FAVORITE FOOD: POPCORN
NAUGHTIEST DEED: IGNORING DELLA
KNOWN ACCOMPLICES: WINERY GUESTS
FAVORITE PASTIME: PLAYING WITH CHILDREN

VERAMAR VINEYARD BERRYVILLE, VA | SHIH TZU, 6 | OWNER: DELLA BOGATY

FAVORITE TOYS: SLIPPERS AND ROCKS
FAVORITE FOOD: STEAK BONES FROM BARBARA
PET PEEVE: OTHER DOGS THAT HAVE A BAD AURA
FAVORITE PASTIMES: GREETING CUSTOMERS AND GETTING TUMMY RUBS
NAUGHTIEST DEEDS: SLEEPING ON FLOWERS AND PAWING DOOR TO GET IN

CASSIE

SHADOW

FAVORITE FOOD: STEAK
FAVORITE TOY: JACK'S DUCK
KNOWN ACCOMPLICES: STEVE AND CAROLE
FAVORITE PASTIMES: EATING AND SLEEPING
PET PEEVE: BEING PUT IN THE KENNEL FOR VACATION
NAUGHTIEST DEED: DOING SOMETHING WRONG AND BLAMING YOUNGER DOGS

PET PEEVE: FOUR-WHEELERS
FAVORITE FOOD: T-BONE STEAK
FAVORITE TOY: SQUEAKY HEDGEHOG
KNOWN ACCOMPLICE: GEORGIA THE CAT
FAVORITE PASTIME: CHASING SQUIRRELS
NAUGHTIEST DEED: PASSING GAS THEN LEAVING THE ROOM

NICK

OWNER: SETH MILLER | WEIMARANER, 3 | **KEN WRIGHT CELLARS** CARLTON, OR | 293

PICO

KNOWN ACCOMPLICE: CRAIG
PET PEEVE: HAVING TOENAILS CLIPPED
FAVORITE TOYS: CORKS, SOCKS AND CAT TOYS
FAVORITE FOODS: CHEERIOS, ROCKS AND CARROTS
NAUGHTIEST DEED: CHASING AND COLLIDING WITH A CAR
FAVORITE PASTIME: EATING LUNCH WITH THE PRODUCTION CREW

SCHRAMSBERG VINEYARDS CALISTOGA, CA | PUG, 3 | OWNER: MEGAN BESS

LUCY

KNOWN ACCOMPLICE: JOEY
FAVORITE TOY: A TENNIS BALL
PET PEEVE: OTHER ALPHA DOGS
NAUGHTIEST DEED: CLEANING THE CAT BOX
FAVORITE FOOD: VANILLA ICE-CREAM CONES
FAVORITE PASTIME: BUG PATROL IN THE POOL

KNOWN ACCOMPLICE: LUCY
FAVORITE TOY: KATIE THE KITTEN
NAUGHTIEST DEED: EATING KRISTEN'S BIRTHDAY
ROAST CHICKEN AND CUPCAKES
FAVORITE PASTIME: PARTICIPATING IN CONVERSATIONS

BODOG

WINE DOGS OF THE WORLD
by Ralph Steadman

In every winery there is a dog...

...not necessarily a nice dog, but always an integral part of the daily life and running of the winery. Not every dog makes me nervous, but I always treat each one with extreme caution. I never go to stroke a dog, but offer the back of my hand to be smelled, licked, and savored, like a fine wine. Winemakers want you to appreciate their dogs – just as much as their wines – as possessing pedigree of the highest kind. I offer for your experienced palates a selection of grand cru mutts.

LOUIS of MANKA's INVERNESS LODGE

WINE DOGS of the WORLD. No.1 CLOVIS DAURÉ

Clovis after a hard day, at the Château de JAU Winery crushing grapes.

Undiscovered pedigree breeds are impossible to find in the rarefied arena of the purebred dog world.

But, in the world of wine, many factors conspire to produce breeds that are impossible to imagine anywhere else. When a puppy is brought in to live as pet and guard dog among the yeast spores that proliferate around a winery, something strange happens.

Although not yet accepted by the International Federation of Cynology, and outlawed by the Rabies Ordinance of 1926, these dogs find themselves maturing into full-fledged aberrations not seen anywhere but in the modern world of wine-breeding.

The smell of dog has become synonymous, to some nasally educated vignerons, with the solid bass notes of a good farmyard burgundy. There are, of course, variations. They are predominantly white, scruffy, and wine-stained, with tannic tinges in the ears.

Laid-back Wine DOG No.5. Bolinas, California   *Ralph Steadman '01*

Occasionally, black ones emerge, and sometimes, spotted black and white, but the nose of a dog bears no comparison to the nose of a Château Beychevelle 1971. Except, perhaps, that every nose on every dog in every winery is shiny and wet.

RALPH STEADMAN HAS ILLUSTRATED MANY BOOKS, INCLUDING HUNTER S. THOMPSON'S *FEAR AND LOATHING IN LAS VEGAS* AND THE FIFTIETH-ANNIVERSARY EDITION OF GEORGE ORWELL'S *ANIMAL FARM*. HE IS THE AUTHOR OF *THE GRAPES OF RALPH* (FOR WHICH HE WON A GLENFIDDICH FOOD & DRINK AWARD), *UNTRODDEN GRAPES*, *STILL LIFE WITH BOTTLE*, *THE BOOK OF JONES*, AND *GONZO*. HE LIVES IN ENGLAND.

FAVORITE FOOD: STEAK
FAVORITE TOY: STUFFED HEDGEHOG
PET PEEVES: BICYCLES AND MOTORCYCLES
FAVORITE PASTIME: PLAYING IN THE SNOW
KNOWN ACCOMPLICE: 96 YEAR OLD
GRANDMA RAGNHILD CARLBERG
NAUGHTIEST DEED: EATING FRESHLY BAKED,
10-EGG CAKE JUST BEFORE DECORATING

AJAX

CHRISTOPHER BRIDGE OREGON CITY, OR | GREAT SWISS MOUNTAIN DOG, 5 | OWNERS: CHRIS AND SUSANNE CARLBERG

MILO

FAVORITE TOY: A STUFFED COW
FAVORITE FOOD: McDONALD'S APPLE PIES
FAVORITE PASTIME: CHASING GEESE IN THE POND
NAUGHTIEST DEED: STEALING THE GOOSE EGGS OUT
OF THE LAKE HOUSE AND SWIMMING ASHORE TO EAT THEM

BODIE

FAVORITE TOY: STUFFED GOAT
PET PEEVE: BEING LEFT ALONE
NAUGHTIEST DEED: LIFTING HIS
LEG ON CUSTOMERS' CAR TIRES
FAVORITE PASTIME: TEARING UP STUFFED TOYS

GINA

FAVORITE PASTIME: BEGGING FOR FOOD
KNOWN ACCOMPLICES: LUCY, CALI AND TUFF
PET PEEVE: NOT BEING THE CENTER OF ATTENTION
FAVORITE TOY: STUFFED ANIMALS AND GRAPE CANES
NAUGHTIEST DEED: STEALING A VISITOR'S STUFFED BEAR

FAVORITE TOY: SQUEAKY DUCK
KNOWN ACCOMPLICES: HIS FAMILY
NAUGHTIEST DEED: PEEING ON SUIT JACKET
PLACED ON CHAIR, SO THE OWNER COULD NOT LEAVE
FAVORITE FOOD: SPAGHETTI WITH MEATBALLS
PET PEEVE: THE FARM MANAGER'S NEW TRUCK
FAVORITE PASTIME: RIDING IN THE TRUCK, JEEP OR MOTORBIKE

SCOOTER

SOPHIE

PET PEEVE: OTHER DOGS
KNOWN ACCOMPLICE: GINA
FAVORITE FOOD: TABLE SCRAPS
FAVORITE PASTIMES: PATROLLING
THE BORDERS AND HARASSING SKUNKS
NAUGHTIEST DEED: GETTING SPRAYED BY SKUNKS

PET PEEVE: FIREWORKS
KNOWN ACCOMPLICE: TASHA
FAVORITE FOOD: THE NEIGHBOR'S TRASH
FAVORITE PASTIME: GUARDING THE FRONT PORCH
NAUGHTIEST DEED: NUMBER TWOS IN THE GARDEN
FAVORITE TOY: ANYTHING HE CAN STEAL AND TAKE HOME

COBY

BACO NOIR

PET PEEVE: BEES
KNOWN ACCOMPLICES:
SHADOW AND THE KIDS
FAVORITE FOOD: CHEESE
FAVORITE TOYS: BALL AND KONG
NAUGHTIEST DEED: RUNNING AWAY WITH SHADOW
FAVORITE PASTIMES: PLAYING BALL AND EATING GRAPES

FAVORITE FOOD: LAMB
FAVORITE TOY: ANYTHING FLUFFY THAT SQUEAKS
PET PEEVES: RAINY DAYS AND FLIES IN THE HOUSE
FAVORITE PASTIMES: SNIFFING OUT BAD CORKS AND IDENTIFYING TCA
NAUGHTIEST DEED: EATING A CHECKBOOK, A DISH SPONGE AND A CALCULATOR

MISS LOUISA-BELLE

DARWIN

PET PEEVES:
CATS, LOUD NOISES
AND FIREWORKS

FAVORITE TOY:
HIS SISTER SHELBY

FAVORITE FOOD: TASTING ROOM CRACKERS

FAVORITE PASTIME: RUNNING AFTER RABBITS

NAUGHTIEST DEED: OPENING DOORS ON
PEOPLE'S RVS AND CLIMBING INTO THE CAPTAIN'S SEAT

FAVORITE FOOD: CHEESECAKE
FAVORITE TOY: A TENNIS BALL
PET PEEVE: BEING LEFT ALONE
KNOWN ACCOMPLICE: SCOOTER
NAUGHTIEST DEED: EATING A BOX OF VANILLA OREOS
FAVORITE PASTIME: TAKING LONG WALKS IN THE VINEYARD

TOOKIE

KNOWN ACCOMPLICE: AMELIA
PET PEEVES: GUNS AND FIREWORKS
FAVORITE TOY: PLAYING WITH THE CHILDREN
FAVORITE PASTIME: WORKING IN THE VINEYARD
NAUGHTIEST DEED: PULLING OUT HER STITCHES

KNOWN ACCOMPLICE: SHADOW
PET PEEVE: REALLY FAST RABBITS
FAVORITE FOOD: PINOT NOIR GRAPES
NAUGHTIEST DEED: EATING TOO MANY PINOT NOIR GRAPES
FAVORITE PASTIME: CHASING JACK RABBITS IN THE VINEYARD

MARA

FAVORITE TOY: A STICK
KNOWN ACCOMPLICE: COLBY
NAUGHTIEST DEED: RUNNING
INSIDE COVERED IN MUD
FAVORITE FOOD: LARGE BONES
PET PEEVE: GERMAN SHEPHERDS
FAVORITE PASTIME: EATING GRAPES

ROCKY

PET PEEVE: BATHS
FAVORITE TOY: BLAKESLEY'S HAIR
FAVORITE FOOD: BUTTERED WAFFLES
FAVORITE PASTIME: BASKING IN THE SUN
NAUGHTIEST DEED: TAKING EVERYTHING OFF THE KITCHEN COUNTER

OMAR

BUCK

FAVORITE FOOD: YES PLEASE!
FAVORITE TOY: BALL
NAUGHTIEST DEED: SNIFFING CROTCHES
KNOWN ACCOMPLICE: JAKE THE SNAKE
FAVORITE PASTIMES: SWIMMING AND BEING PETTED

BERINGER VINEYARDS ST. HELENA, CA │ LABRADOR, 4 │ OWNER: RON SCHRIEVE

FAVORITE TOY: BALL
PET PEEVE: HAVING NO FOOD
NAUGHTIEST DEED: PUTTING HER
NOSE ON THE DINNER TABLE
FAVORITE PASTIME: PLAYING FETCH
KNOWN ACCOMPLICE: JAKE THE SNAKE

LU LU

GOOBER

PET PEEVE: OTHER DOGS
FAVORITE TOY: A TENNIS BALL
FAVORITE PASTIMES: SLEEPING AND EATING
KNOWN ACCOMPLICES: NONE – HE WORKS ALONE
NAUGHTIEST DEED: TURNING OVER GARBAGE CANS

BENZIGER FAMILY WINERY GLEN ELLEN CA

FAVORITE TOY: WILD TURKEYS
FAVORITE FOOD: RIB EYE STEAK
PET PEEVE: BROKEN WINE GLASSES
NAUGHTIEST DEED: JUMPING IN WINERY VISITORS' CARS
KNOWN ACCOMPLICES: JAKE, SHASTA, RUDY AND HER SISTER TILLY
FAVORITE PASTIME: CHASING WILD TURKEYS OUT OF THE VINEYARDS

FANCY

DAISY

FAVORITE FOOD: EVERYTHING
FAVORITE TOY: SQUEAKY SNAKE
NAUGHTIEST DEED: PEEING INSIDE
KNOWN ACCOMPLICES: HOLLY AND ODE
FAVORITE PASTIME: PLAYING CHASE WITH THE CHILDREN

FAVORITE TOY: SQUEAKY TOY LOG
FAVORITE FOOD: ANYTHING FROM THE TABLE
KNOWN ACCOMPLICES: GRAY AND CHRISTIAN
PET PEEVES: FLASHLIGHTS AND LAWNMOWERS
FAVORITE PASTIME: CHASING GROUNDHOGS AND HARES
NAUGHTIEST DEED: CHALLENGING COYOTES AROUND THE FARM

SKIPPER

TRIGGER

PET PEEVE: THE HOSE
KNOWN ACCOMPLICE: BART
FAVORITE TOY: TENNIS BALL
FAVORITE FOOD: WHATEVER IS IN HER MOUTH
FAVORITE PASTIMES: CHASING BALLS AND SWIMMING
NAUGHTIEST DEED: EATING SAM'S RUBBER DINOSAUR

CASA NUESTRA WINERY AND VINEYARDS ST. HELENA, CA | LABRADOR Y. 2 | OWNER: STEPHANIE ZACHARIA

CHATEAU
POTELLE

3875

FAVORITE TOY: BED
NAUGHTIEST DEED: BEGGING
FAVORITE FOOD: PICNIC FOOD
KNOWN ACCOMPLICES: MIMIE AND CASPER
PET PEEVE: VISITORS BRINGING THEIR PETS
FAVORITE PASTIMES: GREETING GUESTS AND SLEEPING BY THE FIRE

OPUS

SHELBY

FAVORITE TOY: ROPE
KNOWN ACCOMPLICE: DARWIN
FAVORITE PASTIME: CHASING ANYTHING THAT MOVES
PET PEEVES: CATS AND BEING AWAY FROM THE FAMILY
FAVORITE FOODS: GRAPES, STRAWBERRIES AND DOG BONES

SUNSTONE VINEYARDS AND WINERY SANTA YNEZ, CA | AUSTRALIAN SHEPHERD ♀ | OWNERS: THE RICE FAMILY

FAVORITE TOY: GLOVES
KNOWN ACCOMPLICE: MATTIE
NAUGHTIEST DEEDS: DIGGING FOR GOPHERS AND STEALING GLOVES
PET PEEVE: 28 ACRES NOT BEING LARGE ENOUGH
FAVORITE PASTIME: WALKING ALONGSIDE THE VINEYARD TRACTOR

BENTLEY

FEBEE

FAVORITE TOY: A TENNIS BALL
PET PEEVE: BEING SMELLED BY OTHER DOGS
KNOWN ACCOMPLICES: COOPER, BANDIT AND BEATTY
FAVORITE PASTIMES: SWIMMING AND PLAYING IN WATER
NAUGHTIEST DEED: CHEWING THROUGH A COUCH AND BOAT WIRING

FAVORITE FOOD: PICNICS
KNOWN ACCOMPLICE: ANNIE
FAVORITE TOY: STUFFED KITTEN TOY
PET PEEVES: WOODCHUCKS, CATS AND STRANGERS AFTER DARK
FAVORITE PASTIME: KEEPING THE WINERY PREMISES FREE OF UNWANTED VARMINTS
NAUGHTIEST DEED: TEARING A HOLE IN THE BOTTOM OF A HOT TUB WHILE CHASING CRITTERS

SHADOW

CASEY

FAVORITE FOOD: PRIME RIB EYE
FAVORITE PASTIME: CHASING SQUIRRELS
FAVORITE TOYS: RAWHIDE AND CHEW BONE
KNOWN ACCOMPLICES: GREG, LEIGH AND ARNOLD
PET PEEVE: TALL MEN WEARING HATS AND SUNGLASSES
NAUGHTIEST DEED: RUNNING AWAY AND RETURNING AT MIDNIGHT, STINKY

FAVORITE TOY: STUFFED FROGGY
PET PEEVE: SHINY METAL OBJECTS
KNOWN ACCOMPLICE: TATUM THE CAT
FAVORITE PASTIME: RIDING IN THE CAR
FAVORITE FOODS: BROCCOLI AND GRANNY SMITH APPLES
NAUGHTIEST DEED: BARKING AT THE ANIMALS ON THE TV

TUCKER

FAVORITE FOOD: AHI TUNA
FAVORITE TOY: GAIL'S SOCKS
KNOWN ACCOMPLICE: LULU
PET PEEVE: FEET MONSTERS
NAUGHTIEST DEED: RUNNING
AFTER WILMA, THE 24-YEAR-OLD CAT
FAVORITE PASTIME: BEING GAIL'S SHADOW

MISSY

FAVORITE TOY: CASHMERE BLANKET
FAVORITE PASTIME: JUMPING IN THE POND
PET PEEVES: BATHS AND THE GARDEN HOSE
KNOWN ACCOMPLICES: JYOMO AND POSSUM
FAVORITE FOOD: TOSSED SALAD WITH ASPARAGUS
NAUGHTIEST DEED: EATING AN ENTIRE BAG OF
DOG FOOD THEN BEING TAKEN TO THE VET

MAX

LUCY

KNOWN ACCOMPLICES:
COCO AND RUFF

FAVORITE PASTIME: SUNBATHING

FAVORITE TOY: WINE CORKS

NAUGHTIEST DEED: FINDING MUD
PUDDLES AFTER A SPRING RAIN

PET PEEVE: NON-DOG-FRIENDLY STORES

FAVORITE TOY: TENNIS BALL
FAVORITE PASTIME: RUNNING
FAVORITE FOOD: DRIED CHICKEN LIVERS
KNOWN ACCOMPLICES: GINA, SOPHIE, TUFF AND CALI
NAUGHTIEST DEED: BARKING AT VISITORS WHO COME TO THE FRONT DOOR

LUCY

*"I wonder if other dogs think poodles
are members of a weird religious cult."*

——— **RITA RUDNER**

CHEF CHIEN
by Joshua Greene

A MOSTLY TRUE STORY OF SPOT

Spot was the runt of the litter. *By the time his sister Mocha left for a new home, she weighed in at fourteen pounds. His brother Bull was next to go, the biggest of the boys at 15 pounds. Spot, an eight-pound, leggy black pup, was the only one of his siblings with a little tuft of white hair on his chest. Nobody wanted him.*

So we kept Spot, much to the initial disdain of his mother, who required us to get a separate dog bed for her son. He grew leggier as he grew up, and must have reminded mama of the tall show champion who had been forced upon her against her will. Soon, he stood much taller than she, with a longer snout and a sleek coat. Not that Lady Charlemagne wasn't a beauty herself, but she'd been bred as a huntress, while Spot had the show-off instincts of his father. It was apparent in the way each of them would approach a frisbee. Charley bolted after it, a low bullet charging across the field, leaping into the air to grab it as she might a falling bird in a former life. Spot, learning a thing or two from his mother, soon caught onto the frisbee game, but his gait was more of a prance, no matter how fast or far the frisbee went. Somehow, effortlessly, he would be there where the disk was beginning to coast into range, ready to rise up on his hind legs and pluck the frisbee from its hovering post, as if to take a martini glass from a silver tray.

By the time Spot was two, his charm, together with his talent at frisbee, had spread far and wide, catching the attention of the art director at a national wine magazine. She was planning a photo shoot, and needed a dog star. It happened that Spot and Charley spent most of their days at the office with that same art director, Johanna, and her own two pups. When she put out the casting call, a stack of beauty shots arrived.

She narrowed it down to local talent, and dogs arrived from every surrounding town, from dachshunds to Great Danes, ready to audition for the shot. They came into her studio, one by one, and posed on their haunches while the photographer's assistant held a fishing rod with a bone on the end of the line just high enough above to be out of range.

Spot and Charley watched them pass through the office to Johanna's studio. His mother barely acknowledged the small dogs, and dismissed the larger beasts after a quick sniff; Spot would sit at Johanna's door and watch. The auditions all began with the dog sitting patiently, then the bone would get too close. One standard schnauzer stood on his hind legs, trying to snatch the bone. A chihuahua leapt and yelped. A collie rolled onto his back, long nose pointed toward the bone as if to tempt it further.

Each dog was dismissed with a "We'll call you" from Johanna. As the assistant began to reel in the bone for the day, Spot made his move. He nudged open Johanna's door with his snout, and walked over to her for a pat on the head.

"Do you want to audition?" Johanna asked. Spot let out a deep groan of pleasure in thanks for the ear rub he was soon receiving, then walked over to the set and sat down where all the other dogs had sat. Out came the fishing rod again, down came the bone, and Spot sat transfixed, his eyes on the bone. The bone came to an inch over his head. He sat still and watched.

"He's the man," the photographer's assistant said. And so Spot began to prepare for his moment in the spotlights.

He set himself on a regimen of running an extra mile every day, cutting back on those extra portions of rice he so loved with his dinner, insisting on an extra long brushing at night to prepare for his beauty rest.

By the day of the shoot, he was fit and trim, his coat shinier than ever. The photographer's studio was an old converted barn, and though it had been decades since animals had lived there, Spot felt right at home in the big, open space. There was a table with a brown paper bag filled with groceries on the set; it turned out that Spot's role was to sit looking at the bag, and not to jump it.

The assistant had a box of small dog bones, one of which dangled from the fishing pole, to focus Spot's attention upward while the photographer took the shot. It all went smoothly, and Johanna decided to style a more ambitious photo for the opening spread of the story. It was a feature on value wines, the sort you might bring home with the groceries for Sunday night dinner. So Johanna decided that Spot should be the chef. She arranged a wine bottle, heads of lettuce and garlic, ripe tomatoes, purple eggplants and a baguette on the table. Then she scattered a few bones behind them, to tempt Spot up onto his hind legs. He stood behind the table as if he were giving a cooking class.

For the first few takes, Spot was more than willing to stand, but for a fee, which amounted to at least six of the small bones. Soon the bone was dangling from the pole again, to focus his attention up. But between the smell of all the food and the proximity of the little bones, his nose kept taking him back to the tabletop. Within half an hour, Spot had eaten an entire box of bones and was starting in on the second.

By the end of the shoot, Spot was beginning to slow down. And by the time he arrived home, he'd lost some of his labrador smile. Soon enough, it became clear that all the preparation Spot had taken upon himself, the dieting and exercise, had backfired. The evidence was everywhere, for days. Spot sulked, as his pride turned to embarrassment. We all agreed that Spot's modeling days were numbered.

But his days on earth were not so quickly curtailed. While his siblings' early glory faded (Mocha, we learned, suffered from a skin condition and other ailments, and didn't survive past ten; Bull, christened Pétrus at his Westchester home, took off after a car and met its tires instead), Spot lived on.

Finally, just before his sixteenth birthday, he suffered a stroke and started walking sideways; we had to make a difficult decision to put him down. He rallied, of course, and in three days he looked perky again. But he knew his time had come when I cooked up a plate of bacon and eggs and gave it to him – before it was ever touched by a human. We sat in front of a roaring fire while Spot the labrador chef ate his last supper.

WHEN NOT BREEDING LABRADORS, JOSHUA GREENE IS THE PUBLISHER AND EDITOR OF *WINE & SPIRITS MAGAZINE*, BASED IN NEW YORK. WWW.WINEANDSPIRITSMAGAZINE.COM

FAVORITE FOOD: STEAK
FAVORITE TOY: OAK LIMBS
PET PEEVE: GATOR, HIS PREDECESSOR
NAUGHTIEST DEED: STEALING WINERY
EQUIPMENT FROM THE CELLAR
KNOWN ACCOMPLICES: ANYA AND GUNDA
FAVORITE PASTIME: KEEPING AN EYE ON EVERYONE

BRUTUS

MAGGIE

NAUGHTIEST DEED: EATING
LEFTOVER FOOD IN THE CAR

KNOWN ACCOMPLICES:
DEKE TIDWELL AND FEDEX DRIVER

FAVORITE PASTIME: DUCK HUNTING

FAVORITE TOY: TOY STUFFED DUCK

PET PEEVE: UPS DELIVERY DRIVERS

FAVORITE TOY: YELLOW TENNIS BALLS
PET PEEVES: DEER AND HAVING A BATH
FAVORITE FOOD: BONES FROM THE BUTCHER
KNOWN ACCOMPLICE: EMMY THE SCAREDY CAT
FAVORITE PASTIME: CHASING EMMY UP A POST
AND STARING AT HER FOR HOURS
NAUGHTIEST DEED: CHEWING UP AND DESTROYING BEDS

GRACIE

LOOKSHA

KNOWN ACCOMPLICE: LOUIS
FAVORITE TOY: EMPTY LABEL SPOOLS
NAUGHTIEST DEED: EATING A
WHOLE BLOCK OF TALEGGIO CHEESE
PET PEEVES: UMBRELLAS, BEAVER
SCULPTURES AND CANOE RIDES
FAVORITE PASTIME: CHASING CHIPMUNKS
FAVORITE FOOD: WINE, PREFERABLY STICKY

FAVORITE TOY: A SLIPPER
PET PEEVE: BEING LEFT ALONE
FAVORITE PASTIME: CHASING RABBITS
FAVORITE FOODS: GOUGERES OR THE CAT'S FOOD
NAUGHTIEST DEED: HAVING TOO MUCH ENTHUSIASM
KNOWN ACCOMPLICES: MAGGIE, JACK AND TALISKER

MIA

KNOWN ACCOMPLICE: ROSEY

FAVORITE PASTIMES: CHASING
CHIPMUNKS AND SWIMMING

FAVORITE TOYS: STICKS AND PINE CONES

PET PEEVE: NOT BEING ABLE TO CATCH THE
RACCOONS THAT GET IN HER DOG FOOD AT NIGHT

NAUGHTIEST DEED: TERRORIZING THE NEIGHBOR'S CHICKENS AND GOATS

FAVORITE FOOD: CHEESE
PET PEEVE: FAST-MOVING TRUCKS
KNOWN ACCOMPLICES: MURRY, RUBY AND KAT
FAVORITE PASTIME: CHASING RABBITS AND BIRDS
FAVORITE TOY: A STUFFED CHIRPING EASTER CHICKY
NAUGHTIEST DEED: STEALING GLOVES AND CHEWING THEM TO BITS

ARGUS

MATTIE

PET PEEVE: GOPHERS
FAVORITE TOY: JACK RABBITS
KNOWN ACCOMPLICES: HOLLY, DAISY AND LAYLA
FAVORITE PASTIME: CHASING RABBITS IN THE VINEYARD
NAUGHTIEST DEED: JUMPING OVER THE TASTING
ROOM COUNTER, KNOCKING OVER SEVERAL BOTTLES

PET PEEVE: HORSES
FAVORITE PASTIME: CHEWING
FAVORITE TOY: STUFFED SQUIRREL
FAVORITE FOOD: SLICED DELI HAM
KNOWN ACCOMPLICES: MARCO AND LUCA
NAUGHTIEST DEED: CHEWING UP VERY EXPENSIVE SANDALS

PRIMO

BANDIT

FAVORITE FOOD: VENISON
PET PEEVE: VACUUM CLEANERS
FAVORITE TOY: ANYTHING WITH A SQUEAK
FAVORITE PASTIME: CHASING BUTTERFLIES
NAUGHTIEST DEED: EATING ONE OF MARK'S SHOES
KNOWN ACCOMPLICES: ERNIER, NICK AND IRIS

FAVORITE TOY: A TENNIS BALL
KNOWN ACCOMPLICE: STRIKER
FAVORITE FOODS: SPAGHETTI
AND PIZZA CRUSTS
PET PEEVE: BEING LEFT AT HOME
NAUGHTIEST DEED: TEARING UP 15
BAGS OF PACKING PEANUTS
FAVORITE PASTIME: GETTING MUDDY
AT THE FOOTBALL FIELD

COPPER

TRUMAN

FAVORITE TOY: DINOSAUR
PET PEEVE: HOT WEATHER
KNOWN ACCOMPLICE: CALI
NAUGHTIEST DEED: DIGGING IN THE GARDEN
FAVORITE PASTIMES: DIGGING AND SWIMMING
FAVORITE FOOD: ANYTHING THAT HITS THE FLOOR

FAVORITE FOOD: T-BONES
FAVORITE TOY: STUFFED FISH
PET PEEVE: BEING SQUIRTED WITH WATER
KNOWN ACCOMPLICES: ROCKY AND MR. B
NAUGHTIEST DEED: STEALING MIKE'S LUNCH OUT OF HIS TRUCK
FAVORITE PASTIME: RIDING DOWN TO THE BUS STOP TO PICK UP MARK

JESS

MOOKA

KNOWN ACCOMPLICE: TIKKA
FAVORITE FOOD: CORN CHIPS
NAUGHTIEST DEED: RUNNING AWAY
FAVORITE PASTIMES: HANGING OUT WITH BUDDIES
AND STEALING FOOD FROM THE KITCHEN

PET PEEVE: CATS
FAVORITE FOOD: CAT FOOD
KNOWN ACCOMPLICE: DAN DEE
FAVORITE TOY: BARNEY
THE STUFFED ANIMAL
FAVORITE PASTIME: RUNNING
AFTER BIKE TIRES
NAUGHTIEST DEED: DIGGING UP
THE GARDEN AND FLOWERS

STAR

FREDDIE

PET PEEVE: VISITING THE VET
FAVORITE TOY: RAWHIDE BONE
FAVORITE FOOD: BARBECUE PORK
FAVORITE PASTIME: BEGGING FOR TREATS
KNOWN ACCOMPLICES: BARNEY AND JASMINE
NAUGHTIEST DEED: RUNNING AWAY WITH BARNEY

FAVORITE TOY: *LEASH*
KNOWN ACCOMPLICE: *TULIP*
FAVORITE FOOD: *EGG YOLKS*
PET PEEVE: *BEING CONFINED TO HER PEN*
FAVORITE PASTIME: *DIGGING FOR MOLES*
NAUGHTIEST DEED: *STEALING GOOSE EGGS*

SOPHIE

LUCIA

FAVORITE FOOD: CRACKERS
PET PEEVE: BEING LEFT AT HOME
KNOWN ACCOMPLICE: LUCKY THE WINERY CAT
FAVORITE TOYS: SOFT STUFFED PUG OR TAXI
FAVORITE PASTIME: SLEEPING UNDER BILL'S DESK
NAUGHTIEST DEED: ROLLING IN
UNMENTIONABLE THINGS IN THE VINEYARD

FAVORITE FOOD: STEAK
FAVORITE TOY: SQUEAKY FROG
PET PEEVE: DEER IN THE VINEYARD
FAVORITE PASTIME: CHEWING CORKS
KNOWN ACCOMPLICE: EUTOPIA THE CAT
NAUGHTIEST DEED: DESTROYING IMPORTANT PAPERS

CORKY

BOOMER

FAVORITE TOY: ATV
KNOWN ACCOMPLICE: BILL
FAVORITE FOOD: WOODCHUCKS
PET PEEVE: HAVING HER PHOTO TAKEN
NAUGHTIEST DEED: CATCHING A SKUNK
FAVORITE PASTIME: WOODCHUCK HUNTING

KNOWN ACCOMPLICE: JASMINE
FAVORITE TOY: SQUEAKY HOT DOG
FAVORITE FOOD: ANYTHING ANYONE ELSE IS EATING
FAVORITE PASTIME: LAYING ON THE FLOOR DIRECTLY
BEHIND THE VISITORS AT THE TASTING BAR
PET PEEVE: NOT GETTING PETTED BY WINERY VISITORS
NAUGHTIEST DEED: JUMPING INTO WINERY VISITORS' CARS

SAGE

OWNERS: LOREE AND PAT SPANGLER | GERMAN SHEPHERD X, 2 | SPANGLER VINEYARDS ROSEBURG, OR | 357

LUCY

FAVORITE FOOD: TABLE SCRAPS
FAVORITE PASTIME: LAYING AROUND
FAVORITE TOY: RAWHIDE DOUGHNUTS
KNOWN ACCOMPLICE: MICHAEL BAZACO
NAUGHTIEST DEED: ROLLING IN COW MANURE
PET PEEVES: BATH TIME AND REMOTE CONTROL CARS

WINDHAM WINERY PURCELLVILLE, VA | LABRADOR, 7 | OWNER: NICKI BAZACO

DUJAC

FAVORITE TOY: DEAD VOLES
KNOWN ACCOMPLICE: ROMEO
PET PEEVE: UPS DELIVERY MAN
FAVORITE PASTIME: GREETING GUESTS OF THE WINERY,
PARTICULARLY THOSE WEARING WHITE PANTS
FAVORITE FOOD: RIPE OREGON PINOT NOIR GRAPES
NAUGHTIEST DEED: CHEWING UP THREE DIFFERENT IRRIGATION SETS

OWNERS: LYNN AND RON PENNER-ASH | LABRADOR, 7 | **PENNER-ASH WINE CELLARS** NEWBERG, OR

BUCK

FAVORITE FOOD:
CHICKEN STRIPS

FAVORITE PASTIME:
WAITING FOR A
TOOTSIE ROLL POP

KNOWN ACCOMPLICE: PEPPER

NAUGHTIEST DEED: POOPING IN THE DRIVEWAY

PET PEEVE: PEPPER BLOCKING HIM FROM GETTING TO HIS MASTER

NOBLE ESTATE VINEYARD AI

PET PEEVE: TICKS
FAVORITE FOOD: CHEESE
FAVORITE TOY: YOUR PATTING HAND
NAUGHTIEST DEED: GETTING CAUGHT
BY THE DOG CATCHER
FAVORITE PASTIME: LYING AT PEOPLE'S
FEET BY THE PICNIC TABLE
KNOWN ACCOMPLICES: FLINT, BAYLEY AND SURF

BABETTE

SYRAH

KNOWN ACCOMPLICE: MINNIE
FAVORITE TOY: STUFFED HEDGEHOG
FAVORITE FOOD: ANYTHING SHE CAN GET
NAUGHTIEST DEED: GETTING INTO THE GARBAGE
FAVORITE PASTIME: WRESTLING WITH NICHOLAS AND ANDREW

FAVORITE PASTIME: CHASING THE BALL
PET PEEVE: HAVING TO GET OFF THE COUCH
FAVORITE TOYS: SQUEAKY DUCK AND KONG DISC
FAVORITE FOODS: PEOPLE FOOD AND COTTAGE CHEESE
KNOWN ACCOMPLICES: JASON AND ALL OF HIS BUDDIES
NAUGHTIEST DEED: STEALING A WHOLE COOKED CHICKEN
AND PRIME RIB OFF THE KITCHEN COUNTER

LUCIE BELL

SIENNA

FAVORITE FOOD: HOT DOGS
KNOWN ACCOMPLICES: COYOTES
FAVORITE TOYS: VINES AND STICKS
PET PEEVE: STUSSY, THE VINEYARD CAT
NAUGHTIEST DEED: DIGGING UP PLANTS AROUND THE HOUSE
FAVORITE PASTIME: HUNTING MICE AND GROUND SQUIRRELS

FAVORITE FOOD: SMOKED TURKEY
PET PEEVE: THE VACUUM CLEANER
FAVORITE TOYS: STUFFED ANIMALS
KNOWN ACCOMPLICES: BRAD AND CASEY
FAVORITE PASTIME: CHASING RABBITS AND BIRDS
NAUGHTIEST DEED: CHASING A DUCK FOR OVER 100 METERS INTO SENECA LAKE

ARNOLD

RASCAL

FAVORITE FOOD: VOLES

PET PEEVE: BETSY'S ANTICS

FAVORITE TOY: LIVE VOLES

FAVORITE PASTIME:
CHASING BIRDS

NAUGHTIEST DEED: EATING
THE CHRISTMAS HAM

FAVORITE FOOD: HOT DOGS
PET PEEVES: BATHS AND RAIN
FAVORITE PASTIME: PLAYING FETCH
FAVORITE TOY: PLASTIC SQUEAKY BALL
KNOWN ACCOMPLICES: MICKEY AND FEBEE
NAUGHTIEST DEED: BEING AN ESCAPE ARTIST

BANDIT

OSO

PET PEEVE: THUNDER
FAVORITE TOY: RABBITS
FAVORITE FOOD: PEDIGREE
KNOWN ACCOMPLICE: CHACAL
NAUGHTIEST DEED: WEEING IN THE LUNCH BOX
FAVORITE PASTIME: CHASING RABBITS AND COYOTES

PET PEEVE: CATS
FAVORITE TOY: OLD ROPES
FAVORITE FOOD: SMOKED PIG EARS
FAVORITE PASTIME: DUCK HUNTING
NAUGHTIEST DEED: EATING DRIP IRRIGATION
KNOWN ACCOMPLICES: ROSIE, MISHA AND SALLY

CABERNET

GUARDIAN OF THE CABERNET
by Bruce Cass

I show up a little late *for my appointment with the winemaker. The winery really is way the hell up in the mountains and I've been lost most of the day. As I get out of the car, I spot a charming young girl across the parking lawn. She's about four. All curls, shy and shimmering summer dresses. She's backlit by the sun, with yellow flowers all around.*

I wave at her. You know, one hand, fingers vertical, modified typing pantomime in front of my eyes. She's not sure if she should respond. Just then, this ginormous alsatian-husky-type animal appears from behind a bush. He probably outweighs me. He's got one blue eye and one green one. He cocks the green one at me, and steps in front of the little girl. She grabs him by the ear. Has to reach up to do it. Way up. I blink. The dog flickers his lips. Just a ripple. As if I couldn't have guessed he's got teeth.

"She belongs with me," *he says.*

"Indeed," *I say out loud, my voice pitched somewhat higher than normal.*

She smiles at me. Great.

"Don't even think about it," *the animal snarls.*

She giggles. I'm starting to sweat, profusely.

I look over at the winery. It's about forty yards away. I couldn't have made it even in the flower of my youth.

"You look guilty," *the dog says, slightly bemused. Fantastic. He's a mind reader into the bargain.*

"You talkin' to me?" *I ask, putting a brave face on things.*

Really there's nothing for it. I might as well get back in the car. Drive through the screen door into the winery. I sit down and hit the All Lock button on the door. Dial the winemaker on my cell phone.

"Where are you?" he asks.

"Out in the parking lot," I tell him. "I'm looking at this 400-pound beast. He's tasting me with his eyes."

"Thurber?" the winemaker asks. "He's just a big woosey. Scratch his ears. He'll melt. He loves everybody."

Ain't that just like these back-to-the-earth winemakers in the Sierra Foothills? Now I think they're trying to take all their frustration about the process of objective wine critique out on me. Thurber, my ass! Dog probably hasn't eaten in six weeks.

I drive home. Give that clown's cabernet an 87.

Two years later I'm back. Winery's been selling cabernet for $1,500 a bottle. I've got a gaggle of hedge-fund managers from Connecticut in tow. They're all 30-something with trophy wives and new, 8,000-sq-ft homes. Just put in 5,000-bottle cellars. Need to fill 'em up. They're paying me a small fortune to get them this appointment.

Of course my hedge-fund guys don't really like wine. I asked what they've enjoyed recently, and got the cliché response, "Silver Oak." When I took them to the first winery this morning, the hostess poured us all a sauvignon blanc.

"What am I going to do with this?" one of the wives asked. "It's 10.30 in the morning."

"Spit it out in the shrubbery," I suggest.

Not likely. Princesses from Connecticut don't spit things in the shrubbery.

By early afternoon half the group is drunk. Everybody's cranky. We get off the bus. Thurber lopes out to greet us. One of the princesses freaks. More sympathetic I could not be.

"You need to lock that dog up," the lead princess orders the winemaker. Clearly this chick is used to calling the shots.

"But this is his home," the winemaker says.

"Then we're leaving," the Connecticut group declares in unison. They get back on the bus.

"Who knew," I shrug at the winemaker, making a face that on a baby would indicate gas.

On the way back down the hill, I sit next to one of the hedge-fund guys.

"How much would that winery have cost him to build?" he asks me.

"Oh, $30 or $40 million," I opine wildly.

"So, he's not really wealthy," the hedge-fund guy says, absently. Only in America I'm thinking.

These days Thurber and I get together every now and then. We drink good wine. We tell stories. We laugh.

BRUCE CASS BEGAN TEACHING WINE IN THE SAN FRANCISCO BAY AREA IN 1972. NOW 33 YEARS AND 9000+
HAPPY STUDENTS LATER, HE HAS FOUNDED THE BRUCE CASS WINE LAB. INTERNATIONALLY RECOGNIZED FOR
HIS EXPERTISE ON SMALL-VOLUME CALIFORNIA WINE PRODUCERS, BRUCE HAS EARNED ACCOLADES FOR HIS WORK
AS A WINE EDUCATOR, EDITOR, FREELANCE WINE WRITER AND WINE JUDGE. WWW.BRUCECASSWINELAB.COM

PET PEEVE: *HIS VET*
FAVORITE TOY: *JOE*
KNOWN ACCOMPLICE: *JOE*
FAVORITE PASTIMES: *EATING SNACKS
AND RIDING IN THE CAR*
FAVORITE FOOD: *PORK NECK BONES*
NAUGHTIEST DEED: *BARFING AFTER
STUFFING HIMSELF*

HERSHY

DAPHNE

PET PEEVE: CATS
NAUGHTIEST DEED: CHASING CATS
FAVORITE TOY: ANYTHING SHE CAN CHEW ON
FAVORITE PASTIME: RACING THE 4-WHEELER
FAVORITE FOOD: EATING GRAPES OFF THE VINE
KNOWN ACCOMPLICES: HANNA, PARKER AND TUCKER

PET PEEVE: WILD TURKEYS
FAVORITE TOY: A PINK BALL
FAVORITE FOOD: LAMB CHOPS
FAVORITE PASTIME: CHEWING DOG BONES
KNOWN ACCOMPLICES: CHARDONNAY AND RASCAL
NAUGHTIEST DEED: EATING LAMB CHOPS, PACKAGE INCLUDED

SYRAH

LADY

FAVORITE TOY: A STICK
FAVORITE FOOD: GRAPES
NAUGHTIEST DEED: JUMPING ON PEOPLE
PET PEEVE: BEING SQUIRTED WITH THE HOSE
FAVORITE PASTIME: SPYING ON THE NEIGHBORS
KNOWN ACCOMPLICES: PAUL, LYNN AND MAJOR

FAVORITE TOY: HIS BONE
PET PEEVE: GETTING OUT OF THE TRUCK
FAVORITE FOODS: DOG TREATS AND COOKIES
FAVORITE PASTIME: GREETING VISITORS AND FRIENDS
KNOWN ACCOMPLICES: BUZZARDS, QUAIL, DEER, RACCOONS, POSSUM AND WILD TURKEY
NAUGHTIEST DEEDS: CHASING THE FOUR CATS AND TRYING TO EAT GRAPES DURING HARVEST

MERLE

BÄRLI

FAVORITE TOY: A LARGE BONE
FAVORITE PASTIME: CHEWING UP EVERYTHING
KNOWN ACCOMPLICES: FREDDIE AND JONATHAN
PET PEEVES: STRONG PERFUMES AND HOT WEATHER
NAUGHTIEST DEED: EATING FOOD FROM THE COUNTER

PET PEEVE: BEING RIDICULED
FAVORITE FOOD: CHEESE AND CRACKERS
KNOWN ACCOMPLICES: JOYCE AND BÄRLI
FAVORITE PASTIME: RIDING IN THE TRUCK
NAUGHTIEST DEED: CHEWING UP A GOOD COUCH

GUS

PET PEEVE: CAMERAS
FAVORITE TOY: THE CAT
KNOWN ACCOMPLICE: THE CAT
FAVORITE FOOD: ANYTHING FROM THE BBQ
FAVORITE PASTIME: STARING OFF INTO SPACE
NAUGHTIEST DEED: EATING TOR'S BEST CABERNET GRAPES

HONEY

OWNERS: THE KENWARD FAMILY | GOLDEN RETRIEVER X, 20 | **TOR KENWARD FAMILY WINES** ST. HELENA, CA

PET PEEVE: BEING LEFT ALONE
FAVORITE TOY: LOUD SQUEAKY TOYS
FAVORITE FOODS: FISH AND VEGETABLES
NAUGHTIEST DEED: SWIMMING IN THE CREEK
KNOWN ACCOMPLICES: JULIANE AND ISABEL
FAVORITE PASTIME: PLAYING WITH THE CHILDREN AND DOGS

SOLEIL

BOXWOOD WINERY MIDDLEBURG, VA | BORDER COLLIE, 8 MONTHS | OWNER: RACHEL MARTIN

PET PEEVE: CATS
FAVORITE FOOD: CHEESE
FAVORITE TOY: TUG ROPE
FAVORITE PASTIME: CHASING WILDLIFE
KNOWN ACCOMPLICES: SYRAH AND RASCAL
NAUGHTIEST DEED: EATING GRAPES FROM THE HARVEST BASKET

CHARDONNAY

TEDDY

FAVORITE FOOD: PRETZELS
PET PEEVE: THUNDERSTORMS
KNOWN ACCOMPLICE: GOBLIN THE WINERY CAT
NAUGHTIEST DEED: VISITING NEIGHBORS TO BEG FOOD
FAVORITE PASTIME: BEGGING WINERY PRETZELS FROM GUESTS

FAVORITE TOY: TENNIS BALLS

KNOWN ACCOMPLICES: SONNY,
BOY, RUSTY AND SIENNA

NAUGHTIEST DEED: CHEWING
PATTY'S FAVORITE SHOES

FAVORITE FOOD: MEXICAN FOOD

PET PEEVE: PATTY NOT BEING AROUND

FAVORITE PASTIME: DRIVING THE FORKLIFT

STELLA

APRIL

FAVORITE FOOD: KIBBLE
KNOWN ACCOMPLICE: KEVIN
FAVORITE TOYS: BASKETBALL
AND AN OLD GLOVE
FAVORITE PASTIMES: FETCHING
STICKS AND ROLLING BALLS
PET PEEVE: HAVING NOTHING TO PLAY WITH

FAVORITE TOY: PET FROG
PET PEEVE: BEING LEFT ALONE
FAVORITE FOOD: EUKANUBA DRIED
KNOWN ACCOMPLICES: PICO AND BRUTUS
FAVORITE PASTIME: CHEWING ON HER FROG
NAUGHTIEST DEED: RUNNING OFF TO THE VINEYARDS

STACEY

ZEUSS

FAVORITE FOOD: STEAK
PET PEEVE: SQUIRRELS IN THE BACKYARD
FAVORITE PASTIMES: EXERCISING SQUIRRELS
AND WOODCHUCK HUNTING
NAUGHTIEST DEED: KILLING THE NEIGHBOR'S CAT

FAVORITE TOY: STICKS
FAVORITE FOOD: BONES
KNOWN ACCOMPLICE: BUSTER
PET PEEVE: BEING SURPRISED
FAVORITE PASTIME: SUNBATHING
NAUGHTIEST DEED: BURYING BONES IN THE VINEYARD

ANNIE

SHOOBOX CHARLIE

FAVORITE TOY: A BALL
PET PEEVE: THE FEDERAL EXPRESS MAN
KNOWN ACCOMPLICES: AUGUST AND MATTHIAS
FAVORITE PASTIMES: SWIMMING AND FETCHING
NAUGHTIEST DEED: CHASING THE FEDERAL EXPRESS MAN
FAVORITE FOODS: ROAST CHICKEN, BROCCOLI AND EPOISSE

THE FIRST WINE DOGS:

THE DOGS OF CANIS VENATICI

by Craig McGill

Icarius never realized it at the time, *but his first meeting with Bacchus, the god of wine and ecstasy, would ultimately lead to his own death. It all started innocently enough as Icarius unwittingly offered Bacchus a tour of his vineyard with his two vineyard dogs, Asterion and Chara. Bacchus was traveling incognito and was dressed head to toe in black Dolce & Gabbana and a pair of Wayfarer sunglasses. If you didn't know by now, Bacchus was cool. Way cool and of course wasn't recognized by Icarius.*

The tour concluded with the Scott Henry trellis system that Icarius had adopted in the vineyard. He was so impressed with the quality of his grapes, Bacchus offered to show Icarius how to make wine. Icarius was delighted by this offer as his pinot noir grapes were previously only ever used as table grapes.

After what seemed like a short time, Icarius was ready to release his first vintage – a delightfully full-bodied, tasty little number that rivaled the best of Burgundy. To share his heavenly delights, he decided to have a party and invited the entire local neighborhood to taste his liquid gold.

The party was a great success and continued into the early hours of the morning, until the cops were called for a third time. Under the influence of the pinot noir, most of the guests were already asleep. However, when they awoke the next morning, the guests were suffering from hangovers and thumping headaches.

Never previously experiencing this, they all gathered to discuss what had happened the night before. None of them could remember a thing, so collectively they decided that Icarius must have poisoned them all.

They overpowered Icarius in his sleep, killing him and discarding his body in a ditch. Deep in despair from separation anxiety, Asterion and Chara began to search for Icarius. When they found him they both jumped into the ditch to die with their master.

If that wasn't depressing enough – Icarius' pinot noir went on to win a gold medal in the local agricultural show that summer.

And the moral of the story is: your newfound wine friends will never be as loyal as a wine dog.

FAVORITE TOY: RUBBER BONE
KNOWN ACCOMPLICES: COYOTES
FAVORITE FOOD: ALPO GRAVY MIX
FAVORITE PASTIME: PLAYING WITH COYOTES
NAUGHTIEST DEED: CHEWING UP WORK BOOTS
PET PEEVE: STRANGERS COMING TO THE HOUSE

TRIXIE

PANCHITA

KNOWN ACCOMPLICE: PILOT
FAVORITE TOY: PINK FRISBEE
FAVORITE FOOD: DOG BISCUITS
NAUGHTIEST DEED: ROLLING IN THE MUD AFTER A BATH
PET PEEVE: ACCIDENTALLY BEING LOCKED IN THE WINERY
FAVORITE PASTIME: RUNNING IN CIRCLES AROUND TOUR GUESTS

PET PEEVE: COLD DAYS
KNOWN ACCOMPLICE: SYRAH
FAVORITE TOY: OLD GRAPE VINES
NAUGHTIEST DEED: BEING CAMERA SHY
FAVORITE FOOD: VITABONES DOG COOKIES
FAVORITE PASTIME: EATING GRAPES OFF THE VINE

MINNIE

FAVORITE FOOD: STEAK
FAVORITE TOY: A TENNIS BALL
KNOWN ACCOMPLICE: MARLYN ALLEN
PET PEEVES: GROUNDHOGS AND THUNDER
NAUGHTIEST DEED: HEELING A DELIVERY MAN
FAVORITE PASTIME: WATCHING FOR AIRPLANES

PET PEEVE: BEING BRUSHED
FAVORITE PASTIME: WALKING
NAUGHTIEST DEED: EATING BUTTER
OFF THE BUTTER DISH
KNOWN ACCOMPLICES: MOJO AND SOPHIE
FAVORITE TOYS: SQUEAKY TOYS AND THE CAT

GABI

DALLAS

PET PEEVE: BATH TIME
FAVORITE FOOD: CHICKEN
NAUGHTIEST DEED: STEALING SHOES
FAVORITE PASTIME: PLAYING WITH WAFFLES AND TEDDY
KNOWN ACCOMPLICES: DENNY, LINDSEY, ABBEY AND JAXSON

NAUGHTIEST DEED: STEALING
A LAMB STEAK FROM THE BBQ
FAVORITE FOOD: KOSHER HOT DOGS
PET PEEVE: BARRY MANILOW MUSIC
KNOWN ACCOMPLICES: PRINCESS ZINA AND HERO
FAVORITE PASTIME: CHASING WATER FROM A RUNNING HOSE
FAVORITE TOYS: SQUARE TENNIS BALL AND SHEEPSKIN BLANKET

BEAR

PET PEEVE: SKUNKS
FAVORITE TOY: A BALL
KNOWN ACCOMPLICES: SUNNY AND MAX
FAVORITE FOOD: GRAPES DURING CRUSH
FAVORITE PASTIMES: SLEEPING AND EATING
NAUGHTIEST DEED: TRYING TO STEAL TREATS

RUFF

FAVORITE TOY: MIA
FAVORITE FOOD: FRESH EGGS
KNOWN ACCOMPLICES: MIA AND NICO
PET PEEVE: MEN IN HATS OR WEARING BEARDS
FAVORITE PASTIMES: WATCHING CHICKENS AND HIDING
NAUGHTIEST DEED: SNEAKING INTO THE BATHROOM TO WATCH

SOCA

EMMA

KNOWN ACCOMPLICE: ROMEO
FAVORITE TOY: WOODEN BARREL BUNGS
NAUGHTIEST DEED: DUMPING IN THE WINERY
FAVORITE PASTIME: GREETING TASTING ROOM CUSTOMERS

WINNIE-MAE

PET PEEVE: COLD NIGHTS
FAVORITE FOOD: PRO PLAN
KNOWN ACCOMPLICE: STORM
FAVORITE PASTIME: WRESTLING
FAVORITE TOY: MARROW BONES
NAUGHTIEST DEED: CHEWING ON STORM

OWNER: LOIS BOECKMANN | GOLDEN RETRIEVER, 8 MONTHS | **BEDELL CELLARS** CUTCHOGUE, NY | 401

FAVORITE FOOD: CHEESE
PET PEEVES: GOPHERS AND MOLES
KNOWN ACCOMPLICES: UVA AND RICO
FAVORITE PASTIME: SLEEPING ON THE COUCH
FAVORITE TOY: UVA THE MOTHER-IN-LAW'S DOG
NAUGHTIEST DEED: STEALING TOOLS WHILE YOU ARE USING THEM

VINO

NAMASTÉ VINEYARDS DALLAS, OR | STANDARD POODLE, 4 | OWNER: CHRIS MILLER

FAVORITE TOY: BABY THE STUFFED CAT
PET PEEVE: VINEYARD WORKERS IN HATS
FAVORITE FOOD: ANYTHING, ESPECIALLY GRAPES
NAUGHTIEST DEED: EATING NEW MANOLO BLAHNIK SHOES
FAVORITE PASTIMES: LOUNGING, BARKING AND WAGGING HIS TAIL

WINSTON

OWNERS: CHRISTOPHER AND KRISTINE WILLIAMS | LABRADOR, 12 | **WATTLE CREEK WINERY** CLOVERDALE, CA

FAVORITE FOOD: PIZZA
PET PEEVES: BATHS AND HAIRCUTS
FAVORITE PASTIME: CHASING RABBITS
FAVORITE TOY: ANY OF ADRIAN'S DOLLS
KNOWN ACCOMPLICES: BISON, BENTLEY AND OZ
NAUGHTIEST DEED: BRINGING A RABBIT CARCASS INTO THE HOUSE

MAX

STRYKER SONOMA GEYSERVILLE, CA | LABRADOR / POODLE X, 2 | OWNER: CRAIG MACDONALD

PET PEEVE: HERBAL SMOKE
FAVORITE TOY: QUACKING DUCK
NAUGHTIEST DEED: PEEING ON THE CARPET
FAVORITE FOODS: BANANAS AND TOMATOES
KNOWN ACCOMPLICES: BUSTER, TURBO AND CHAMP
FAVORITE PASTIMES: EATING PIG EARS AND SWIMMING IN THE RIVER

BELLA ISADORA

ABBEY

KNOWN ACCOMPLICE: AILEEN
FAVORITE TOY: SQUEAKY TOYS
PET PEEVE: WALKING IN THE RAIN
NAUGHTIEST DEED: EATING AILEEN'S SHOES
FAVORITE PASTIME: RUNNING FREE WITHOUT A LEASH

PET PEEVE: JELL-O
FAVORITE FOOD: FORTUNE COOKIES
FAVORITE TOY: CAT FRIEND "CHEWEY"
KNOWN ACCOMPLICES: SKEETER AND CHEWEY
FAVORITE PASTIME: HAVING BELLY RUBBED BY ANYONE
NAUGHTIEST DEED: EATING A DEAD RODENT IN FRONT OF THE PHOTOGRAPHER

BELLA

KIRI TE KANAWA

FAVORITE FOOD: MEXICAN TORTILLAS
KNOWN ACCOMPLICE: RUSKA THE CAT
PET PEEVE: BEING LOCKED IN A ROOM
NAUGHTIEST DEED: EATING RED GRAPES ON A WHITE CARPET
FAVORITE PASTIMES: CHASING BIRDS AND RABBITS OUT OF THE VINEYARDS
AND GREETING CUSTOMERS IN THE TASTING ROOM

FAVORITE TOY: FRED
PET PEEVE: BEING ALONE
FAVORITE FOOD: VANILLA ICE-CREAM
NAUGHTIEST DEED: PICKING ALL THE TULIPS
KNOWN ACCOMPLICES: SCOOBY AND SCRAPPY
FAVORITE PASTIME: NIBBLING FINGERS AND TOES

PEPPER

ETHEL

PET PEEVE: BATHS
KNOWN ACCOMPLICE: FRED
FAVORITE FOOD: EVERYTHING
FAVORITE PASTIME: RUNNING FREE
NAUGHTIEST DEED: CHEWING FENCES

CHARDONNAY

FAVORITE TOY: A BALL
PET PEEVE: LOUD NOISES
KNOWN ACCOMPLICE: MERLOT
FAVORITE PASTIME: PLAYING BALL
FAVORITE FOODS: CHICKEN AND RICE
NAUGHTIEST DEED: JUMPING ON THE COUCH

LIZZY

FAVORITE TOY: FRISBEE
FAVORITE FOOD: CARRION
NAUGHTIEST DEED: EATING CARRION
FAVORITE PASTIME: PLAYING WITH THE KIDS
PET PEEVE: ANY LIVING THING ON THE WRONG SIDE OF HER INVISIBLE FENCE
KNOWN ACCOMPLICES: ANY LIVING THING ON THE RIGHT SIDE OF HER INVISIBLE FENCE

HANSEL

PET PEEVE: CATS
FAVORITE FOOD: VENISON
FAVORITE TOY: TENNIS BALLS
FAVORITE PASTIME: CHASING CATS
NAUGHTIEST DEED: RUNNING AWAY AND GETTING ARRESTED

PET PEEVE: RAIN
FAVORITE TOY: SLIPPERS
KNOWN ACCOMPLICE: HANSEL
FAVORITE PASTIMES: RUNNING AND PULLING
FAVORITE FOOD: ANYTHING INCLUDING POTATO PEELS

GRETL

CHARLIE

FAVORITE FOOD: YAMS
NAUGHTIEST DEED: EATING THE IRS FORMS
FAVORITE TOYS: CHEW STICKS AND TENNIS BALLS
KNOWN ACCOMPLICES: DICK, JOAN, MEG AND ZIGGIE
FAVORITE PASTIMES: CHASING THE BALL AND BITING THE HAND THAT FEEDS HIM

FAVORITE FOOD: CHEESE
KNOWN ACCOMPLICE: JAY
NAUGHTIEST DEED: DIGGING
FAVORITE PASTIME: SWIMMING
FAVORITE TOY: BILL CLINTON DOLL
PET PEEVES: GOING TO THE VET
AND A CAT CALLED TACKLE

CORKY

BUSTER

FAVORITE TOY: ANNIE
FAVORITE FOOD: BONES
KNOWN ACCOMPLICE: ANNIE
NAUGHTIEST DEED: CHASING THE ATV
PET PEEVE: UNANNOUNCED VISITORS
FAVORITE PASTIME: FOLLOWING THE MOST INTERESTING WORKER

PET PEEVE: BEING ALONE
FAVORITE FOODS: GOPHERS AND MOLES
KNOWN ACCOMPLICES: ABBY AND MISSY
NAUGHTIEST DEED: BEING AN ENERGETIC BARKER
FAVORITE PASTIME: CATCHING GOPHERS AND MOLES

TERI

SOPHIE

FAVORITE TOY: A BASEBALL
PET PEEVE: THE SOUND OF GUNS
FAVORITE FOOD: KITCHEN SCRAPS
NAUGHTIEST DEED: CHASING ANIMALS
KNOWN ACCOMPLICES: THE WINERY CHICKENS
FAVORITE PASTIME: SLEEPING IN THE SHADE OF THE BARN

PET PEEVE: GOPHERS
FAVORITE TOY: GLOVES
FAVORITE PASTIME: DIGGING FOR GOPHERS
NAUGHTIEST DEED: THE GOPHER DIGGING THING
KNOWN ACCOMPLICES: ROWDY, SASSY, MATTIE AND SATIE

GHOST

SUNNY

PET PEEVE: SKUNKS
FAVORITE FOOD: CHICKEN
FAVORITE TOY: A PIECE OF WOOD
KNOWN ACCOMPLICES: RUFF AND MAX
FAVORITE PASTIME: CARRYING AROUND BIG STICKS
NAUGHTIEST DEED: STEALING FOOD FROM UNSUSPECTING GUESTS

PET PEEVE: RAINY DAYS
KNOWN ACCOMPLICE: MARA
FAVORITE TOY: VINE CLIPPINGS
FAVORITE PASTIME: CHASING MARA
NAUGHTIEST DEED: ANNOYING MARA
FAVORITE FOOD: CHARDONNAY GRAPES

SHADOW

OWNER: ANA KELLER | GERMAN SHEPHERD, 10 | **KELLER ESTATE WINERY** PETALUMA, CA | 421

LIBERTY

FAVORITE TOY: BALL
FAVORITE FOOD: CANTALOUPE
PET PEEVE: NOT BEING ALLOWED TO PLAY
FAVORITE PASTIME: CHASING STICKS IN THE CREEK
KNOWN ACCOMPLICES: SADIE, SHU-SHU AND RUBY
NAUGHTIEST DEEDS: TEARING UP THE BACKYARD AND DROPPING EVERY TOY IN THE CREEK

RAYMOND VINEYARDS ST. HELENA, CA | LABRADOR, 3 | OWNERS: CRAIG AND MARGARET RAYMOND

FAVORITE FOOD: EVERYTHING
FAVORITE PASTIME: SLEEPING
PET PEEVE: THE VACUUM CLEANER
KNOWN ACCOMPLICE: LACEY THE HORSE
FAVORITE TOY: DENISE'S 3-YEAR-OLD SON
NAUGHTIEST DEED: STEALING THE BABY'S FOOD

BUDDY

TY

PET PEEVE: MEN
FAVORITE TOY: SICK MONKEY
FAVORITE FOOD: EVERYTHING
KNOWN ACCOMPLICES: RINGO AND SHADOW
FAVORITE PASTIME: AVOIDING HIS BROTHER RINGO
NAUGHTIEST DEED: DESTROYING REMOTE CONTROLS

FAVORITE TOY: PLATYPUS
PET PEEVE: ANYTHING OVERHEAD
NAUGHTIEST DEED: DESTROYING THE
'WINERIES OF NORTH AMERICA' BOOK
KNOWN ACCOMPLICES: SHADOW AND TY
FAVORITE PASTIME: PLAYING WITH HIS BROTHER TY

RINGO

TARARA WINERY LEESBURG, VA | MINIATURE SCHNAUZERS, 3 AND 2 | OWNERS: ROB AND MARNIE WARREN

FAVORITE FOOD: CHEESE
PET PEEVE: BEING LEFT ALONE
FAVORITE PASTIME: WRESTLING
NAUGHTIEST DEED: DESTROYING CLOTHING
KNOWN ACCOMPLICE: SOLTICE THE PIT BULL,
HIS WRESTLING PARTNER
FAVORITE TOY: KENNY AND HEATHER'S CLOTHING

AZUL

VINNY

PET PEEVE: TAKING PILLS
FAVORITE FOOD: BANANAS
FAVORITE TOY: RAWHIDE BONE
NAUGHTIEST DEED: TAKING THE GRANDCHILDREN'S TOYS
KNOWN ACCOMPLICES: CLYDE, RALPH, LIVIE AND ERIN
FAVORITE PASTIME: WALKS IN THE SONOMA PLAZA TO MEET VISITORS

PET PEEVE: THE CAT
FAVORITE TOY: THE CAT
KNOWN ACCOMPLICE: SQUIRE
FAVORITE PASTIME: HERDING
SQUIRE ON THE 4WD MOTORCYCLE

SAMMY

FAVORITE TOY: PEOPLE
KNOWN ACCOMPLICE: SUNNY
FAVORITE FOOD: TABLE SCRAPS
NAUGHTIEST DEED: CHASING GEESE
PET PEEVE: WHEN AL AND CINDY LEAVE THE HOME
FAVORITE PASTIMES: RACING WITH CARS AND LAYING BY THE POND

KESWICK VINEYARDS KESWICK, VA | LABRADOR X. 3 | OWNERS: AL AND CINDY SCHORNBERG

PET PEEVE: GUNSHOTS
FAVORITE TOY: A TENNIS BALL
KNOWN ACCOMPLICE: HOUDINI
FAVORITE FOOD: SAMMY SNACKS
NAUGHTIEST DEED: CHEWING UP A PILLOW
FAVORITE PASTIME: GREETING FOLKS WITH A BALL IN HIS MOUTH

MACK

OWNER: AMANDA GEE-TAYLOR | LABRADOR, 4 | **KING FAMILY VINEYARDS** CROZET, VA | 429

SAVANA

FAVORITE TOY: FRISBEE
FAVORITE FOOD: EVERYTHING
PET PEEVE: AGGRESSIVE CHILDREN
FAVORITE PASTIME: CATCHING FRISBEES
KNOWN ACCOMPLICES: BASIL AND ABBEY

KLUGE ESTATE WINERY AND VINEYARD CHARLOTTESVILLE, VA | LABRADOR 1 | OWNER: JUDITH DICKINSON

KNOWN ACCOMPLICE: DIEGO
PET PEEVE: HAVING TO STAY INDOORS
FAVORITE FOOD: ANY TYPE OF CHEESE
FAVORITE TOY: BLUE SQUEAKY DONUT
NAUGHTIEST DEED: BREAKING INTO THE
BEDROOM TO FIND SHOES TO CHEW ON
FAVORITE PASTIME: HUNTING FOR RABBITS

CALAFIA

OWNERS: DOUG AND ANGELA BRAUN | LABRADOR 2 | PRESIDIO WINERY LOMPOC CA 431

ABBY

FAVORITE TOY: HER BED
PET PEEVE: MISSING DINNER
KNOWN ACCOMPLICE: TAWNY PORT
FAVORITE PASTIME: JUMPING IN THE DITCH
FAVORITE FOOD: HOMEMADE ABBEY STEW

KNOWN ACCOMPLICE: ABBY
FAVORITE FOOD: PARMESAN CHEESE RIND
PET PEEVE: LEAVING THE RIVERS OR LAKES
FAVORITE TOY: HER STUFFED ANIMAL MONKEY
NAUGHTIEST DEED: SPILLING AND DRINKING BEER
FAVORITE PASTIMES: CATCHING ROCKS AND BREAKING TEETH

TAWNY

EDENVALE WINERY MEDFORD, OR | GOLDEN RETRIEVERS, 3 | OWNERS: THE ROOT AND CAMPANELLA FAMILIES

PET PEEVE: THE VET
FAVORITE TOY: PEOPLE
NAUGHTIEST DEED: EATING
THE BEST FURNITURE
KNOWN ACCOMPLICES: HUCK,
MUDDY, BISCUIT AND PEPPER
FAVORITE FOOD: PEOPLE FOOD

TURK

AGGIE

PET PEEVE: THE CAMERA
KNOWN ACCOMPLICE: FRED
NAUGHTIEST DEED: ROLLING IN COW DUNG
FAVORITE PASTIME: GREETING TASTING ROOM VISITORS

FAVORITE TOY: ANY STICK
FAVORITE FOOD: MILK BONE
FAVORITE PASTIME: FETCHING
PET PEEVE: BILLY'S CALCULATOR WIRE
KNOWN ACCOMPLICES: SHASTA AND FANCY
NAUGHTIEST DEED: CHASING EVAN THE CAT

JAKE

OWNERS: MARK AND TRACY BURNINGHAM | LABRADOR 3 | BENZIGER FAMILY WINERY GLEN ELLEN CA | 435

MAGGIE

FAVORITE FOOD: ANYTHING
PET PEEVE: BEING LEFT ALONE
FAVORITE TOY: SQUEAKY DUCK
NAUGHTIEST DEED: WHERE DO I START?
FAVORITE PASTIME: GETTING INTO TROUBLE

LANGE ESTATE *DUNDEE, OR* | *GOLDEN RETRIEVER, 6 MONTHS* | *OWNER: JESSE LANGE*

FER SERUADOU

FAVORITE FOOD: MEAT
KNOWN ACCOMPLICE: TREIXADURA
FAVORITE PASTIME: PLAYING FETCH
PET PEEVE: BEING LEFT ALONE INSIDE THE HOUSE
NAUGHTIEST DEED: LEAVING MESS IN THE WINERY
FAVORITE TOYS: CORKS, MAGNOLIA SEED PODS AND SOCCER BALLS

JOSIE

FAVORITE FOOD: PICNICS
NAUGHTIEST DEED: DIGGING
KNOWN ACCOMPLICE: LIZZIE
PET PEEVES: EXERCISE AND HAVING A BATH
FAVORITE PASTIMES: SLEEPING AND SWIMMING
FAVORITE TOY: DEAD FISH FROM THE RESERVOIR

PET PEEVE: DEER
FAVORITE TOY: TILDA
KNOWN ACCOMPLICE: TILDA
FAVORITE PASTIME: CLEANING HER FEET
FAVORITE FOOD: HORSE HOOF TRIMMINGS
NAUGHTIEST DEED: PIERCING HER SISTER SYD'S EAR

RIA

"My dog is worried about the economy
because Alpo is up to $3 a can.
That's almost $21 in dog money."

———————— **JOE WEINSTEIN**

THE STORY OF MOOSE
by Dan Berger

He's a breed apart, as the saying goes, and clearly it was an accident that fortuitously gave Bruce Cohn his beloved Moose.

"I was breeding English bulldogs," said Bruce, owner of the B.R. Cohn Winery in Glen Ellen. "I had a white and brindle bulldog by the name of Maggie Mae and we also had a yellow lab around here.

"Well, one day, one of my sons left the gate open, and that's how we got Moose."

The fascinating cross of labrador retriever and English bulldog would normally make a mix with numerous problems, and in the litter of six only two survived. Bella was adopted and Moose stayed.

Moose is a sweet, affectionate greeter for guests to the ranch, and often wanders into the tasting room, offering an unsolicited paw and posing to be petted.

At age 8, Moose is an institution here, and regulars anticipate his friendly face and sincere eyes. His 93 pounds is deceiving. He's very mellow, sleeps a lot in the heat of the afternoon, and lets little children poke and pound him.

Moose has become such a fixture in the newly redesigned tasting room because his picture is now on a Meritage-type cabernet sauvignon blend called Moose's Red.

A portion of the $40 per bottle fee is donated to Pets Lifeline, a local animal shelter. The winery also offers T-shirts, sweatshirts, and dog cookies that honor Moose.

Although both English bulldogs and labs are prone to various ailments, the mellow Moose seems to enjoy the best traits of both breeds. He likes the water, and often swims in the family pool and takes dips in a local creek. And Bruce often takes Moose out in his water-ski boat, wearing an adult life vest.

His large, thick, short and stocky frame and large paws make him seem a bit like a bull-mastiff, and almost daily a visitor asks, "What is he?"

"I call him a Blab," said Bruce.

DAN BERGER IS A NATIONALLY SYNDICATED WINE COLUMNIST WHO ALSO PUBLISHES A WEEKLY NEWSLETTER ON WINE, VINTAGE EXPERIENCES, AND IS EDITOR-AT-LARGE FOR *APPELLATION AMERICA*.

FAVORITE TOY: PLATYPUS
FAVORITE PASTIME: SLEEPING
KNOWN ACCOMPLICE: SAYLOR
FAVORITE FOOD: PEPPERONI STICKS
NAUGHTIEST DEED: STEALING FOOD
PET PEEVE: PEOPLE IN UNIFORMS AND TRUCKS

RUSTY

SHADOW

FAVORITE FOOD: CHEESE
FAVORITE PASTIME: FETCHING STICKS
IN THE LAKE AND POTOMAC RIVER
PET PEEVE: NOT HAVING PEOPLE AROUND
FAVORITE TOY: CHEESE-SCENTED CHEW BONE
NAUGHTIEST DEED: TAKING A LOAF OF FRENCH BREAD FROM A GUEST'S PICNIC

FAVORITE TOY: FRISBEE
FAVORITE PASTIME: OCEAN SWIMS
PET PEEVE: UNSAVORY CHARACTERS
KNOWN ACCOMPLICES: KAILA AND HADLEY
FAVORITE FOOD: "BREATHIES" CHICKEN JERKY
NAUGHTIEST DEED: EATING USED KLEENEX FROM OUT OF THE GARBAGE

KAHLUA

CHIANTI

FAVORITE FOOD: RAWHIDES
NAUGHTIEST DEED: DROOLING
PET PEEVES: LIGHTNING AND THUNDER
FAVORITE TOY: SQUIRREL SQUEAKY TOY
FAVORITE PASTIME: SINGING WITH DOUGLAS

DOMAINE LA DUE NAPA, CA │ GOLDEN RETRIEVER, 5 │ OWNERS: DOUGLAS AND ANGELA DUE

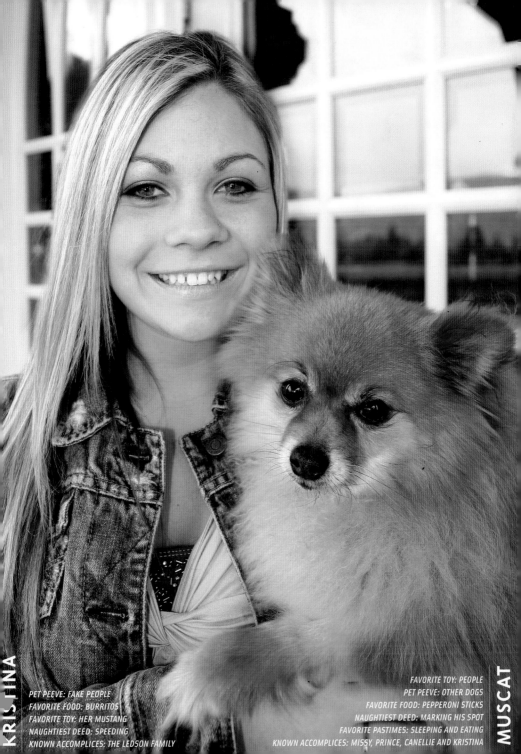

KRISTINA

MUSCAT

PET PEEVE: FAKE PEOPLE
FAVORITE FOOD: BURRITOS
FAVORITE TOY: HER MUSTANG
NAUGHTIEST DEED: SPEEDING
KNOWN ACCOMPLICES: THE LEDSON FAMILY

FAVORITE TOY: PEOPLE
PET PEEVE: OTHER DOGS
FAVORITE FOOD: PEPPERONI STICKS
NAUGHTIEST DEED: MARKING HIS SPOT
FAVORITE PASTIMES: SLEEPING AND EATING
KNOWN ACCOMPLICES: MISSY, PRINCE, CANELLIE AND KRISTINA

FAVORITE FOOD: STEAK
FAVORITE TOY: FRISBEE
PET PEEVE: PEOPLE WITH HATS ON
NAUGHTIEST DEED: JUMPING AND
PLAYING IN THE WINERY FOUNTAIN
KNOWN ACCOMPLICE: JIMMY THE COCKATIEL
FAVORITE PASTIME: RUNNING IN THE VINEYARDS

PRINCE

PRINCE

MATTIE

FAVORITE TOY: DUCK

FAVORITE PASTIME: SCOUTING THE TRAIL
FOR HER EQUINE BUDDIES, PEARL AND PAL

FAVORITE FOOD: ARTISANAL GOAT'S CHEESE

PET PEEVE: GANGS OF SQUIRRELS TAUNTING HER

NAUGHTIEST DEED: KILLING ELEVEN
SEATBELTS IN SIX DIFFERENT VEHICLES

FAVORITE TOY: KONG
FAVORITE FOOD: STEAK
KNOWN ACCOMPLICES: LUCY, GINA AND SOPHIE
FAVORITE PASTIME: SWIMMING IN THE RANCH POOL

FAVORITE TOY: FRISBEE
FAVORITE FOOD: GRAPES
NAUGHTIEST DEED: CHASING THE CAT
FAVORITE PASTIME: SWIMMING IN THE RANCH POOL

UFF

CALI

PET PEEVE: OTHER DOGS
FAVORITE FOOD: PICNICS
KNOWN ACCOMPLICE: JOSIE
FAVORITE TOY: DEAD FISH FROM THE RESERVOIR
NAUGHTIEST DEED: CONFRONTING UPS DELIVERY PEOPLE

ZZIE

FAVORITE PASTIME: EATING
FAVORITE FOOD: SHEEP POOP
PET PEEVE: NOT GETTING HIS WAY
NAUGHTIEST DEED: GOING TO HOSPITAL
AFTER EATING TOO MANY GRAPES
KNOWN ACCOMPLICES: ORSON AND THE LAMBS

OLLIE

BRUTUS

FAVORITE FOOD: PEOPLE FOOD
FAVORITE TOY: STUFFED ROOSTER
FAVORITE PASTIME: CHASING STICKS
PET PEEVE: PUTTING ON HIS SHOCK COLLAR
KNOWN ACCOMPLICES: STACY AND THE THREE CATS
NAUGHTIEST DEED: EATING TWO BOXES OF SEE'S CANDY AT CHRISTMAS

FAVORITE TOY: BALLS
PET PEEVE: STRANGERS
KNOWN ACCOMPLICE: ROCKY
NAUGHTIEST DEED: CHASING AND
CUTTING IN FRONT OF CARS
FAVORITE FOOD: RAW HAMBURGERS
FAVORITE PASTIME: STARING DOWN VEHICLES

COLBY

BULLET

FAVORITE FOOD: VENISON
KNOWN ACCOMPLICE: ALLY
FAVORITE TOY: DEAD RABBIT
PET PEEVE: EMPTY FOOD BOWL
NAUGHTIEST DEED: HUMPING THE NEIGHBOR'S CAT
FAVORITE PASTIMES: SWIMMING AND PLAYING TUG OF WAR

PET PEEVE: RAIN
FAVORITE TOY: CHEW BONE
FAVORITE FOOD: ICE-CREAM
KNOWN ACCOMPLICE: SPENCER
FAVORITE PASTIME: DRINKING FROM THE TOILET BOWL
NAUGHTIEST DEED: TEACHING HERSELF HOW TO OPEN THE FRIDGE

SOPHIE

BUSTER

FAVORITE TOY: A STICK
KNOWN ACCOMPLICE: HIS BROTHER DIESEL
PET PEEVES: FIREWORKS AND LOUD NOISES
FAVORITE FOODS: CAT FOOD AND WHITE WINE GRAPES
FAVORITE PASTIME: NEVER LEAVING HIS MASTER'S SIDE
NAUGHTIEST DEED: SNEAKING INTO THE HOUSE TO NAP ON THE SOFA

PET PEEVE: BATHS
FAVORITE TOY: A TENNIS BALL
FAVORITE PASTIME: SWIMMING
FAVORITE FOOD: EGGS AND TOAST
NAUGHTIEST DEED: PLAYING WITH SKUNKS

SOLO

PATCHES

FAVORITE TOY: BALLS
PET PEEVE: LOUD TRUCKS
FAVORITE PASTIMES: SLEEPING
AND CHASING SQUIRRELS
FAVORITE FOODS: DOG FOOD AND MEAT
NAUGHTIEST DEED: EXPOSING HERSELF

FAVORITE FOOD: CHEESE
KNOWN ACCOMPLICE: BILL
FAVORITE TOYS: TOWELS AND DEAD RABBITS
PET PEEVES: BEING LEFT AT HOME AND THE LEAF BLOWER
FAVORITE PASTIMES: RUNNING MARATHONS AND SWIMMING
NAUGHTIEST DEEDS: BITING WINEMAKERS AND CHASING COYOTES

EARL

OWNER: JAINE VINEYARDS NAPA, CA

FAVORITE TOY: HEDGEHOG
FAVORITE FOOD: CHICKEN SATAY STICKS
KNOWN ACCOMPLICE: AUNT CAROLINE
PET PEEVE: HAVING HIS NAILS TRIMMED
FAVORITE PASTIMES: CHASING RABBITS AND SLEEPING IN THE SUN
NAUGHTIEST DEED: RETRIEVING THANKSGIVING TURKEY CARCASS FROM THE TRASH

ATALON WINERY OAKVILLE, CA | LABRADOR / GREAT DANE X, 8 | OWNER: HOLLY EVANS

FAVORITE FOOD: PIG EARS
KNOWN ACCOMPLICE: RIPPLE
FAVORITE TOY: A TENNIS BALL
PET PEEVE: GETTING A BATH
AFTER SHE ROLLS IN DEER POOP
FAVORITE PASTIME: FINDING MICE
NAUGHTIEST DEED: ROLLING IN DEER POOP

WILLOW

RUFUS

PET PEEVE: DECAF COFFEE
FAVORITE PASTIME: KISSING
FAVORITE TOY: JIMMY CHOO SHOES
KNOWN ACCOMPLICES: BARBARA AND CHARLES
FAVORITE FOODS: COFFEE, HOT DOGS AND CROISSANTS WITH JAM
NAUGHTIEST DEED: PULLING HAIR ORNAMENTS OUT OF LADIES' PONYTAILS

FAVORITE TOY: CHOPPER
FAVORITE FOOD: PEOPLE FOOD
PET PEEVE: BIRDS IN THE VINEYARD
NAUGHTIEST DEED: CHASING TRUCKS
FAVORITE PASTIME: CHASING FROGS IN THE POND
KNOWN ACCOMPLICES: CHOPPER, JENNY AND DAD

MOJO

RIPPLE

FAVORITE TOY: MERLOT CANES
FAVORITE FOOD: DINNER SCRAPS
PET PEEVES: CROWDS AND
THE FOURTH OF JULY
NAUGHTIEST DEED: CHEWING
UP ALL THE CAT'S TOYS
KNOWN ACCOMPLICES:
WILLOW AND ANNA BELLE

DOGSTROLOGY VINTAGE 2007

WITH MADAM NYAM NYAM AND HER CRYSTAL DECANTER

ARIES

*COME ON, COME HERE? COME HERE! AS ARIES, YOU DOGGIES ARE THE NATURAL BORN 'LEADERS OF THE PACK' OF THE ZODIAC. DOG OWNERS AROUND THE WORLD ARE FOOLED INTO BELIEVING THEY ARE ACTUALLY TAKING YOU OUT FOR A WALK BUT THIS IS NEVER REALLY THE CASE. BEING ON THE LEAD HAS A TOTALLY DIFFERENT MEANING TO YOU, AND YOU GUYS NEED TO THINK ABOUT WHO'S THE BOSS SOMETIMES. ALRIGHT ALREADY, SO IT'S YOU, BUT WE WON'T TELL, SO LONG AS YOU PLAY DEAD ON OCCASION AND DO THOSE SILLY TRICKS THAT SEEM TO AMUSE ANYBODY WILLING TO WORSHIP YOUR GREATNESS. **DRINK THIS MONTH** – PULL ONE OF YOUR KEEPERS OUT OF THE KENNEL. A CABERNET WITH WOOF! YOU ARE SO SONOMA.*

TAURUS

*CONTRARY TO YOUR SIGN, THERE'S NO BULL WITH YOU LOT, UNLESS OF COURSE YOU ARE A BULLDOG, A NATURAL TENDENCY OF TAUREANS. FIERCELY LOYAL, AND SOMETIMES A TOUCH ON THE STUBBORN SIDE, YOU GUYS LOVE TO EAT GRASS AND THEN REGURGITATE IT BY YOUR OWNER'S FEET. OF COURSE SOMETIMES THIS AFFECTION IS A LITTLE MISUNDERSTOOD, BUT THOSE BEAUTIFUL PUPPY EYES COULD MELT THE HEART OF THE MOST DISPLEASED DOG OWNER. JUST REMEMBER THAT BEING ASKED TO DEMONSTRATE OBEDIENCE CAN OFTEN MEAN A LITTLE TREAT ON OCCASION, AND THAT BEING TOLD WHAT TO DO CAN ALSO HAVE ITS OWN REWARDS. JUST SIT AND BEAR IT I SAY. **DRINK THIS MONTH** – SOMETHING BULLISH AND OFF THE LEASH. ZINFANDEL.*

GEMINI

*YOU GUYS ARE TWICE THE FUN AND TWICE THE DOG, AND HAVE A HABIT OF CONFUSING THE HECK OUT YOUR OWNER BECAUSE YOU ALWAYS SEEM TO BE IN TWO PLACES AT ONCE. JUST WHEN THEY THOUGHT YOU'D GONE OUTSIDE, YOU'RE ACTUALLY INSIDE HAVING YET ANOTHER CHEW ON THE TOILET ROLL IN THE WC, OR KNOCKING OVER THE RUBBISH BIN TO SEE IF THERE'S ANYTHING INSIDE. DOUBLE TROUBLE SHOULD BE YOUR REAL ZODIAC NAME. YOU ARE THE MONKEY OF THE DOG WORLD; FAST, CHATTY AND LIABLE TO SWING FROM ONE NAUGHTY ACTIVITY TO THE NEXT. SLOW DOWN AND SMELL THE ROSES INSTEAD OF DIGGING THEM UP OK? MAYBE PETER PUPPY PAN, IT'S TIME YOU GREW UP. **DRINK THIS MONTH** – SOMETHING SUPPLE AND PRETTY FROM SANTA BARBARA. PINOT.*

CANCER

*IT HAS TO BE SAID THAT YOU GUYS ARE KNOWN FOR YOUR CRABBINESS AT BEING MADE TO GO OUTSIDE TO PEE AT NIGHT. BEING SNAPPY MAY END UP NOT WORKING IN YOUR FAVOUR, OR YOUR OWNER'S GREATER INTERESTS. LEAVING A LITTLE BIT OF YOURSELF INSIDE AS A GIFT MAY NOT BE THE SOLUTION EITHER. YOU GUYS NEED TO REMEMBER NOT TO BITE THE HAND THAT FEEDS YOU, NO MATTER WHETHER IT'S BELOW ZERO OR RAINING CATS AND DOGS, WHEN THE CALL OF NATURE BECKONS. AS A WATER SIGN, YOU NEED TO GO AND TAKE TIME OUT AT THE BEACH OCCASIONALLY. NOT ONLY WILL THE FRESH AIR BE GOOD FOR YOU, SHAKING YOUR SALT-WATER AND SAND-LADEN COAT ALL OVER YOUR OWNER SURELY DEMONSTRATES JUST HOW MUCH YOU DO LOVE THEM. **DRINK THIS MONTH** – SOMETHING FIZZY WITH BITE. CARNEROS IS YOUR CAPER.*

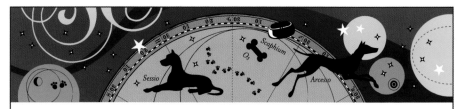

LEO

♌

DRAMA QUEENS BY NATURE, YOU GUYS ASSUME THAT YOU ARE NATURAL BORN ROYALTY AND LET EVERYBODY KNOW IT. AFGHAN HOUNDS AND CORGIS ARE OFTEN BORN UNDER THIS SIGN. WHETHER IT'S THE WAY YOU STRUT WHEN YOU GO WALKIES OR YOUR CAPACITY TO LOOK REGAL, EVEN AFTER THAT UNFORTUNATE NEUTERING OPERATION, YOU GUYS LEAVE ANY MONARCH FOR DEAD. PEOPLE OFTEN COMMENT ON YOUR WELL-GROOMED GOOD LOOKS, WHICH BEGS THE QUESTION OF JUST HOW YOU GUYS DEAL WITH ALL THAT ATTENTION. DON'T FORGET THE LITTLE GUYS TOO, ESPECIALLY THOSE CHIHUAHUAS, AND REMEMBER THAT IN ORDER TO RULE, YOU MUST ALWAYS MAKE SURE YOUR SUBJECTS ADORE YOU. THAT WAY, A LIFELONG SUPPLY OF BONES IS A SURE THING AND ALL YOU HAVE TO DO IS LOOK GOOD (DOG). **DRINK THIS MONTH** – LEADERS OF THE PACKS NEED SOMETHING LOADED FROM LODI.

VIRGO

♍

OK, SO WHAT'S ALL THE FUSS ABOUT YOU GUYS, AND WHY IS IT, JUST FOR ONCE, YOU CAN'T TRY SOME DOG FOOD THAT ISN'T YOUR ABSOLUTE FAVORITE? YOU PUPPIES ARE LIKE THE WINE AND FOOD CRITIC OF THE DOG WORLD AND COLLECT BONES FOR CELLARING LIKE IT'S GOING OUT OF STYLE! SO WHAT IF THE DAFFODILS HAVE TO MAKE ROOM FOR YOUR 2005 VINTAGE OR THE NEWLY PLANTED LEMON TREE IS DUG UP FOR THE PURPOSES OF MATURATION. IF ONLY YOUR OWNERS COULD UNDERSTAND THE VALUE OF RESEARCH AND COLLECTION OF BONES THAT IS SO IMPORTANT TO A DOG LIKE YOU. PERHAPS YOU COULD TEACH THEM A THING OR TWO ABOUT AGING WINE, INSTEAD OF WATCHING WITH DOGGED DISMAY AS THEY KNOCK BACK YET ANOTHER BOTTLE WITHOUT A THOUGHT FOR GIVING IT A CHANCE TO LAY DOWN AND IMPROVE SOMEWHERE IN THE GARDEN. **DRINK THIS MONTH** – OH SO FASHIONABLE VIOGNIER FROM PASO ROBLES.

LIBRA

♎

PEACE LOVING AND DIPLOMATIC, IF THERE WAS A UN IN DOG WORLD, YOU GUYS WOULD STAFF IT. YOU REMIND YOUR OWNER THAT EVEN AFTER EATING THE ROAST THAT WAS LEFT OUT FOR DINNER, FORGIVENESS IS NEXT TO 'DOGLINESS'. SO WHAT IF YOU ATE THE APPLE PIE, ICE-CREAM AND AFTER-DINNER MINTS THAT WERE ALSO HANGING AROUND. IT'S YOUR JOB TO MAKE SURE ALL FOOD IS SAFE AND FIT FOR HUMAN CONSUMPTION; SUCH IS YOUR BELIEF IN SHARING. JUST REMEMBER THAT CREATING A PLEASANT ENVIRONMENT FOR HUMANS TO LIVE IN MAY MEAN OCCASIONALLY GETTING OFF THE COUCH, AFTER YOU HAVE SO KINDLY WARMED IT FOR THEM. **DRINK THIS MONTH** – BALANCE BABY, BALANCE. OREGON RIESLING, OR PINOT GRIS OR …

SCORPIO

♏

SCORPIOS KNOW THE MEANING OF REVENGE. HOW MANY CUSHIONS, CURTAINS, AND OCCASIONAL SOFAS, HAVE BEEN CHEWED TO BITS WHEN YOU HAVE BEEN LEFT AT HOME ALONE! YOU GUYS NEED TO LEARN THAT REVENGE IS A DISH BEST SERVED COLD. TRY INSTEAD LEAVING A WELL-CHILLED (PREFERABLY BURIED AND LEFT OUTSIDE FOR A GOOD THREE TO TEN MONTHS) BONE UNDER THE FRESHLY LAUNDERED BED LINEN. A FECUND BONE SMELLS A THOUSAND WORDS I LIKE TO SAY, AND REVENGE SHOULD NEVER BE SWEET - IT SHOULD BE EXTREMELY RANCID. CUTTING THE CHEESE AND LEAVING THE ROOM QUICKLY WHILST YOUR HUMAN COMPANIONS ARE HAVING A DINNER PARTY, OR WHILST THEY'RE OPENING / DECANTING A DECENT BOTTLE SHOULD ALSO BE CONSIDERED. **DRINK THIS MONTH** – A WOOFY SYRAH FROM WASHINGTON.

SAGITTARIUS

YOU GUYS ARE THE HALF AND HALF OF THE ZODIAC AND ARE OFTEN DEMONSTRATED BY THE 57 HEINZ VARIETY OF THE DOG WORLD. MANY HALF WOLFHOUND, HALF TERRIER ARE BORN UNDER THIS SIGN. YOU GUYS LIKE TO BELIEVE THAT SPREADING YOUR SEED AROUND THE NEIGHBORHOOD WILL GUARANTEE THE SURVIVAL OF THE SPECIES. AS A CONSEQUENCE, YOU TEND TO OUTLIVE MOST BREEDS AND OFTEN ENJOY A LIFE OF LONGEVITY, AND EVEN HIGH INTELLIGENCE. YOUR PHYSICAL QUIRKINESS ENDEARS YOU TO OWNERS THE WORLD OVER. NOW IF ONLY ALL THE OTHER DOGS COULD 'KETCHUP'... **DRINK THIS MONTH** – ANY MERITAGE OR RHONE RANGER OR BOTH BLENDED.

CAPRICORN

YOUR MOTTO IS SLOW AND STEADY WINS THE RACE, WHICH MEANS HAVING LOTS OF DOG NAPS. LIKE THE HARDY GOAT YOUR SIGN EMBODIES, YOU ARE INCLINED TO EAT ANYTHING INCLUDING SHOES, PLANTS, TREES AND GARDEN HOSES. CAPRICORN TENDS TO RULE LABRADORS AND ROTTWEILERS, WHOSE NATURAL INSTINCT TO TRY CONSUMING ANYTHING ONCE, FORTUNATELY STOPS AT YOUNG CHILDREN UNDER THE AGE OF FIVE. FAITHFUL, COMMITTED, AND ALWAYS RELIABLE, YOUR STOIC CAPACITY FOR LOVING THE HUMAN RACE SHOULD BE REWARDED BOTH IN THIS LIFE AND THE NEXT. JUST REMEMBER THAT WHEN IN DOUBT, SLEEP IT OUT. **DRINK THIS MONTH** – A CUDDLY CALIFORNIAN CHARDONNAY.

AQUARIUS

ALWAYS OUT THERE, IN FACT YOU DON'T HAVE DOG TRAINERS, YOU HAVE DOG GURUS. 'DOG FRIENDS ARE THE BEST FRIENDS' IS YOUR PERSONAL MOTTO, AND YOU ARE KNOWN FOR YOUR CAPACITY TO BE LOVED BY JUST ABOUT EVERYONE, EXCEPT FOR THE OCCASIONAL CAT. YOU JUST DON'T GO OUT FOR WALKIES, YOU GO OUT TO SEND THE MESSAGE. WHAT YOU NEED TO REALIZE IS THAT A GOOD BONE ISN'T THE SECRET TO LONG LIFE, AS FAR AS THE REST OF THE WORLD IS CONCERNED. YOUR DOWNWARD DOG POSE IS A CREDIT TO THE YOGA MASTER THAT YOU ONCE CHARMED THE ASHRAM OFF OF. **DRINK THIS MONTH** – MONTEREY MERLOT .

PISCES

YOU LOT ARE THE PUSSYCATS OF THE ZODIAC. SO INCREDIBLY SENSITIVE, YOU CAN EMOTE AT THE DROP OF A BONE; LASSIE MOVIES WERE PROBABLY WRITTEN BY YOU. WHEN YOUR OWNERS LEAVE YOU ALONE IN THE HOUSE, YOU HOWL DOWN THE NEIGHBORHOOD FOR HOURS, AND MANY CALLS ARE MADE TO 911 IN THE BELIEF THAT SOMEBODY HAS DIED. OF COURSE ONCE YOUR OWNERS HAVE RETURNED, THE AFFECTION DELIVERED BY WET LICKS AND CONTINUOUSLY RUNNING LAPS AROUND THE COFFEE TABLE MAKE UP FOR ANY BAD BEHAVIOR, SAY FOR EXAMPLE, THE DIGGING UP OF YOUR OWNER'S CAR KEYS THAT MYSTERIOUSLY WENT MISSING THE LAST TIME YOU WERE LEFT HOME ALONE. PERHAPS YOUR 'KEY' TO HAPPINESS IS TO STOP HOUNDING PEOPLE. **DRINK THIS MONTH** – WHITE ZINFANDEL BUT DON'T DRINK WITH FISH – THEY ALWAYS WIN.

THE MADAME WAS AIDED AND ABETTED BY SALLY ASHTON AND ZAR BROOKS. SALLY IS THE PROUD OWNER OF TWO BOY BASENJIS, NYAM NYAM AND ZEBEDEE, WHOSE CAPACITY TO DISTRACT HER WHILST SHE IS WRITING IS MATCHED ONLY BY THEIR ABILITY TO CHEW HER FAVORITE BOOKS. SUCH IS LIFE IN A WORLD WHERE HER DOGS ALWAYS HAVE THE LAST WORD! SALLY@STRANGERANDSTRANGER.BIZ; ZAR IS THE PRINCIPAL SOPHIST OF WINE INDUSTRY CONSULTANTS STRANGER & STRANGER, IE. A TYPIST WHO DRINKS. HE IS OFTEN WALKED BY THE ABOVEMENTIONED CORK HOUNDS. ZAR@STRANGERANDSTRANGER.BIZ

SCOOBY

FAVORITE TOYS: HIS SOCCER BALL
AND ANYTHING THAT MAKES A NOISE
FAVORITE FOODS: TOSTADAS AND CANDY
FAVORITE PASTIMES: RUNNING AND SLEEPING
PET PEEVE: PEOPLE BLOWING AIR ON HIS FACE

PAPAPIETRO PERRY WINERY HEALDSBURG, CA | CHIHUAHUA, 5 MONTHS | OWNER: ESTEBAN GARCIA

KNOWN ACCOMPLICES: EMMA,
SHADOW, TREVOR AND MIKE
NAUGHTIEST DEED: EATING THE
NEIGHBOR'S KIDS' CATCHER'S MITT
PET PEEVE: NOT BEING FED TREATS
FAVORITE FOOD: GRAPES FROM THE VINE

DIETER

FAVORITE FOOD: DOG FOOD
PET PEEVE: NOT BEING ABLE TO RUN
KNOWN ACCOMPLICE: ESTHER THE HAWK
FAVORITE PASTIME: HUNTING WITH ESTHER
FAVORITE TOY: FRANKENSQUEEKER, HIS SQUEAKY TOY
NAUGHTIEST DEED: JUMPING ON THE HOOD OF A NEW CAR
OWNERS: ROB BELL AND CHRYSTI VAN ECKHARDT-BELL

FAVORITE FOOD: RAW FOOD
KNOWN ACCOMPLICE: JOSIE
FAVORITE TOY: SQUEAKY TOYS
PET PEEVES: RAISED VOICES AND NOISE
FAVORITE PASTIMES: SHEEP HERDING AND BEACH RUNS

HANNAH

JOSIE

PET PEEVE: BATHS
FAVORITE FOOD: RAW FOOD
KNOWN ACCOMPLICE: HANNAH
FAVORITE PASTIME: BEACH RUNS
FAVORITE TOYS: BALLS AND STICKS
NAUGHTIEST DEED: STEALING SACK LUNCHES

FAVORITE FOOD: LEFTOVERS
KNOWN ACCOMPLICE: JASON
PET PEEVE: BEING ON A LEASH
FAVORITE TOY: RUBBER CHICKEN
FAVORITE PASTIME: STARING AT HER OWNERS
NAUGHTIEST DEED: STEALING TWO FILET MIGNON FROM THE COUNTER

MABLE

RUBY

KNOWN ACCOMPLICES:
SCOOBY AND LUKE
FAVORITE FOOD: MEAT
PET PEEVE: SWEARING
FAVORITE TOY: TENNIS BALL
FAVORITE PASTIME: PLAYING WITH TENNIS BALLS
NAUGHTIEST DEED: STEALING MEAT OFF THE COUNTER

NAUGHTIEST DEED: CHASING AFTER CATS
FAVORITE FOOD: PEOPLE FOOD OF COURSE
FAVORITE PASTIME: NAPPING UNDER THE VALLEY OAK
PET PEEVE: STAYING AT HOME WHILE BRIAN GOES TO WORK
KNOWN ACCOMPLICE: SAGE THE GAL FROM ARMIDA WINERY

DANTE

MADISON

PET PEEVES: TICKS AND FLEAS
KNOWN ACCOMPLICE: DALLAS
FAVORITE PASTIME: CHASING HER TAIL
FOR TASTING ROOM GUESTS
FAVORITE TOYS: HEADLESS STUFFED
ANIMALS LEFT ALL OVER THE VINEYARD
NAUGHTIEST DEED: EATING THE CHRISTMAS EVE LEG OF LAMB
FAVORITE FOODS: PIZZA CRUSTS AND HER MORNING BANANA

FAVORITE TOY: GLOVES
FAVORITE PASTIME: DIGGING FOR GOPHERS
FAVORITE FOOD: PEOPLE FOOD OR HORSE MANURE
NAUGHTIEST DEED: STEALING AND BURYING GLOVES
KNOWN ACCOMPLICES: ROWDY, SASSY, MATTIE AND SATIE

BINGO

MAX

FAVORITE PASTIMES: SLEEPING IN
THE SUN AND CHASING SQUIRRELS
FAVORITE FOODS: STEW AND WINE
PET PEEVES: SQUIRRELS AND SKUNKS
NAUGHTIEST DEED: CHASING TRUCKS
KNOWN ACCOMPLICES: SUNNY AND RUFF
FAVORITE TOYS: SOCCER BALL AND TRUCKS

LARSON FAMILY WINERY SONOMA, CA | GERMAN SHEPHERD X, 7 | OWNERS: TOM AND BECKY LARSON

NAUGHTIEST DEED: WALKING MUDDY
FEET THROUGH TASTING ROOM

PET PEEVE: HAVING HIS TAIL PULLED

FAVORITE PASTIME:
CHASING RABBITS AND BIRDS

KNOWN ACCOMPLICES:
LESLIE, CRYSTAL AND JORGE

FAVORITE FOOD: CHICKEN JERKY

OREO

MAX

NAUGHTIEST DEED: CHASING THE NEIGHBOR'S BULL
FAVORITE TOY: YELLOW STUFFED CHICKEN
FAVORITE FOOD: T-BONE STEAK BONES
FAVORITE PASTIME: CHASING THE CAT
KNOWN ACCOMPLICE: ALEXANDER
PET PEEVE: BEING LEFT ALONE

FAVORITE TOY: OLD BALL
NAUGHTIEST DEED: JUMPING
KNOWN ACCOMPLICE: BRANDY
PET PEEVES: BATHING AND BEING LEFT OUTSIDE
FAVORITE PASTIME: CHASING AFTER ANYTHING
FAVORITE FOOD: ANYTHING, INCLUDING GRAPES

CHICO

MAURITSSON FAMILY WINERY HEALDSBURG, CA | LABRADOR, 3 | OWNERS: CLAY AND CARRIE MAURITSSON

SOHO

FAVORITE FOOD: GREENIES
FAVORITE TOY: BARREL BUNG
FAVORITE PASTIME: PLAYING TUG OF WAR
PET PEEVE: ANY WATER THAT COMES OUT OF A HOSE
NAUGHTIEST DEED: STEALING BARREL BUNGS OUT OF BARRELS

CARRIE

FAVORITE TOY: HER HUSBAND, CLAY
NAUGHTIEST DEED: NOT THAT NAUGHTY
PET PEEVE: THE ALL BLACKS RUGBY TEAM
FAVORITE PASTIME: TRAVELING AND DRINKING WINE

FAVORITE TOY: 20-FOOT ROPE
PET PEEVE: BEING ON A LEASH
FAVORITE FOOD: SCOOBY SNACKS
KNOWN ACCOMPLICES: ZACH AND ABBY
NAUGHTIEST DEED: SPILLING A BAG OF
BIRDSEED ALL THROUGH THE HOUSE
FAVORITE PASTIMES: CHEWING SHOES
AND CHASING CATS

ZOE

FAVORITE FOOD: PIG EARS
PET PEEVE: NOT GOING TO WORK
FAVORITE TOYS: TENNIS BALL AND FRISBEE
FAVORITE PASTIMES: RIDING ON THE ATV AND JET SKI
NAUGHTIEST DEED: EATING TRI-TIP OFF THE PICNIC TABLE
KNOWN ACCOMPLICES: GRANDMA, MACKENZIE, COURTNEY AND JEREMY

EARNHARDT

COBBER DE VINO

KNOWN ACCOMPLICE: JOAN
FAVORITE FOOD: CHICKEN AND RICE
FAVORITE TOY: CRAZY BOUNCING DOG BALL
NAUGHTIEST DEED: POOPING ON THE LAWN
PET PEEVE: OTHER DOGS POOPING ON THE LAWN
FAVORITE PASTIME: TRYING TO HERD THE HORSES

FAVORITE FOOD: DAN'S
PET PEEVE: OTHER PUPPIES
FAVORITE TOY: ANYTHING THAT SQUEAKS
KNOWN ACCOMPLICES: THE NEIGHBOR'S DOGS
NAUGHTIEST DEED: SWEEPING THE COFFEE TABLE WITH HIS TAIL
FAVORITE PASTIMES: CHASING RABBITS IN THE VINEYARD AND CAR RIDES

RILEY

OWNER: DAN KOSTA | LABRADOR, 7 | **KOSTA BROWNE WINERY** SEBASTOPOL, CA

ROXANNE

FAVORITE TOY: A BALL

PET PEEVE: JACK RABBITS

FAVORITE FOOD: TWO SCRAMBLED
EGGS WITH NIGHTLY DINNER

FAVORITE PASTIME: SWIMMING IN
THE RANCH IRRIGATION LAKES

NAUGHTIEST DEED: JUMPING INTO
THE NEIGHBOR'S CHICKEN RUN

PET PEEVE: BEING PATTED
FAVORITE FOOD: DOG FOOD
FAVORITE PASTIMES: CHASING
RABBITS AND SLEEPING
NAUGHTIEST DEED: HOME GARDENING
KNOWN ACCOMPLICES: DAISY AND ODE
FAVORITE TOY: STUFFED SQUEAKY SNAKE

HOLLY

MOLLY

PET PEEVE: FIREWORKS
FAVORITE FOOD: PEANUT BUTTER
FAVORITE TOY: GIANT STUFFED LABRADOR
KNOWN ACCOMPLICES: BASIL, GINGER AND ARAGORN
NAUGHTIEST DEED: HAVING A MUD BATH BEFORE ENTERING HOUSE
FAVORITE PASTIME: TRYING TO CARRY MORE THAN THREE BALLS IN HER MOUTH AT SAME TIME

FAVORITE TOY: OLD BONE
FAVORITE FOODS: CHEESE AND SAUSAGES
KNOWN ACCOMPLICES: TOM, CASSIDY AND COOPER
PET PEEVES: BEING ALONE AND HYPERACTIVE DOGS
NAUGHTIEST DEED: KNOCKING OVER EXPENSIVE WINE
FAVORITE PASTIMES: DIGGING AND FOLLOWING HIS NOSE

WINSTON

CHECKERS

FAVORITE TOY: A BALL
PET PEEVE: LIGHTNING
FAVORITE FOOD: CARROTS
KNOWN ACCOMPLICE: CASSIDY
FAVORITE PASTIME: PLAYING BALL

PET PEEVE: GROOMING
FAVORITE FOOD: CHEESE
FAVORITE TOY: ANYTHING THAT SQUEAKS
FAVORITE PASTIME: CHASING EVERYTHING
NAUGHTIEST DEED: LAPPING UP THE DRIPPINGS
FROM THE WINE FILTER THEN SLEEPING IT OFF
KNOWN ACCOMPLICES: SCHATSIE, AMELIA AND STANZIE THE CAT

PENNY

KEN

PET PEEVE: FROST
FAVORITE FOOD: THAI FOOD
FAVORITE PASTIME: TRAVELING
FAVORITE TOY: THE GRAPE HOE
NAUGHTIEST DEED: SPEEDING
KNOWN ACCOMPLICES: PAIGE AND KELLY

PET PEEVE: GUNSHOTS
FAVORITE TOY: ANTLERS
FAVORITE PASTIME: SUNBATHING
FAVORITE FOODS: POPCORN AND SQUASH
NAUGHTIEST DEED: WEEDING THE GARDEN
KNOWN ACCOMPLICES: ZOEY AND CRAMER

PAIGE

FAVORITE TOY: ROCKS
NAUGHTIEST DEED: GETTING
INTO GARBAGE – EVERY DAY
KNOWN ACCOMPLICE: CALLISTO
FAVORITE FOODS: BREAD AND CRACKERS
FAVORITE PASTIMES: EATING GARBAGE AND
BEFRIENDING PICNICKERS AT THE WINERY
PET PEEVE: A CERTAIN COLLEGE PROFESSOR

EMMY LOU

PET PEEVE: CATS
KNOWN ACCOMPLICE: KATY RU
FAVORITE FOOD: PEANUT BUTTER
FAVORITE TOY: ANYTHING THAT SQUEAKS
NAUGHTIEST DEED: GETTING INTO THE GARBAGE
FAVORITE PASTIME: GOING TO THE BEACH TO DIG AND ROLL IN THE SAND

FAVORITE FOOD: EVERYTHING
FAVORITE TOY: A TENNIS BALL
KNOWN ACCOMPLICES: RUBEE AND EMMY LOU
FAVORITE PASTIMES: PLAYING FETCH AND SLEEPING
NAUGHTIEST DEED: DESTROYING EMMA'S OFFICE DOOR WHILE LEFT ALONE

B

YAHI

PET PEEVE: DRUNKS
FAVORITE TOY:
JIM'S MIND
FAVORITE FOOD: GOPHERS
KNOWN ACCOMPLICES: JIM AND QUEENIE
FAVORITE PASTIME: PATROLLING THE VINEYARD

THAT'S A 100-POINT BURGER

by Craig McGill

Big, lean, uncomplicated, *uncompromising, mouth-fill of intense, unparalleled flavour. Not to stick in the fridge but to consume now. You could be excused for thinking that some of that tasting room jargon has rubbed off on me and that I'm describing one of my favorite pinot noirs. But no, I'm talking about the 100-point burger.*

Let's face it. The USA is the undisputed king of the hamburger. There are burgers everywhere and most of them are damn good. I'd worked my way around ten states photographing for the Wine Dogs book and managed to sample burgers almost everywhere I went. Burgers were big news over here. But it didn't strike me until the last week of the trip, that all of these famous people that I'd met in the wine industry weren't that interested in talking about wine or dogs. It was burgers that they craved. It was this culinary delight that was every decent wine-maker's holy grail – they all want to find the 100-point burger.

Robert Parker's love of the mighty American hamburger is legendary. It was in fact Robert who tempted me to keep searching for the 100-point burger. After photographing his two dogs, Buddy and Hoover, the conversation mysteriously turned to burgers. Maybe Robert could smell my love of burgers – after all I had so many burgers over in the US that I was beginning to look like one. After I had left New York and was driving to Maryland to see Robert, I had decided that I'd eaten enough burgers for a lifetime. But Robert had different ideas. First, he described the In-N-Out burger as one of the country's finest. But don't order off the menu, he cautioned. Just walk up to the counter and order double, double animal style. It's not on the menu but it's fantastic. It was like a burger subculture with its own language. Well, I just had to have one.

I informed Robert that I was flying to Santa Barbara in the morning and that hopefully I'll grab an In-N-Out burger when I arrive. Robert's eyes lit up and he told me that he'd just returned from Santa Barbara and I must eat the pièce de résistance of burgers – The Kobe Burger. The Kobe Burger can be found at The Wine Cask in Fess Parker's Inn. It's sensational! Well, I didn't need any better critique than that, so next day I was hoofing down a Kobe Burger. I can tell you now that it was every bit as tasty as Robert described. The highest-quality certified Wagyu beef, caramelised onions, grilled white cheese, fresh tomatoes and crisp lettuce. Cooked to perfection. I devoured it and proclaimed to the staff that it should be renamed the 100-point burger. They all happily agreed but this may have just been a ploy to get me to leave quicker. Who knows?

I didn't know it until the next day, but the 100-point burger was my undoing. I awoke that morning with no idea of the events that were about to unfold. I arrived at my first photo-shoot for the day at Carhartt Vineyards and was greeted by Mike and Brooke Carhartt and an excitable rat terrier named Buddy. Buddy proved to be a difficult customer to photograph and was a bit over me telling him to sit all the time without sharing that dog treat I kept waving in front of the camera. So, I decided to squat down a bit closer to Buddy's height. It was at this very moment that an almighty roar ripped through the air, reminiscent of perhaps the terrifying noise experienced in the great quake of 1906 or, worse still, the after-fart from eating all of those burgers. At this time the Carhartts, simultaneously, silently and politely, took a few steps backwards and Buddy's tail began to wag furiously and he sat with unbridled enthusiasm not seen to this point.

But much to my embarrassment, it was neither an earthquake nor a fart but the noise made as I split my pants when I squatted to photograph Buddy. I got some good shots of Buddy and quickly left for my next appointment.

Unfortunately, I had to return to the scene of the misdemeanor only a few minutes later with my tail between my legs, as I had left my only copy of the Australian Wine Dogs book there. Not a word was mentioned about my indiscretion as I returned. As polite as Mike and Brooke are, I have a sneaking suspicion that when they read this story it may be the first time they realise what events actually took place that day.

As I write this story, true to my word, I have not eaten another burger since the 100-point burger. But what I don't understand is – surely it can't be the pinot noir I'm consuming giving me all this wind!

SUSAN ELLIOTT

SYDNEY, NSW

Stella and Sue

SUSAN IS A MULTI-SKILLED ARTIST WITH A BACKGROUND IN FINE ART, ILLUSTRATION AND PRINTMAKING. AFTER COMPLETING TWO YEARS OF A PSYCHOLOGY DEGREE, SUE CHANGED TO A CAREER IN ART. SHE GRADUATED FROM THE CITY ART INSTITUTE IN 1986, MAJORING IN DRAWING, PRINTMAKING AND PAINTING.

AFTER TWO YEARS LIVING ABROAD, SUE RETURNED TO AUSTRALIA AND EXHIBITED HER GRAPHIC ART AND SCREENPRINTS EXTENSIVELY AROUND SYDNEY WHILE ALSO WORKING IN A NUMBER OF SMALL DESIGN STUDIOS. SHE HAS DEVELOPED INTO AN AWARD-WINNING GRAPHIC DESIGNER WITH OVER 17 YEARS OF EXPERIENCE IN THE INDUSTRY.

SUE JOINED McGILL DESIGN GROUP IN 1999 AS CO-OWNER AND CREATIVE DIRECTOR. SHE IS ALSO CO-FOUNDER AND PRINCIPAL OF THE GIANT DOG PUBLISHING HOUSE, WHICH IS RESPONSIBLE FOR PRODUCING A NUMBER OF BEST-SELLING BOOKS INCLUDING THE WINE DOGS AND FOOTY DOGS TITLES.

FAVORITE FOOD: NOODLES
FAVORITE PASTIME: WATCHING MOVIES WITH STELLA
NAUGHTIEST DEED: TEASING HUSKIES
KNOWN ACCOMPLICES: CRAIG, TOK, TARKA AND STELLA
OBSESSIONS: BATH SALTS AND FOOTBALL MULLETS OF THE '80s
PET PEEVE: WHISTLING

SUE'S KNOWLEDGE OF DOGS IS UNPARALLELED AND IN THE PAST HAS ALSO FOUND TIME TO BE A SUCCESSFUL SIBERIAN HUSKY BREEDER. SHE IS CONSIDERED AMONGST THE PACK TO BE A GREAT OWNER. SUE IS A LOVER OF ALL WHITE WINE AND USUALLY REACHES FOR HER FAVORITE RIESLING WHEN FEELING A LITTLE HUSKY.

GIANT DOG PUBLISHING

GIANT DOG IS A NICHE INDEPENDENT PUBLISHING HOUSE SPECIALIZING IN PRODUCING BENCHMARK QUALITY DESIGN AND ART BOOKS. RECENT PUBLICATIONS INCLUDE *WINE DOGS: ORIGINAL EDITION*, *WINE DOGS DELUXE EDITION*, *FOOTY DOGS* AND *WINE DOGS: USA EDITION*. www.giantdog.com.au

CRAIG McGILL

SYDNEY, NSW

ORIGINALLY FROM SHEPPARTON, VICTORIA, CRAIG IS A SELF-TAUGHT DESIGNER AND ILLUSTRATOR WHO STARTED HIS OWN DESIGN BUSINESS IN MELBOURNE AT 18 YEARS OF AGE. DURING THAT TIME HE WAS APPOINTED AS A DESIGN CONSULTANT TO THE RESERVE BANK OF AUSTRALIA.

HIS DESIGNS AND ILLUSTRATIONS HAVE GRACED BANKNOTES THROUGHOUT THE WORLD, INCLUDING THE AUSTRALIAN BICENTENARY TEN-DOLLAR NOTE. HIS WORK APPEARS ON THE ORIGINAL AUSTRALIAN $100 NOTE, PAPUA NEW GUINEA KINA, COOK ISLAND DOLLARS AND ENGLISH POUND TRAVELLER'S CHEQUES. CRAIG WAS ALSO INVOLVED IN THE DESIGN AND ILLUSTRATION OF MANY COUNTRIES' SECURITY DOCUMENTS SUCH AS PASSPORTS, BONDS AND TRAVELLER'S CHEQUES.

AT THE AGE OF 23 HE DESIGNED THE ENTIRE SERIES OF THE COOK ISLAND BANKNOTES AND IT IS BELIEVED THAT HE WAS THE WORLD'S YOUNGEST DESIGNER TO DESIGN A COUNTRY'S COMPLETE CURRENCY. IN 1991, CRAIG MOVED TO SYDNEY WHERE HIS ILLUSTRATIONS WERE REGULARLY COMMISSIONED BY AGENCIES AND DESIGNERS BOTH IN AUSTRALIA AND AROUND THE WORLD.

Tok, Craig and Tarka

DATE OF BIRTH: DEAD IN DOG YEARS

FAVORITE FOOD: ROAST DUCK AND PINOT NOIR

FAVORITE PASTIMES: VENTRILOQUISM AND BEING A BIG KID

NAUGHTIEST DEED: CHASING HUSKIES WHILE STARK NAKED

OBSESSIONS: BEER, WINE AND COLLECTING USELESS THINGS

KNOWN ACCOMPLICES: SUE, TOK, TARKA AND STELLA

PET PEEVE: UNORIGINAL IDEAS

HE IS NOW WIDELY KNOWN AS AUSTRALIA'S ONLY FREELANCE CURRENCY DESIGNER. CRAIG HAS ALSO DESIGNED AND ILLUSTRATED FIVE STAMPS FOR AUSTRALIA POST.

CRAIG HAS BEEN CREATIVE DIRECTOR OF HIS OWN AGENCY, McGILL DESIGN GROUP, FOR OVER TWENTY-THREE YEARS.

HAVING GROWN UP WITH A SUCCESSION OF BEAGLES, CRAIG IS NOW OWNED BY THREE SIBERIAN HUSKIES. www.realnasty.com.au

McGILL DESIGN GROUP

McGILL DESIGN GROUP WAS FORMED IN 1981 AND SPECIALIZES IN PROVIDING A WIDE RANGE OF QUALITY GRAPHIC DESIGN SERVICES. THE STUDIO HAS PRODUCED NUMEROUS FINE WINE LABELS AND PACKAGING AS WELL AS CORPORATE IDENTITIES, ADVERTISING, PUBLICATIONS AND TELEVISION COMMERCIALS. www.mcgilldesigngroup.com

PHOTOGRAPHERS

Tok McGill

CRAIG McGILL (AKA 'THE DOG WHISPERER') SHOOTS EXCLUSIVELY FOR GIANT DOG PUBLISHING. HE CREDITS HIS SUCCESS TO HIS MATADOR-LIKE SKILLS WITH A SCHMACKO. www.winedogs.com

Front cover of Jojo Maximus, back cover of Ruby, title page of Pixie and pages 2, 9, 10, 11, 13, 16, 17, 18, 20, 21, 22, 23, 25, 26, 27, 29, 30, 31, 32, 33, 36, 37, 38, 39, 40, 41, 42, 44, 46, 47, 48, 52, 53, 54, 55, 56, 59, 62, 63, 64, 66, 67, 68, 69, 71, 72, 75, 77, 78, 79, 80, 82, 83, 84, 85, 86, 88, 89, 90, 91, 92, 93, 97, 98, 99, 101, 102, 104, 105, 106, 116, 117, 118, 119, 120, 121, 122, 123, 124, 125, 127, 135, 136, 137, 138, 139, 140, 142, 143, 144, 145, 146, 149, 150, 151, 153, 154, 155, 156, 157, 163, 166, 167, 168, 175, 176, 177, 179, 180, 182, 184, 185, 187, 188, 189, 196, 198, 200, 201, 203, 204, 205, 209, 213, 214, 219, 220, 221, 222, 223, 224, 225, 226, 229, 232, 233, 234, 235, 236, 238, 239, 240, 241, 243, 244, 247, 248, 250, 252, 253, 256, 257, 259, 260, 265, 267, 277, 278, 279, 282, 284, 287, 291, 292, 301, 302, 303, 304, 306, 307, 308, 309, 311, 314, 315, 316, 317, 318, 322, 323, 324, 326, 329, 330, 331, 332, 337, 339, 344, 346, 349, 350, 355, 362, 365, 367, 375, 376, 379, 381, 384, 391, 393, 397, 398, 399, 400, 405, 407, 415, 417, 419, 421, 426, 427, 431, 435, 438, 440, 443, 445, 447, 448, 449, 451, 452, 456, 457, 459, 460, 462, 463, 464, 466, 470, 476, 477, 481, 482, 484, 485, 487, 488, 489, 490, 491, 492, 493, 496, 497, 498, 499, 500 and 506. ALL IMAGES © CRAIG McGILL 2006

PAGE 197: PATCH FROM MUTT LYNCH, SONOMA CA COURTESY OF KEVIN JUDD © 2006

PAGE 211: SPOT FROM PACIFIC STAR WINERY, FORT BRAGG CA COURTESY OF SUZETTE COOK © 2006

PAGE 388: SHOOBOX CHARLIE FROM SINE QUA NON, OAK VIEW CA COURTESY OF KATY OVERSTREET © 2006

PAGE 442: MOOSE FROM B.R. COHN WINERY, GLEN ELLEN CA COURTESY OF MARTY COHN © 2006

Maisy Boddington

JAMES BODDINGTON HAS OVER 19 YEARS EXPERIENCE AS A PROFESSIONAL PHOTOGRAPHER. HE IS RECOGNIZED AS ONE OF AUSTRALIA'S LEADING PORTRAIT AND REPORTAGE PHOTOGRAPHERS. JAMES CONTINUES TO FREELANCE FOR AN EVER-INCREASING DIVERSITY OF EDITORIAL, CORPORATE AND ADVERTISING CLIENTS. HIS WORK CAN ALSO BE SEEN IN THE BOOKS, *WINE DOGS: DELUXE EDITION* AND *FOOTY DOGS*. JAMES ENTHUSIASTICALLY TRAVELED AROUND THE USA WITHOUT BEING BITTEN ONCE! www.jamesboddington.com

Pages 14, 15, 19, 24, 28, 34, 35, 43, 45, 50, 51, 58, 60, 61, 65, 70, 73, 74, 87, 94, 95, 96, 100, 103, 114, 115, 126, 129, 130, 131, 132, 133, 134, 147, 148, 152, 158, 159, 160, 161, 162, 164, 165, 174, 178, 181, 183, 186, 190, 191, 192, 193, 194, 195, 199, 202, 206, 207, 208, 210, 212, 218, 227, 230, 231, 237, 242, 245, 246, 249, 251, 254, 255, 258, 264, 266, 268, 269, 270, 271, 272, 273, 274, 275, 276, 280, 281, 283, 285, 286, 288, 289, 290, 293, 294, 295, 300, 305, 310, 312, 313, 319, 320, 321, 325, 327, 328, 338, 340, 341, 342, 343, 345, 347, 348, 351, 352, 353, 354, 356, 357, 358, 359, 360, 361, 363, 364, 366, 368, 369, 373, 374, 377, 378, 380, 382, 383, 385, 386, 387, 392, 394, 395, 396, 401, 402, 403, 404, 406, 408, 409, 410, 411, 412, 413, 414, 416, 418, 420, 422, 423, 424, 425, 428, 429, 430, 432, 433, 434, 436, 437, 439, 444, 446, 450, 453, 454, 455, 458, 461, 465, 471, 472, 473, 474, 475, 478, 479, 480, 483, 486, 494, 495 and 507. ALL IMAGES © JAMES BODDINGTON 2006

WINERY AND VINEYARD LISTINGS

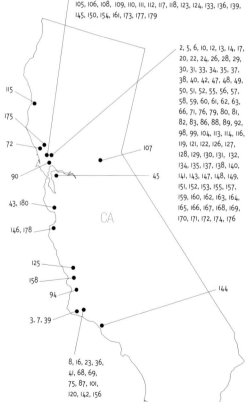

1, 4, 9, 11, 15, 18, 19, 21, 25, 27, 32, 44, 46, 53, 54, 64, 65, 67, 70, 73, 74, 77, 78, 84, 85, 91, 93, 95, 96, 97, 100, 102, 103, 105, 106, 108, 109, 110, 111, 112, 117, 118, 123, 124, 133, 136, 139, 145, 150, 154, 161, 173, 177, 179

2, 5, 6, 10, 12, 13, 14, 17, 20, 22, 24, 26, 28, 29, 30, 31, 33, 34, 35, 37, 38, 40, 42, 47, 48, 49, 50, 51, 52, 55, 56, 57, 58, 59, 60, 61, 62, 63, 66, 71, 76, 79, 80, 81, 82, 83, 86, 88, 89, 92, 98, 99, 104, 113, 114, 116, 119, 121, 122, 126, 127, 128, 129, 130, 131, 132, 134, 135, 137, 138, 140, 141, 143, 147, 148, 149, 151, 152, 153, 155, 157, 159, 160, 162, 163, 164, 165, 166, 167, 168, 169, 170, 171, 172, 174, 176

115

175

72

90

43, 180

146, 178

125

158

94

3, 7, 39

107

45

144

CA

8, 16, 23, 36, 41, 68, 69, 75, 87, 101, 120, 142, 156

CALIFORNIA

1. A. Rafanelli Vineyard and Winery PAGE 301
4685 W. Dry Creek Rd,
Healdsburg CA 95448
Ph: 707 433 1385 Fax: 707 433 3836
Email: garden2view@aol.com
Web: www.arafanelliwinery.com

2. Altamura Vineyards and Winery PAGE 277
1700 Wooden Valley Rd, Napa CA 94558
Ph: 707 253 2000 Fax: 707 255 8987
Email: altamurawinery@aol.com
Web: www.altamura.com

3. Ampelos Cellars and Vineyards
PAGES 66, 188, 247
7253 Santos Rd, Lompoc CA 93436
Ph: 805 736 9957 Fax: 805 456 0461
Email: info@ampeloscellars.com
Web: www.ampeloscellars.com

4. Arista Winery PAGE 330
7015 Westside Rd, Healdsburg CA 95448
Ph: 707 473 0606 Fax: 707 473 0635
Email: info@aristawinery.com
Web: www.aristawinery.com

5. Atalon Winery PAGE 462
7600 St. Helena Hwy, Oakville CA 94562
Ph: 707 948 2640 Fax: 707 948 4114
Email: info@atalon.com
Web: www.atalon.com

6. August Briggs PAGE 150
333 Silverado Trail, Calistoga CA 94515
Ph: 707 942 4912 Fax: 707 942 5854
Email: beth@augustbriggswines.com
Web: www.augustbriggswines.com

7. Babcock Winery & Vineyards PAGE 204
5175 E. Hwy 246, Lompoc CA 93436
Ph: 805 736 1455 Fax: 805 736 3886
Email: info@babcockwinery.com
Web: www.babcockwinery.com

8. Beckmen Vineyards PAGE 225
2670 Ontiveros Rd, Los Olivos CA 93441
Ph: 805 688 8664 Fax: 805 688 9983
Email: info@beckmenvineyards.com
Web: www.beckmenvineyards.com

9. Belvedere Winery PAGE 248
4035 Westside Rd, Healdsburg CA 95448
Ph: 707 431 4440 Fax: 707 433 4927
Email: belvedere@hwines.com
Web: www.belvederewinery.com

10. Bennett Lane Winery PAGE 327
3340 Hwy 128, Calistoga CA 94515
Ph: 1877 629 6272 Fax: 707 942 6482
Email: info@bennettlane.com
Web: www.bennettlane.com

11. Benziger Family Winery
PAGES 106, 149, 250, 267, 316, 317, 435, 443
1883 London Ranch Rd, Glen Ellen CA 95442
Ph: 707 935 4046 Fax: 707 935 3018
Email: greatwine@benziger.com
Web: www.benziger.com

12. Beringer Vineyards PAGES 314, 315
2000 Main St, St. Helena CA 94974
Ph: 707 963 7115
Email: beringer@beringer.com
Web: www.beringer.com

13. Blackbird Vineyards PAGE 280
5033 Big Ranch Rd, Napa CA 94558
Ph: 707 252 4444 Fax: 707 252 9999
Email: info@blackbirdvineyards.com
Web: www.blackbirdvineyards.com

14. Bouchaine Vineyards PAGES 423, 461
1075 Buchli Station Rd, Napa CA 94558
Ph: 707 252 9065 Fax: 707 252 0401
Email: info@bouchaine.com
Web: www.bouchaine.com

15. B.R. Cohn Winery PAGE 442
15000 Sonoma Hwy, Glen Ellen CA 95442
Phone: 800 330 4064 Fax: 707 938-4585
Email: info@brcohn.com
Web: www.brcohn.com

16. Bridlewood Estate
BACK COVER, PAGES 78, 236
3555 Roblar Ave, Santa Ynez CA 93460
Ph: 508 688 9000 Fax: 805 688 2443
Email: info@bridlewoodwinery.com
Web: www.bridlewoodwinery.com

17. Brookdale Vineyards PAGE 235
4006 Silverado Trail, Napa CA 94558
Ph: 707 258 1454 Fax: 707 255 8561
Email: info@brookdalewine.com
Web: www.brookdalewine.com

18. Bucklin PAGES 88, 89
8 Old Hill Ranch Rd, Glen Ellen CA 95442
Ph: 707 933 1726 Fax: 707 938 9169
Email: Kin@BuckZin.com
Web: www.buckzin.com

19. Buena Vista Winery PAGE 391
27000 Ramal Rd, Sonoma CA 95476
Ph: 707 252 7117 Fax: 707 252 0392
Email: TastingRoom@buenavista
carneros.com
Web: www.buenavistacarneros.com

20. Cain Vineyard and Winery PAGE 268
3800 Langtry Rd, St. Helena CA 94574
Ph: 707 963 9155 Fax: 707 963 9502
Email: winery@cainfive.com
Web: www.cainfive.com

21. Camellia Cellars PAGE 152
57 Front St, Healdsburg CA 95448
Ph: 707 433 1290 Fax: 707 433 1290
Email: chris@camelliacellars.com
Web: www.camelliacellars.com

22. Cardinale PAGE 22
7600 St. Helena Hwy, Oakville CA 94562
Ph: 800 588 0279 Fax: 707 944 2824
Email: info@cardinale.com
Web: www.cardinale.com

**23. Carhartt Vineyard
and Winery** PAGE 232
1691 Alamo Pintado Rd, Solvang CA 93463
Ph: 805 688 0685 Fax: 805 688 3004
Email: info@carharttvineyard.com
Web: www.carharttvineyard.com

24. Carlo Mondavi Cellars PAGE 264
PO Box 2, Oakville CA 94562
Ph: 310 205 9907 Fax: 310 205 9909
Email: carlo.mondavi@daviskin.com
Web: www.davigroup.com

25. Carol Shelton Wines PAGE 191
P.O. Box 755, Windsor CA 95492
Ph: 707 575 3441 Fax: 707 575 0245
Email: zin@carolshelton.com
Web: www.carolshelton.com

**26. Casa Nuestra Winery
and Vineyards** PAGE 320
3451 Silverado Trail North,
St. Helena CA 94574
Ph: 707 963 5783 Fax: 707 693 3174
Email: info@casanuestra.com
Web: www.casanuestra.com

27. Castle Vineyards & Winery PAGE 151
122 W. Spain St, Sonoma CA 95476
Ph: 707 996 1966 Fax: 707 996 1582
Email: Susan@CastleVineyards.com
Web: www.castlevineyards.com

28. Ceja Vineyards PAGE 281
1016 Las Amigas Rd, Napa CA 94558
Ph: 707 255 3954 Fax: 707 253 7998
Email: wine@cejavineyards.com
Web: www.cejavineyards.com

**29. Chappellet Vineyards
and Winery** PAGES 14, 313
1581 Sage Canyon Rd, St. Helena CA 94574
Ph: 707 968 7136 Fax: 707 967 9424
Email: info@chappellet.com
Web: www.chappellet.com

30. Chateau Montelena PAGE 15
1429 Tubbs Ln, Calistoga CA 94515
Ph: 707 942 5105 Fax: 707 942 4221
Email: customer-service@montelena.com
Web: www.montelena.com

31. Chateau Potelle Winery
PAGES 95, 100, 321
3875 Mt. Veeder Rd, Napa CA 94558
Ph: 707 255 9440 Fax: 707 255 9444
Email: info@chateaupotelle.com
Web: www.chateaupotelle.com

32. Chateau St. Jean PAGE 406
8555 Sonoma Hwy, Kenwood CA 95452
Ph: 707 833 4134
Web: www.chateaustjean.com

33. Clark-Claudon Vineyards PAGE 342
305 Brookside Dr, Angwin CA 94508
Ph: 707 965 9393 Fax: 707 965 1135
Email: info@clarkclaudon.com
Web: www.clarkclaudon.com

34. Cliff Lede Vineyards PAGES 26, 257, 307
1473 Yountville Cross Rd,
Yountville CA 94599
Ph: 707 944 8642 Fax: 707 754 1613
Email: Info@CliffLedeVineyards.com
Web: www.cliffledevineyards.com

35. Clos Du Val PAGES 220, 221, 223
5330 Silverado Trail, Napa CA 94558
Ph: 707 259 2200 Fax: 707 252 4125
Email: hospitality@closduval.com
Web: www.closduval.com

36. Consilience PAGE 253
2933 Grand Ave, Los Olivos CA 93441
Ph: 805 691 1020 Fax: 805 691 1018
Email: Mambo@consiliencewines.com
Web: www.consiliencewines.com

37. Crichton Hall Vineyards PAGE 271
1150 Darms Ln, Napa CA 94558
Ph: 707 224 4200 Fax: 707 224 4218
Email: info@crichtonhall.com
Web: www.crichtonhall.com

38. Crocker & Starr Wines PAGE 21
415 Dowdell Ln, St. Helena CA 94574
Ph: 707 967 9111 Fax: 707 967 9611
Email: office@crockerstarr.com
Web: www.crockerstarr.com

39. Curran Wines PAGES 84, 85
4435 Santa Rosa Rd, Lompoc CA 93436
Ph: 805 736 5761 Fax: 805 736 5761
Email: info@curranwines.com
Web: www.curranwines.com

40. Cuvaison Estate Wines PAGES 1, 17
4550 Silverado Trail North,
Calistoga CA 94515
Ph: 707 942 6266 Fax: 707 942 5732
Email: info@cuvaison.com
Web: www.cuvaison.com

41. Daniel Gehrs Wines PAGE 407
2939 Grand Ave, Los Olivos CA 93441
Ph: 805 693 9686 Fax: 805 693 0750
Email: info@dgwines.com
Web: www.dgwines.com

42. Darioush Winery
PAGES 20, 80, 256, 292, 332
4240 Silverado Trail, Napa CA 94558
Ph: 707 257 2345 Fax: 707 257 7056
Email: em-info@darioush.com
Web: www.darioush.com

43. David Bruce Winery PAGES 136, 137
21439 Bear Creek Rd, Los Gatos CA 95033
Ph: 408 354 4214 Fax: 408 395 5478
Email: dbw@davidbrucewinery.com
Web: www.davidbrucewinery.com

44. Davis Bynum Winery PAGE 266
8085 Westside Rd, Healdsburg CA 95448
Ph: 707 433 5852 Fax: 707 433 4309
Email: marketing@davisbynum.com
Web: www.davisbynum.com

45. Dee Vine Wines PAGE 135
Pier 19 The Embarcadero,
  San Francisco CA 94111
Ph: 415 398 3838 Fax: 415 788 9463
Email: info@dvw.com
Web: www.dvw.com

46. Deerfield Ranch Winery PAGE 279
10210 Sonoma Hwy, Kenwood CA 95452
Ph: 707 833 5215 Fax: 707 833 1312
Email: winery@deerfieldranch.com
Web: www.deerfieldranch.com

47. Delectus Winery PAGE 258
908C Enterprise Way, Napa CA 94558
Ph: 707 255 1252 Fax: 707 226 5412
Email: admin@delectuswinery.com
Web: www.delectuswinery.com

48. Diamond Creek Vineyards PAGE 18
1500 Diamond Mountain Rd,
  Calistoga CA 94515
Ph: 707 942 6924 Fax: 707 942 6936
Email: zina@diamondcreekvineyards.com
Web: www.diamondcreekvineyards.com

49. Diamond Terrace PAGE 61
1391 Diamond Mountain Rd,
  Calistoga CA 94515
Ph: 707 942 1189 Fax: 707 942 1372
Email: info@diamondterrace.com
Web: www.diamondterrace.com

50. Domaine Chandon PAGES 244, 456
1 California Dr, Yountville CA 94599
Ph: 707 944 8844 Fax: 707 944 1123
Web: www.chandon.com

**51. Domaine Charbay Winery
and Distillery** PAGE 19
4001 Spring Mountain Rd,
  St. Helena CA 94574
Ph: 707 963 9327
Web: www.charbay.com

52. Domaine La Due PAGE 446
1623 Bryce Ct, Napa CA 94558
Ph: 707 258 2561 Fax: 707 252 0565
Email: info@domaineladue.com
Web: www.domaineladue.com

53. Dry Creek Vineyard PAGES 148, 348
3770 Lambert Bridge Rd,
  Healdsburg CA 95448
Ph: 707 433 1000 Fax: 707 433 5329
Email: dcv@drycreekvineyard.com
Web: www.drycreekvineyard.com

54. DuNah Vineyard & Winery PAGE 377
2436 Blucher Valley Rd,
  Sebastopol CA 95472
Ph: 707 829 9666 Fax: 707 829 2447
Email: info@dunahwinery.com
Web: www.dunahwinery.com

55. Dunn Vineyards PAGE 23
PO Box 886, Angwin CA 94508
Ph: 707 965 3642 Fax: 707 965 3805
Email: dunnvineyards@sbcglobal.net

56. Dutch Henry Winery PAGE 194
4310 Silverado Trail, Calistoga CA 94515
Ph: 707 942 5771 Fax: 707 942 5512
Email: info@dutchhenry.com
Web: www.dutchhenry.com

57. Dynamite Vineyards PAGE 130
1695 St. Helena Hwy, St. Helena CA 94574
Ph: 707 968 3633 Fax: 707 968 3632
Email: Dynamite.info@dynamite
  vineyards.com
Web: www.dynamitevineyards.com

58. Ehlers Estate PAGE 165
3222 Ehlers Ln, St. Helena CA 94574
Ph: 707 963 5972 Fax: 707 963 7512
Email: rzuidema@ehlersestate.com
Web: www.ehlersestate.com

59. El Molino PAGES 120, 121, 122, 123
1478 Railroad Ave, St. Helena CA 94574
Ph: 707 963 1257 Fax: 707 963 1647
Email: info@elmolinowinery.com
Web: www.elmolinowinery.com

60. Elan Vineyards PAGE 131
4500 Atlas Peak Rd, Napa CA 94558
Ph: 707 252 3339 Fax: 707 252 4996
Email: ElanWine@aol.com
Web: www.elanvineyards.com

61. Elkhorn Peak Cellars PAGE 181
200 Polson Rd, Napa CA 94558
Ph: 707 255 0504 Fax: 707 258 9564
Email: epcellars@aol.com
Web: www.elkhornpeakcellars.com

62. Elyse Winery PAGES 134, 242
2100 Hoffman Ln, Napa CA 94558
Ph: 707 944 2900 Fax: 707 945 0301
Email: info@elysewinery.com
Web: www.elysewinery.com

63. Etude Wines PAGE 206
1250 Cuttings Wharf Rd, Napa CA 94558
Ph: 707 257 5300 Fax: 707 257 6022
Web: www.etudewines.com

64. Everett Ridge PAGE 282
435 West Dry Creek Rd,
   Healdsburg CA 95448
Ph: 707 433 1637 Fax: 707 433 7024
Email: info@everettridge.com
Web: www.everettridge.com

65. F. Teldeschi PAGE 167
3555 Dry Creek Rd, Healdsburg CA 95448
Ph: 707 433 6626 Fax: 707 433 3077
Email: dteldeschi@neteze.com
Web: www.teldeschi.com

66. Far Niente PAGES 209, 457
1350 Acacia Dr, Oakville CA 94562
Ph: 707 944 2861 Fax: 707 944 2312
Email: info@farniente.com
Web: www.farniente.com

**67. Ferrari-Carano Vineyards
and Winery** PAGE 288
8761 Dry Creek Rd, Healdsburg CA 95448
Ph: 707 433 6700 Fax: 707 431 1742
Email: info@ferrari-carano.com
Web: www.ferrari-carano.com

68. Fess Parker Winery PAGE 229
6200 Foxen Canyon Rd, Los Olivos CA 93441
Ph: 805 488 1545 Fax: 805 686 1130
Email: net@fessparker.com
Web: www.fessparker.com

69. Firestone Vineyard PAGES 438, 452
5000 Zaca Station Rd, Los Olivos CA 93441
Ph: 805 688 3940 Fax: 805 686 1256
Email: info@firestonewine.com
Web: www.firestonewine.com

70. Fisher Vineyards PAGE 289
6200 St. Helena Rd, Santa Rosa CA 95404
Ph: 707 539 7511 Fax: 707 539 3601
Email: info@fishervineyards.com
Web: www.fishervineyards.com

71. Fleury Estate Winery PAGE 127
950 Galleron Rd, Rutherford CA 94573
Ph: 707 967 8333 Fax: 707 967 8281
Email: Brian@fleurywinery.com
Web: www.fleurywinery.com

**72. Flowers Vineyard
& Winery** PAGES 147, 338
28500 Seaview Rd, Cazadero CA 95421
Ph: 707 847 3661 Fax: 707 847 3740
Email: info@flowerswinery.com
Web: www.flowerswinery.com

**73. Forchini Vineyards
& Winery** PAGES 302, 304, 331, 451
5141 Dry Creek Rd, Healdsburg CA 95448
Ph: 707 431 8886 Fax: 707 431 8881
Email: wine@forchini.com
Web: www.forchini.com

74. Forth Vineyards PAGE 341
2335 West Dry Creek Rd,
   Healdsburg CA 95448
Ph: 707 433 1001 Fax: 707 473 0524
Email: jann@forthvineyards.com
Web: www.forthvineyards.com

75. Foxen PAGES 224, 500
7200 Foxen Canyon Rd,
   Santa Maria CA 93454
Ph: 805 937 4251 Fax: 805 937 0415
Email: info@foxenvineyard.com
Web: www.foxenvineyard.com

76. Frazier Winery PAGE 126
40 Lupine Hill Rd, Napa CA 94558
Ph: 707 255 3444 Fax: 707 252 7573
Email: sales@frazierwinery.com
Web: www.frazierwinery.com

77. Frick Winery PAGES 354, 478
23072 Walling Road, Geyserville CA 95441
Ph: 707 857 1980 Fax: 707 857 1980
Email: Frick@frickwinery.com
Web: www.frickwinery.com

**78. GlenLyon Vineyard
& Winery** PAGES 166, 427
2750 John's Hill Rd, Glen Ellen CA 95442
Ph: 707 833 0032 Fax: 707 833 2743
Email: Squire@GlenLyonWinery.com
Web: www.GlenLyonWinery.com

79. Graeser Winery PAGES 208, 210
255 Petrified Forest Rd, Calistoga CA 94515
Ph: 707 942 4437 Fax: 707 942 4437
Email: Info@graeserwinery.com
Web: www.graeserwinery.com

80. Grgich Hills Cellar PAGES 140, 142
1829 Highway 29, Rutherford CA 94515
Ph: 707 963 2784 Fax: 707 963 8725
Email: info@grgich.com
Web: www.grgich.com

**81. Groth Vineyards
and Winery** PAGES 29, 30, 31, 33
750 Oakville Cross Rd, Oakville CA 94562
Ph: 707 944 0290 Fax: 707 944 8932
Email: info@grothwines.com
Web: www.grothwines.com

82. Hendry PAGES 28, 246
3104 Redwood Rd, Napa CA 94558
Ph: 707 226 8320 Fax: 707 226 7549
Email: info@hendrywines.com
Web: www.hendrywines.com

83. Hill Family Estate PAGE 202
Tasting Room at Antique Fair: 6512
    Washington St, Yountville CA 94599
Ph: 707 944 9580 Fax: 707 944 9147
Email: info@hillfamilyestate.com
Web: www.hillfamilyestate.com

84. Huntington PAGE 144
53 Front St, Healdsburg CA 95448
Ph: 707 433 5215 Fax: 707 433 5144
Email: tastingroom@huntingtonwine.com
Web: www.huntingtonwine.com

85. John Tyler Wines PAGE 490
4375 Westside Rd, Healdsburg CA 95448
Ph: 707 473 0123 Fax: 707 473 0825
Email: pamb@johntylerwines.com
Web: www.johntylerwines.com

86. Joseph Phelps Vineyards PAGE 249
200 Taplin Rd, St. Helena CA 94574
Ph: 707 967 3400 Fax: 707 963 4831
Email: jpvwines@aol.com
Web: www.jpvwines.com

87. Kalyra Winery PAGES 318, 344, 491
343 N. Refugio Rd, Santa Ynez CA 93460
Ph: 805 693 8864 Fax: 805 693 8865
Email: info@kalyrawinery.com
Web: www.kalyrawinery.com

88. Keenan Winery PAGES 186, 409
3660 Spring Mountain Rd,
    St. Helena CA 94574
Ph: 707 963 9177 Fax: 707 963 8209
Email: rkw@keenanwinery.com
Web: www.keenanwinery.com

89. Kelham Vineyards
FRONT COVER, PAGES 32, 79
360 Zinfandel Ln, St. Helena CA 94574
Ph: 707 963 2000 Fax: 707 963 2262
Email: info@kelhamvineyards.com
Web: www.kelhamvineyards.com

90. Keller Estate Winery PAGES 311, 421
5875 Lakesville Hwy, Petaluma CA 94954
Ph: 707 765 2117 Fax: 707 765 2118
Email: guenevere@kellerestate.com
Web: www.kellerestate.com

91. Kosta Browne Winery PAGE 489
1300 Montgomery Rd, Sebastopol CA 95472
Ph: 707 290 5704 Fax: 707 823 6835
Email: dkosta@kostabrowne.com
Web: www.kostabrowne.com

92. Kuleto Estate Winery PAGE 392
2470 Sage Canyon Rd, St. Helena CA 94574
Ph: 707 963 9750 Fax: 707 963 4859
Email: info@kuletoestate.com
Web: www.kuletoestate.com

93. Kunde Estate Winery PAGES 481, 487
9825 Sonoma Hwy, Kenwood CA 95452
Ph: 707 833 5501 Fax: 707 833 2204
Email: wineinfo@kunde.com
Web: www.kunde.com

94. Laetitia Vineyard & Winery PAGE 175
453 Laetitia Vineyard Dr,
    Arroyo Grande CA 93420
Ph: 805 481 1772 Fax: 805 473 7215
Email: info@laetitiawine.com
Web: www.laetitiawine.com

95. Landmark Vineyards PAGE 145
101 Adobe Canyon Rd, Kenwood CA 95452
Ph: 707 833 0212 Fax: 707 833 1164
Email: mary@landmarkwine.com
Web: www.landmarkwine.com

96. Larson Family Winery PAGES 398, 420, 480
23355 Millerick Rd, Sonoma CA 95476
Ph: 707 938 3031 Fax: 707 938 3424
Email: becky@larsonfamilywinery.com
Web: www.larsonfamilywinery.com

97. Ledson Winery PAGES 447, 448, 449
7335 Sonoma Hwy, Kenwood CA 95409
Ph: 707 537 3810 Fax: 707 303 3096
Email: info@ledson.com
Web: www.ledson.com

98. Livingston Moffett Winery PAGE 42
1895 Cabernet Ln, St. Helena CA 94574
Ph: 707 963 2120 Fax: 707 963 9385
Email: info@livingstonwines.com
Web: www.livingstonwines.com

99. Long Meadow Ranch PAGE 38
PO Box 477, Rutherford CA 94573
Ph: 707 963 4555 Fax: 707 963 1956
Email: info@longmeadowranch.com
Web: www.longmeadowranch.com

100. Longboard Vineyards PAGE 397
5 Fitch St, Healdsburg CA 95448
Ph: 707 433 3473 Fax: 707 433 3440
Email: kahuna@longboardvineyards.com
Web: www.longboardvineyards.com

101. Margerum Wine Company PAGE 460
5249 Foxen Canyon Rd, Los Olivos CA 93441
Ph: 805 892 9711 Fax: 805 892 9611
Email: doug@winecask.com
Web: www.margerumwinecompany.com

102. Marimar Estate PAGE 483
11400 Graton Rd, Sebastopol CA 94965
Ph: 707 823 3904 Fax: 707 823 4496
Email: marimar@marimarestate.com
Web: www.marimarestate.com

103. Mauritson Family Winery PAGES 484, 485
2859 Dry Creek Rd, Healdsburg CA 95448
Ph: 707 431 0804 Fax: 707 433 5001
Email: info@mauritsonwines.com
Web: www.mauritsonwines.com

104. Merryvale Vineyards PAGES 43, 178
1000 Main St, St. Helena CA 94574
Ph: 707 963 2225 Fax: 707 963 1949
Email: info@merryvale.com
Web: www.merryvale.com

105. Mill Creek Vineyards PAGE 477
1401 Westside Rd, Healdsburg CA 95448
Ph: 707 431 2121 Fax: 707 431 1714
Email: info@millcreekwinery.com
Web: www.millcreekwinery.com

106. Montemaggiore PAGE 164
2355 West Dry Creek Rd,
   Healdsburg CA 95448
Ph: 707 433 9499 Fax: 707 433 1436
Email: info@montemaggiore.com
Web: www.montemaggiore.com

107. Montevina Winery PAGE 384
20680 Shenandoah School Rd,
   Plymouth CA 95669
Ph: 209 245 6942 Fax: 209 245 6617
Email: info@montevina.com
Web: www.montevina.com

108. Moon Mountain Vineyard PAGE 445
1700 Moon Mountain Dr, Sonoma CA 95476
Ph: 707 996 5870 Fax: 707 996 5302
Email: MMNinfo@moonmountain
   vineyard.com
Web: www.moonmountainvineyard.com

109. Moondance Cellars PAGES 419, 479
4901 Blank Rd, Sebastopol CA 95472
Ph: 707 823 0880 Fax: 707 823 0980
Email: info@moondancecellars.com
Web: www.moondancecellars.com

110. Mutt Lynch Winery PAGE 197
1960 Dry Creek Rd, Healdsburg CA
Ph: 707 942 6180 Fax: 707 942 8755
Email: muttlynch@aol.com
Web: wwwmuttlynch.com

111. Nalle Winery PAGES 265, 459
2383 Dry Creek Rd, Healdsburg CA 95448
Ph: 707 433 1040 Fax: 707 433 6062
Email: doug@nallewinery.com
Web: www.nallewinery.com

112. Navillus Birney PAGE 415
8325 Sonoma Mountain Rd,
 Glen Ellen CA 95442
Ph: 707 935 3393 Fax: 707 939 7582
Email: info@navillusbirney.com
Web: www.navillusbirney.com

113. Oakville Ranch PAGES 39, 168
7781 Silverado Trail, Napa CA 94558
Ph: 707 944 9665 Fax: 707 944 9326
Email: info@oakvilleranch.com
Web: www.oakvilleranch.com

114. O'Brien Cellars PAGE 207
1200 Orchard Ave, Napa CA 94558
Ph: 707 252 8463
Email: info@seductionwine.com
Web: www.obriencellars.com

115. Pacific Star Winery PAGE 211
33000 N. Hwy 1, Fort Bragg CA 95437
Ph: 707 964 1155   Fax: 707 964 1105
Email: sally@pacificstarwinery.com
Web: pacificstarwinery.com

116. Palmaz Vineyards PAGE 187
4029 Hagen Rd, Napa CA 94558
Ph: 707 226 5587 Fax: 707 251 0849
Email: contactus@palmazvineyards.com
Web: www.palmazvineyards.com

**117. Papapietro Perry
 Winery** PAGES 470, 476
4791 Dry Creek Rd, Healdsburg CA 95448
Ph: 707 433 0422 Fax: 801 858 2864
Email: info@papapietro-perry.com
Web: www.papapietro-perry.com

118. Passalacqua Winery PAGE 395
3805 Lambert Bridge Rd,
 Healdsburg CA 95448
Ph: 707 433 5550 Fax: 707 433 5575
Email: info@passalacquawinery.com
Web: www.passalacquawinery.com

119. PlumpJack Winery PAGE 177
620 Oakville Cross Rd, Napa CA 94558
Ph: 707 945 1220 Fax: 707 944 0744
Email: winery@plumpjack.com
Web: www.plumpjack.com

120. Presidio Winery PAGES 259, 431
2755 Purisima Rd, Lompoc CA 93436
Ph: 805 740 9463 Fax: 805 740 1720
Email: info@presidiowinery.com
Web: www.presidiowinery.com

121. Provenance Vineyards PAGE 183
1695 St. Helena Hwy, St. Helena CA 94574
Ph: 707 968 3633 Fax: 707 968 3632
Email: info@provenancevineyards.com
Web: www.provenancevineyards.com

122. Quintessa PAGE 234
1601 Silverado Trail, Rutherford CA 94573
Ph: 707 967 1601 Fax: 707 286 2727
Email: receptionist@quintessa.com
Web: www.quintessa.com

123. Quivira PAGE 418
4900 West Dry Creek Rd,
 Healdsburg CA 95448
Ph: 707 431 8333 Fax: 707 431 1664
Email: quivira@quivirawine.com
Web: www.quivirawine.com

124. Rabbit Ridge Winery PAGES 405, 458
3291 Westside Rd, Healdsburg CA 95448
Ph: 707 431 7128 Fax: 707 431 8018
Email: linda_rabbitridge@yahoo.com
Web: www.rabbitridgewinery.com

**125. Rabbit Ridge Winery
 and Vineyards** PAGES 64, 189, 239, 349
1172 San Marcos Rd, Pasa Robles CA 93446
Ph: 805 467 3331 Fax: 805 467 3339
Email: tastingroom@rabbitridgewinery.com
Web: www.rabbitridgewinery.com

126. Raymond Vineyards PAGES 174, 422
849 Zinfandel Ln, St. Helena CA 94574
Ph: 707 963 3141 Fax: 707 963 8498
Email: hospitality@raymondvineyards.com
Web: www.raymondvineyards.com

127. Regusci Winery PAGES 119, 182, 196, 205
5584 Silverado Trail, Napa CA 94588
Ph: 707 254 0403 Fax: 707 254 0417
Email: info@regusciwinery.com
Web: www.regusciwinery.com

128. Reynolds Family Winery PAGES 176, 440
3266 Silverado Trail, Napa CA 94558
Ph: 707 258 2558 Fax: 707 258 9558
Email: info@reynoldsfamilywinery.com
Web: www.reynoldsfamilywinery.com

129. Robert Mondavi Winery
 PAGES 50, 51, 218
7801 St. Helena Hwy, Oakville CA 94562
Ph: 707 968 2200 Fax: 707 968 2208
Email: info@robertmondaviwinery.com
Web: www.robertmondaviwinery.com

**130. Rocca Family
Vineyards** PAGES 46, 47, 254
1130 Main St, Napa CA 94558
Ph: 707 257 8467 Fax: 707 255 2269
Email: maryfran@roccawines.com
Web: www.roccawines.com

131. Rockledge Vineyards PAGE 74
360 Taplin Rd, St. Helena CA 94574
Ph: 707 963 5488 Fax: 707 963 4779
Email: linda@rockledgevineyards.com
Web: www.rockledgevineyards.com

132. Rubicon Estate PAGES 52, 184, 227
1991 St. Helena Hwy, Rutherford CA 94573
Ph: 707 968 1100 Fax: 707 963 9084
Email: info@rubiconestate.com
Web: www.rubiconestate.com

133. Russian Hill Estate PAGE 408
4525 Slusser Rd, Windsor CA 95492
Ph: 707 575 9428 Fax: 707 575 9453
Email: info@russianhillwinery.com
Web: www.russianhillwinery.com

134. RustRidge Vineyards PAGE 60
2910 Lower Chiles Valley Rd,
St. Helena CA 94574
Ph: 707 965 9353 Fax: 707 286 5502
Email: rustridge@rustridge.com
Web: www.rustridge.com

135. Saddleback Cellars PAGES 53, 185
7802 Money Rd, Oakville CA 94562
Ph: 707 944 1305 Fax: 707 944 1325
Email: hillery@saddlebackcellars.com
Web: www.saddlebackcellars.com

136. Saint Helena Road Winery PAGE 417
6995 St. Helena Rd, Santa Rosa CA 95404
Ph: 707 538 8674 Fax: 707 538 7637
Email: sthelenaroad@aol.com
Web: www.sthelenaroadvineyards.com

137. Saintsbury PAGE 75
1500 Los Carneros Ave, Napa CA 94558
Ph: 707 252 0592 Fax: 707 252 0595
Email: info@saintsbury.com
Web: www.saintsbury.com

138. Schramsberg Vineyards
PAGES 294, 385, 454
1400 Schramsberg Rd, Calistoga CA 94515
Ph: 800 877 3623 Fax: 707 942 5943
Email: info1@schramsberg.com
Web: www.schramsberg.com

**139. Sebastiani Vineyards
and Winery** PAGES 44, 426, 498, 499
389 Fourth St East, Sonoma CA 95476
Ph: 707 933 3200 Fax: 707 933 3370
Email: info@sebastiani.com
Web: www.sebastiani.com

140. Sequoia Grove PAGE 63
8338 St. Helena Hwy, Napa CA 94558
Ph: 800 851 7841 Fax: 707 963 9411
Email: info@sequoiagrove.com
Web: www.sequoiagrove.com

141. Shafer Vineyards PAGES 68, 69
6154 Silverado Trail, Napa CA 94558
Ph: 707 944 2877 Fax: 707 944 9454
Email: info@shafervineyards.com
Web: www.shafervineyards.com

142. Shoestring Winery PAGE 303
800 East Hwy 246, Solvang CA 93463
Ph: 800 693 8612 Fax: 805 693 8512
Email: info@shoestringwinery.com
Web: www.shoestringwinery.com

143. Silverado Vineyards PAGE 59
6121 Silverado Trail, Napa CA 94558
Ph: 707 257 1770 Fax: 707 257 1538
Email: info@silveradovineyards.com
Web: www.silveradovineyards.com

144. Sine Qua Non PAGE 388
PO Box 1048, Oak View CA 93022
Ph: 805 649 8901 Fax: 805 649 8902
Email: sqn@sinequanonwines.com

145. Sonoma-Cutrer Vineyards
PAGES 472, 473, 474, 475
4401 Slusser Rd, Windsor CA 95492
Ph: 707 528 1181 Fax: 707 528 1561
Email: info@sonomacutrer.com
Web: www.sonomacutrer.com

146. Southern Latitudes Wines PAGE 278
At the Pine Inn, Lincoln St, Carmel CA 93921
Ph: 831 622 7652 Fax: 831 622 7644
Email: orders@solawines.com
Web: www.solawines.com

147. Spelletich Cellars PAGES 58, 295
880 Vallejo St, Napa CA 94558
Ph: 707 363 0790 Fax: 707 224 5069
Email: info@spellwine.com
Web: www.spellwine.com

**148. Spottswoode Estate Vineyard
& Winery** PAGE 222
1902 Madrona Ave, St. Helena CA 94574
Ph: 707 963 0134 Fax: 707 963 2886
Email: spottswoode@spottswoode.com
Web: www.spottswoode.com

149. St. Clement PAGE 243
2867 St. Helena Highway North,
St. Helena CA 94559
Ph: 800 331 8266 Fax: 707 963 4160
Email: discoverstclement@stclement.com
Web: www.stclement.com

**150. St. Francis Winery
and Vineyards** PAGE 493
100 Pythian Rd, Santa Rosa CA 95409
Ph: 707 833 4666 Fax: 707 833 1813
Email: info@stfranciswine.com
Web: www.stfranciswinery.com

**151. St. Supéry Vineyards
and Winery** PAGES 238, 240, 241
8440 St. Helena Hwy, Rutherford CA 94573
Ph: 707 963 4507 Fax: 707 963 4526
Email: divinecab@stsupery.com
Web: www.stsupery.com

152. Stagecoach Vineyards PAGE 368
3265 Soda Canyon Rd, Napa CA 94558
Ph: 707 226 2215 Fax: 707 256 6198
Email: info@stagecoachvineyard.com
Web: www.stagecoachvineyard.com

153. Stony Hill Vineyard PAGES 155, 200, 201
3331 St. Helena Hwy North,
St. Helena CA 94574
Ph: 707 963 2636 Fax: 707 963 1831
Email: info@stonyhillvineyard.com
Web: www.stonyhillvineyard.com

154. Stryker Sonoma PAGE 404
5110 Hwy 128, Geyserville CA 95441
Ph: 707 433 1944 Fax: 707 433 1948
Email: info@strykersonoma.com
Web: www.strykersonoma.com

155. Sullivan Family Estate PAGE 154
1090 Galleron Rd, Rutherford CA 94573
Ph: 707 963 9646 Fax: 707 963 0377
Email: info@sullivanwine.com
Web: www.sullivanwine.com

**156. Sunstone Vineyards
and Winery** PAGES 308, 322
125 Refugio Rd, Santa Ynez CA 93460
Ph: 805 688 9463 Fax: 805 686 1881
Email: info@sunstonewinery.com
Web: www.sunstonewinery.com

157. Swanson Vineyards PAGE 162
1271 Manley Ln, Rutherford CA 94573
Ph: 707 948 3110 Fax: 707 948 3099
Email: salon@swansonvineyards.com
Web: www.swansonvineyards.com

158. TAZ PAGES 324, 367
45 Main S., Templeton CA 93465
Ph: 805 434 5022 Fax: 805 434 0690
Email: TAZ.info@TAZVineyards.com
Web: www.tazvineyards.com

159. Terra Valentine PAGE 65
3787 Spring Mountain Rd,
St. Helena CA 94574
Ph: 707 967 8340 Fax: 707 967 8342
Email: winemaker@terravalentine.com
Web: www.terravalentine.com

160. The Hess Collection PAGES 138, 203, 251
4411 Redwood Rd, Napa CA 94558
Ph: 707 255 1144 Fax: 707 253 1682
Email: info@hesscollection.com
Web: www.hesscollection.com

161. Thumbprint Cellars PAGE 425
36 North St, Healdsburg CA 95448
Ph: 707 433 2393 Fax: 707 433 2325
Email: lounge@thumbprintcellars.com
Web: www.thumbprintcellars.com

**162. Tokalon Estate /
Traina Vineyards** PAGE 62
c/o Hermosa Vineyards, PO Box 393,
Oakville CA 94562
Ph: 415 810 8738
Email: trevortraina@hotmail.com

163. Tor Kenward Family Wines PAGE 379
1435 Railroad St, St. Helena CA 94574
Ph: 707 963 3100 Fax: 707 963 3114
Email: tor@torwines.com
Web: www.torwines.com

164. Trefethen Vineyards PAGES 48, 252
1160 Oak Knoll Ave, Napa CA 94558
Ph: 707 255 7700 Fax: 707 255 0793
Email: winery@trefethen.com
Web: www.trefethen.com

165. Tres Sabores PAGE 255
1620 S. Whitehall Ln, St. Helena CA 94574
Ph: 707 967 8027 Fax: 707 967 8029
Email: jaj@tressabores.com
Web: www.tressabores.com

166. Turnbull Wine Cellars PAGE 54
8210 St. Helena Hwy, Oakville CA 94562
Ph: 707 963 5839 Fax: 707 963 4407
Email: info@turnbullwines.com
Web: www.turnbullwines.com

167. V. Sattui Winery PAGES 55, 56
1111 White Ln, St. Helena CA 94574
Ph: 707 963 7774 Fax: 707 963 4324
Email: info@vsattui.com
Web: www.vsattui.com

168. Van Der Heyden Vineyards
PAGES 362, 393
4057 Silverado Trail, Napa CA 94558
Ph: 707 257 0130 Fax: 707 257 3311
Email: talig@vanderheydenvineyards.com
Web: www.vanderheydenvineyards.com

169. Varozza PAGE 363
514 Pratt Ave, St. Helena CA 94574
Ph: 707 963 0331 Fax: 707 963 0331
Email: dianna@varozzavineyards.com
Web: www.varozzavineyards.com

170. Veraison PAGES 312, 455
3267 Soda Canyon Rd, Napa CA 94558
Ph: 707 226 2215 Fax: 707 259 6198
Email: jkrupp@veraison.net
Web: www.veraison.net

171. Vinoce PAGES 159, 160, 161
1100 Wall Rd, Napa CA 94558
Ph: 707 944 8717 Fax: 707 944 0145
Email: info@vinoce.com
Web: www.vinoce.com

172. Volker Eisele Family Estate PAGE 158
3080 Lower Chiles Valley Rd,
  St. Helena CA 94574
Ph: 707 965 9485 Fax: 707 965 9609
Email: info@volkereiselevineyard.com
Web: www.volkereiselevineyard.com

173. Wattle Creek Winery PAGE 403
25510 River Rd, Cloverdale CA 95425
Ph: 707 894 5166 Fax: 707 894 2982
Email: info@wattlecreek.com
Web: www.wattlecreek.com

174. Whitehall Lane Winery PAGE 199
1563 St. Helena Hwy, St. Helena CA 94574
Ph: 707 963 9454 Fax: 707 963 7035
Email: greatwine@whitehalllane.com
Web: www.whitehalllane.com

175. Wild Hog Vineyard PAGES 387, 416
PO Box 189, Cazadero CA 95421
Ph: 707 847 3687 Fax: 707 847 3160
Email: wildhog@mcn.org
Web: www.wildhogvineyard.com

176. William Hill Estate PAGE 67
1761 Atlas Peak Rd, Napa CA 94558
Ph: 707 265 3024 Fax: 707 224 4484
Email: tastingroom@williamhillestate.com
Web: www.williamhillestate.com

177. Wilson Winery PAGES 104, 105
1960 Dry Creek Rd, Healdsburg CA 95448
Ph: 707 433 4355 Fax: 707 433 4353
Email: info@wilsonwinery.com
Web: www.wilsonwinery.com

178. Wines of Carmel PAGES 287, 376
11700 Camino Escondido,
  Carmel Valley CA 93924
Ph: 831 659 0750 Fax: 831 659 0750
Email: info@winesofcarmel.com
Web: www.winesofcarmel.com

**179. Yoakim Bridge Vineyard
& Winery** PAGES 98, 99
7209 Dry Creek Rd, Healdsburg CA 95448
Ph: 707 433 8511
Email: virginia@yoakimbridge.com
Web: www.yoakimbridge.com

180. Zayante Vineyard PAGE 339
420 Old Mount Rd, Felton CA 95018
Ph: 831 335 7992 Fax: 831 335 5770
Email: kstarkey@cruzio.com
Web: www.zayantevineyards.com

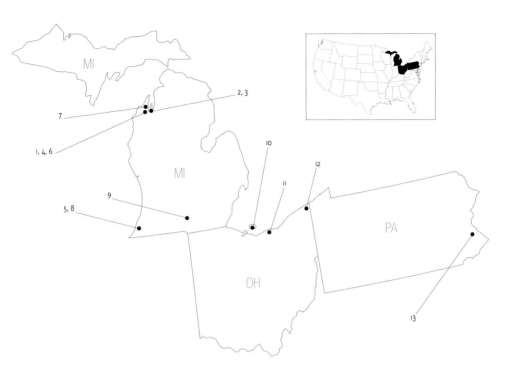

MICHIGAN

1. Bel Lago Winery PAGE 143
6530 South Lake Shore Dr, Cedar MI 49621
Ph: 231 228 4800 Fax: 231 228 4888
Email: info@bellago.com
Web: www.bellago.com

2. Bowers Harbor Vineyards PAGE 16
2896 Bowers Harbor Rd,
  Traverse City MI 49686
Ph: 231 223 7615 Fax: 231 223 7625
Email: info@bowersharbor.com
Web: www.bowersharbor.com

3. Brys Estate Vineyard & Winery PAGE 24
3309 Blue Water Rd, Traverse City MI 49686
Ph: 231 223 9303 Fax: 231 223 9304
Email: bryswine@pentel.net
Web: www.brysestate.com

**4. Chateau Fontaine Vineyards
  and Winery** PAGE 35
2290 S. French Rd, Lake Leelanau MI 49653
Ph: 231 256 0000 Fax: 231 256 9943
Web: www.chateaufontaine.com

5. Domaine Berrien Cellars PAGE 306
398 E. Lemon Creek Rd,
  Berrien Springs MI 49103
Ph: 269 473 9463
Email: winery@domaineberrien.com
Web: www.domaineberrien.com

6. L Mawby PAGE 195
4519 S. Elm Valley Rd, Suttons Bay MI 49682
Ph: 231 271 3522 Fax: 231 271 2927
Email: joni@lmawby.com
Web: www.lmawby.com

7. Leelanau Wine Cellars PAGE 198
5019 Northwest Bayshore Dr,
  Omena MI 49674
Ph: 231 386 5201 Fax: 231 386 9797
Email: lisa@leelanaucellars.com
Web: www.leelanaucellars.com

8. Lemon Creek Winery PAGE 325
533 E. Lemon Creek Rd,
  Berrien Springs MI 49103
Ph: 269 471 1321 Fax: 269 471 1322
Email: winery@lemoncreekwinery.com
Web: www.lemoncreekwinery.com

9. Sandhill Crane Vineyards PAGE 272
4724 Walz Rd, Jackson MI 49201
Ph: 517 764 0679 Fax: 517 764 3260
Email: heather@sandhillcranevineyards.com
Web: www.sandhillcranevineyards.com

OHIO

10. Heineman Winery PAGE 492
1223 Catawba Ave, Put-in-Bay OH 43456
Ph: 419 285 2811 Fax: 419 285 3412
Email: info@HeinemansWinery.com
Web: www.heinemanswinery.com

11. Klingshirn Winery PAGE 351
33050 Webber Rd, Avon Lake OH 44012
Ph: 440 933 6666 Fax: 440 933 7896
Email: info@klingshirnwine.com
Web: www.klingshirnwine.com

12. Tarsitano Winery PAGE 496
4871 Hatch's Corner, Conneaut OH 44030
Ph: 440 224 2444
Email: ken@tarsitanowinery.com
Web: www.tarsitanowinery.com

PENNSYLVANIA

13. Country Creek Winery PAGE 192
133 Cressman Rd, Telford PA 18969
Ph: 215 723 6516 Fax: 215 723 6516
Email: kleinwine4@aol.com
Web: www.countrycreekwinery.com

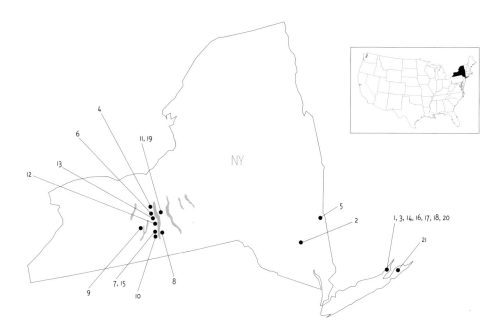

NEW YORK

1. Ackerly Pond Vineyards PAGE 396
1375 Peconic Ln, Peconic NY 11958
Ph: 631 765 6861 Fax: 631 765 3810
Email: rayvin5@aol.com
Web: www.ackerlypondvineyards.com

2. Adair Vineyards PAGES 375, 381
52 Allhusen Rd, New Paltz NY 12561
Ph: 845 255 1377 Fax: 845 691 9584
Email: adairwine@aol.com
Web: www.adairwine.com

3. Bedell Cellars
  PAGES 103, 132, 153, 401, 463, 466
36225 Main Rd, Cutchogue NY 11935
Ph: 631 734 7537 Fax: 631 734 5788
Email: winemail@bedellcellars.com
Web: www.bedellcellars.com

4. Billsboro Winery PAGE 382
4760 W. Lake Rd, Geneva NY 14456
Ph: 315 789 9571
Email: morrisjd@rochester.rr.com
Web: www.billsboro.com

**5. Cascade Mountain Winery
 and Restaurant** PAGE 412
835 Cascade Mt Rd, Amenia NY 12501
Ph: 845 373 9021 Fax: 845 373 7869
Email: cascademt@mohawk.net
Web: www.cascademt.com

6. Fox Run Vineyards PAGE 309
670 Route 14, Penn Yan NY 14527
Ph: 315 536 4616 Fax: 315 536 1383
Email: info@foxrunvineyards.com
Web: www.foxrunvineyards.com

7. Fulkerson PAGE 386
5576 Route 14, Dundee NY 14837
Ph: 607 243 7883 Fax: 607 243 8337
Email: fulkersonwinery@stny.rr.com
Web: www.fulkersonwinery.com

**8. Hazlitt 1852 Vineyards
 and Winery** PAGES 326, 365
5712 Route 414, Hector NY 14841
Ph: 607 546 9463 Fax: 607 546 5712
Email: info@hazlitt1852.com
Web: www.hazlitt1852.com

9. Hunt Country Vineyards PAGE 378
4021 Italy Hill Rd, Branchport NY 14418
Ph: 1800 946 3289 Fax: 315 595 2835
Email: info@huntwines.com
Web: www.huntwines.com

10. Lakewood Vineyards PAGE 310
4024 State Route 14, Watkins Glen NY 14891
Ph: 607 535 9252 Fax: 607 535 6656
Email: wines@lakewoodvineyards.com
Web: www.lakewoodvineyards.com

**11. Lamoreaux Landing
Wine Cellars** PAGE 329
9224 Route 414, Lodi NY 14860
Ph: 607 582 6011 Fax: 607 582 6010
Email: llwc@capital.net
Web: www.lamoreauxwine.com

12. Miles Wine Cellars PAGES 226, 497
168 Randall Crossing Rd, Himrod NY 14842
Ph: 607 243 7742 Fax: 607 243 3827
Email: mileswinecellars@msn.com
Web: www.mileswinecellars.com

13. Prejean Winery PAGE 494
2634 Route 14, Penn Yan NY 14527
Ph: 315 536 7524 Fax: 315 536 7635
Email: wine@prejeanwinery.com
Web: www.prejeanwinery.com

14. Raphael Vineyard PAGE 411
39390 Main Rd, Peconic NY 11958
Ph: 631 765 1100 Fax: 631 765 1991
Email: grandcru@raphaelwine.com
Web: www.raphaelwine.com

15. Rock Stream Vineyards PAGES 11, 13
162 Fir Tree Point Rd, Rock Stream NY 14878
Ph: 607 243 5395
Email: mkarasz@linkny.com
Web: www.rockstreamvineyards.com

16. Sherwood House Vineyards PAGE 464
2600 Oregon Rd, Mattituck NY 11952
Ph: 631 298 2157 Fax: 631 298 2157
Email: info@sherwoodhousevineyard.com
Web: www.sherwoodhousevineyards.com

17. Shinn Estate Vineyards PAGE 34
2000 Oregon Rd, Mattituck NY 11952
Ph: 631 804 0367 Fax: 212 647 9393
Email: shinnvin@optonline.net
Web: www.shinnstatevineyards.com

18. The Old Field Vineyards PAGES 41, 260
59600 Main Rd, Southold NY 11971
Ph: 631 765 0004 Fax: 631 765 3553
Email: livinifera@aol.com
Web: www.theoldfield.com

19. Wagner Vineyards PAGE 356
9322 State Route 414, Lodi NY 14860
Ph: 607 582 6450 Fax: 607 582 6446
Email: orders@wagnervineyards.com
Web: www.wagnervineyards.com

20. Waters Crest Winery PAGE 231
22355 Route 48 Unit 6, Cutchogue NY 11935
Ph: 631 734 5045 Fax: 631 734 5064
Email: jim@waterscrestwinery.com
Web: www.waterscrest.net

21. Wölffer Estate Vineyard PAGE 139
139 Sagg Rd, Sagaponack NY 11962
Ph: 631 537 5106 Fax: 631 537 5107
Email: info@wolffer.com
Web: www.wolffer.com

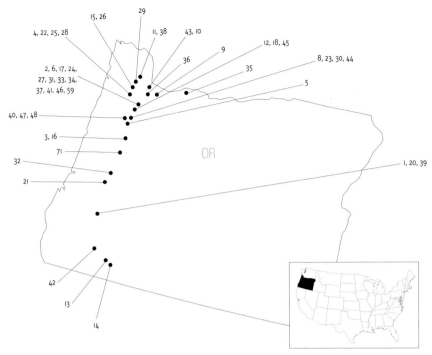

OREGON

1. Abacela Winery PAGES 101, 102
12500 Lookingglass Rd, Roseburg OR 97470
Ph: 541 679 6642 Fax: 541 679 4455
Email: wine@abacela.com
Web: www.abacela.com

2. Adelsheim Vineyard PAGES 94, 97
16800 N.E. Calkins Ln, Newberg OR 97132
Ph: 503 538 3652 Fax: 503 538 2248
Email: info@adelsheim.com
Web: www.adelsheim.com

3. Airlie Winery PAGE 27
15305 Dunn Forest Rd, Monmouth OR 97361
Ph: 503 838 6013 Fax: 503 838 6279
Email: airlie@airliewinery.com
Web: www.airliewinery.com

4. Andrew Rich Wines PAGE 114
801 N. Scott St, Carlton OR 97111
Ph: 503 284 6622 Fax: 503 284 6622
Email: info@andrewrichwines.com
Web: www.andrewrichwines.com

5. Ankeny Vineyard PAGE 373
2565 Riverside Rd. South, Salem OR 97306
Ph: 503 378 1498 Fax: 503 378 0243
Email: ankenyvineyard@hotmail.com
Web: www.ankenyvineyard.com

6. Brick House Vineyards PAGE 213
18200 Lewis Rogers Ln, Newberg OR 97132
Ph: 503 538 5136 Fax: 503 538 5136
Email: info@brickhousewines.com
Web: www.brickhousewines.com

7. Broadley Vineyards PAGE 118
265 S. Fifth Hwy 99, Monroe OR 97456
Ph: 541 847 5934 Fax: 541 847 6018
Email: broadley@peak.org
Web: www.broadleyvineyards.com

8. Bryn Mawr Vineyards PAGE 274
5955 Bethel Hts Rd N.W., Salem OR 97304
Ph: 503 581 4286 Fax: 503 581 4736
Email: davidlj@brynmawrvineyards.com
Web: www.brynmawrvineyards.com

9. Christopher Bridge PAGE 300
12770 S. Casto Rd, Oregon City OR 97045
Ph: 503 263 6267 Fax: 503 263 6267
Email: info@christopherbridgewines.com
Web: www.christopherbridgewines.com

10. Clear Creek Distillery PAGE 219
2389 N.W. Wilson St, Portland OR 97210
Ph: 503 248 9470 Fax: 503 248 0490
Email: rachel@clearcreekdistillery.com
Web: www.clearcreekdistillery.com

11. David Hill Vineyards & Winery PAGE 486
46350 N.W. David Hill Rd,
    Forest Grove OR 97132
Ph: 503 992 8545 Fax: 503 992 8586
Email: davidhill.winery@verizon.net
Web: www.davidhillwinery.com

12. De Ponte Cellars PAGE 179
17545 Archery Summit Rd, Dayton OR 97114
Ph: 503 864 3698 Fax: 503 864 2555
Email: dogs@depontecellars.com
Web: www.depontecellars.com

13. Devitt Winery PAGE 434
11412 Hwy 238, Jacksonville OR 97530
Ph: 541 899 7511
Email: james@devittwinery.com
Web: www.devittwinery.com

14. EdenVale Winery PAGES 116, 233, 237, 432
2310 Voorhies Rd, Medford OR 97501
Ph: 541 512 9463 Fax: 541 512 2957
Email: wines@edenvalewines.com
Web: www.edenvalleyorchards.com

15. Elk Cove Vineyards PAGES 180, 190, 285
27751 N.W. Olson Rd, Gaston OR 97119
Ph: 503 985 7760 Fax: 503 985 3525
Email: info@elkcove.com
Web: www.elkcove.com

**16. Elkhorn Ridge Vineyards
    & Winery** PAGE 37
10895 Brateng Rd, Monmouth OR 97361
Ph: 208 720 3062 Fax: 208 622 8334
Email: cnfoss@earthlink.net
Web: www.elkhornridgevineyards.com

17. Erath Vineyards PAGE 414
9409 N.E. Worden Hill Rd, Dundee OR 97115
Ph: 800 539 9463 Fax: 503 538 1074
Email: info@erath.com
Web: www.erath.com

18. Eyrie Vineyards PAGE 115
935 N.E. 10th Street, McMinnville OR 97128
Ph: 503 472 6315 Fax: 503 472 5124
Email: info@eyrievineyards.com
Web: www.eyrievineyards.com

19. Grochau Cellars PAGE 25
17979 N.E. Lewis Rogers Ln,
    Newberg OR 97132
Ph: 503 522 2455 Fax: 503 286 0560
Email: GCwines@msn.com
Web: www.gcwines.com

20. HillCrest Vineyard PAGE 374
240 Vineyard Ln, Roseburg OR 97470
Ph: 541 673 3709 Fax: 541 957 9063
Email: dyson@hillcrestvineyard.com
Web: www.hillcrestvineyard.com

21. Iris Hill Winery PAGE 36
82110 Territorial (Iris Hill Ln),
    Eugene OR 97405
Ph: 541 345 1617 Fax: 541 895 9879
Email: info@iris-hill.com
Web: www.iris-hill.com

22. J. Daan Wine Cellars PAGE 400
801 N. Scott St, Carlton OR 97111
Ph: 503 807 4435 Fax: 503 472 1852
Email: justin@jdaan.com
Web: www.jdaan.com

23. Kathken Vineyards PAGE 364
5739 Orchard Hts Rd N.W., Salem OR 97304
Ph: 503 316 3911 Fax: 503 399 5476
Email: Kathkenvyd@aol.com
Web: www.kathkenvineyards.com

24. Kelley Family Vineyards PAGES 82, 83
18840 Williamson Rd, Newberg OR 97132
Ph: 503 554 8872 Fax: 503 554 8265
Email: kelleygrapes@aol.com

25. Ken Wright Cellars PAGES 45, 293, 346
263 Kutch St, Carlton OR 97128
Ph: 503 852 7070 Fax: 503 852 7111
Email: cellars@kenwrightcellars.com
Web: www.kenwrightcellars.com

26. Kramer Vineyards PAGE 291
26830 N.W. Olson Rd, Gaston OR 97119
Ph: 503 662 4545 Fax: 503 662 4033
Email: info@kramerwine.com
Web: www.kramerwine.com

27. Lange Estate PAGES 71, 73, 436
18380 N.E. Buena Vista Dr, Dundee OR 97115
Ph: 503 538 6476 Fax: 503 538 1938
Email: wendy@langewinery.com
Web: www.langewinery.com

28. Lemelson Vineyards PAGE 350
12020 N.E. Stag Hollow Rd, Carlton OR 97111
Ph: 503 852 6619 Fax: 503 852 6119
Email: info@lemelsonvineyards.com
Web: www.lemelsonvineyards.com

29. Montinore Estate PAGES 70, 87
3663 S.W. Dilley Rd, Forest Grove OR 97116
Ph: 503 359 5012 Fax: 503 357 4313
Email: info@montinore.com
Web: www.montinore.com

30. Mystic Wines PAGE 40
3995 Deepwood Ln N.W., Salem OR 97304
Ph: 503 581 2769 Fax: 503 581 2894
Email: info@mysticwine.com
Web: www.mysticwine.com

31. Namasté Vineyards PAGE 402
5600 Van Well Rd, Dallas OR 97338
Ph: 503 623 4150 Fax: 503 212 0117
Email: chris@namastevineyards.com
Web: www.namastevineyards.com

32. Noble Estate Vineyard
   & Winery PAGE 360
29210 Gimpl Hill Rd, Eugene OR 97402
Ph: 541 338 3007 Fax: 541 683 9102
Email: wines@nobleestatevineyard.com
Web: www.nobleestatevineyard.com

33. Patricia Green Cellars PAGE 383
15225 N.E. North Valley Rd,
   Newberg OR 97132
Ph: 503 554 0821 Fax: 503 538 3681
Email: winery@patriciagreencellars.com
Web: www.patriciagreencellars.com

34. Penner-Ash Wine Cellars PAGE 359
15771 N.E. Ribbon Ridge Rd,
   Newberg OR 97132
Ph: 503 554 5545 Fax: 503 554 6696
Email: info@pennerash.com
Web: www.pennerash.com

35. Pheasant Valley Vineyard
   & Winery PAGES 86, 328
3890 Acree Dr, Hood River OR 97031
Ph: 541 387 3040 Fax: 541 386 7327
Email: gail@pheasantvalleywinery.com
Web: www.pheasantvalleywinery.com

36. Ponzi Vineyards PAGES 340, 345, 399
14665 S.W. Winery Lane,
   Beaverton OR 97007
Ph: 503 628 1227 Fax: 503 628 0354
Email: info@ponziwines.com
Web: www.ponziwines.com

37. Redhawk Winery PAGE 482
2995 Michigan City Ln N.W.,
   Salem OR 97304
Ph: 503 362 1596 Fax: 503 589 9189
Email: jpatwine@aol.com
Web: www.redhawkwine.com

38. Ruby Carbiener Vineyards
   & Winery PAGE 323
14135 N.W. Timmerman Rd,
   Forest Grove OR 97116
Ph: 503 524 5663 Fax: 503 524 2685
Email: lynn@rcvineyards.com
Web: www.rcvineyards.com

39. Spangler Vineyards PAGE 357
491 Winery Ln, Roseburg OR 97470
Ph: 541 679 9654 Fax: 541 679 3888
Email: info@spanglervineyards.com
Web: www.spanglervineyards.com

40. Stangeland Vineyards
   and Winery PAGE 305
8500 Hopewell Road N.W., Salem OR 97304
Ph: 503 581 0355 Fax: 503 540 3412
Email: stangelandwinery@gotsky.com
Web: www.stangelandwinery.com

41. Torii Mor Winery PAGE 355
18325 N.E. Fairview Dr, Dundee OR 97115
Ph: 503 554 0105 Fax: 503 538 2239
Email: info@toriimorwinery.com
Web: www.toriimorwinery.com

42. Troon Vineyard PAGE 72
1475 Kubli Rd, Grants Pass OR 97527
Ph: 541 846 9900 Fax: 541 846 6096
Email: cmartin@troonvineyard.com
Web: www.troonvineyard.com

43. Urban Wineworks PAGE 347
407 N.W. 16th Ave, Portland OR 97209
Ph: 503 550 9969 Fax: 503 226 9799
Email: info@urbanwineworks.com
Web: www.urbanwineworks.com

44. Van Duzer Vineyards PAGE 337
11975 Smithfield Rd, Dallas OR 97338
Ph: 503 623 6420 Fax: 503 623 4310
Email: kathy@vanduzer.com
Web: www.vanduzer.com

45. Walnut City Wineworks PAGE 91
475 N. 17th St, McMinnville OR 97128
Ph: 503 472 3215 Fax: 503 473 3294
Email: wine@walnutcitywineworks.com
Web: www.walnutcitywineworks.com

46. Wine Country Farm PAGE 488
6855 Breyman Orchards Rd,
*   Dayton OR 97114*
Ph: 503 864 3446
Email: jld@winecountryfarm.com
Web: www.winecountryfarm.com

47. Witness Tree Vineyard PAGES 90, 93
7111 Spring Valley Rd N.W., Salem OR 97304
Ph: 503 585 7874 Fax: 503 362 9765
Email: info@witnesstreevineyard.com
Web: www.witnesstreevineyard.com

48. Youngberg Hill Vineyards
and Inn PAGE 96
10660 S.W. Youngberg Hill,
*   McMinnville OR 97128*
Ph: 503 472 2727 Fax: 503 472 1313
Email: youngberghill@netscape.net
Web: www.youngberghill.com

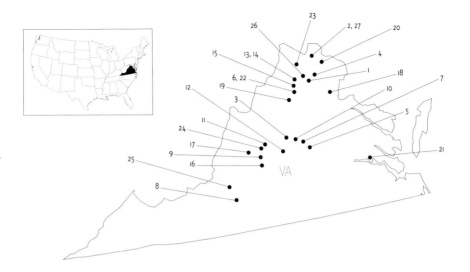

VIRGINIA

1. Boxwood Winery PAGE 380
2042 Burrland Rd, Middleburg VA 20117
Ph: 540 687 8778 Fax: 540 687 8765
Email: rem@boxwoodwinery.com
Web: www.boxwoodwinery.com

2. Breaux Vineyards PAGES 275, 319
36888 Breaux Vineyards Ln,
    Purcellville VA 20132
Ph: 540 668 6299 Fax: 540 668 6283
Email: info@breauxvineyards.com
Web: www.breauxvineyards.com

3. Burnley Vineyards PAGE 276
4500 Winery Ln, Barboursville VA 22923
Ph: 540 832 2828 Fax: 540 832 2280
Email: Info@Burnleywines.com
Web: www.burnleywines.com

4. Chrysalis Vineyards PAGE 437
23876 Champe Ford Rd,
    Middleburg VA 20117
Ph: 540 687 8222 Fax: 540 687 8666
Email: McCloud@ChrysalisWine.com
Web: www.chrysaliswine.com

5. Cooper Vineyards PAGES 129, 230
13372 Shannon Hill Rd, Louisa VA 23226
Ph: 540 894 5253 Fax: 804 560 5848
Email: info@coopervineyards.com
Web: www.coopervineyards.com

6. Farfelu Vineyards PAGE 453
137 Farfelu Ln, Flint Hill VA 22627
Ph: 540 364 2930 Fax: 540 675 3387
Email: sduty@farfeluwine.com
Web: www.farfeluwine.com

7. Gioiosa Vineyards PAGE 433
1890 Poindexter Rd, Louisa VA 23093
Ph: 540 967 9463 Fax: 540 967 0784
Email: lewgioiosa@hotmail.com
Web: www.greenspringswinery.com

**8. Hickory Hill Vineyards
and Winery** PAGE 439
1722 Hickory Cove Ln, Moneta VA 24121
Ph: 540 296 1393 Fax: 540 296 1393
Email: wendy@hickoryhillvineyards.com
Web: www.hickoryhillvineyards.com

**9. Hill Top Berry Farm
and Winery** PAGE 394
2800 Berry Hill Rd, Nellysford VA 22958
Ph: 434 361 1266 Fax: 434 361 1266
Email: hilltop1@ntelos.net
Web: www.hilltopberrywine.com

10. Keswick Vineyards PAGE 428
1575 Keswick Winery Dr, Keswick VA 22947
Ph: 434 244 3341 Fax: 434 244 9976
Email: info@keswickvineyards.com
Web: www.keswickvineyards.com

11. King Family Vineyards PAGE 429
6550 Roseland Farm, Crozet VA 22932
Ph: 434 823 7800 Fax: 434 823 7801
Email: info@kingfamilyvineyards.com
Web: www.kingfamilyvineyards.com

12. Kluge Estate Winery
   and Vineyard PAGE 430
100 Grand Cru Dr, Charlottesville VA 22902
Ph: 434 977 3895 Fax: 434 977 0606
Email: info@klugeestate.com
Web: www.klugeestate.com

13. Linden Vineyards PAGE 353
3708 Harrels Corner Rd, Linden VA 22642
Ph: 540 364 1997 Fax: 540 364 3894
Email: linden@crosslink.net
Web: www.lindenvineyards.com

14. Naked Mountain Vineyard PAGE 352
2747 Leeds Manor Rd, Markham VA 22643
Ph: 540 364 1609 Fax: 540 364 3299
Email: nakedmountain@yahoo.com
Web: www.nakedmtn.com

15. Oasis Winery PAGE 193
14141 Hume Rd, Hume VA 22639
Ph: 540 635 3105 Fax: 540 635 4653
Email: info@oasiswine.com
Web: www.oasiswine.com

16. Rebec Vineyards and Winery PAGE 269
2229 N. Amherst Hwy, Amherst VA 24521
Ph: 434 946 5168
Email: winery@rebecwinery.com
Web: www.rebecwinery.com

17. Rockbridge Vineyard PAGE 366
35 Hill View Lane, Raphine VA 24472
Ph: 1 888 511 9463 Fax: 1 888 511 9463
Email: rockbridge@email.com
Web: www.rockbridgevineyard.com

18. Rogers Ford Farm Winery PAGE 495
14674 Rogers Ford Rd, Sumerduck VA 22742
Ph: 540 439 3707 Fax: 540 439 3757
Email: john@rogersfordwine.com
Web: www.rogersfordwine.com

19. Sharp Rock Vineyard PAGE 471
5 Sharp Rock Rd, Sperryville VA 22740
Ph: 540 987 8020
Email: jeast@sharprockvineyards.com
Web: www.sharprock.com

20. Tarara Winery PAGES 424, 444
13648 Tarara Ln, Leesburg VA 20176
Ph: 703 771 7100 Fax: 703 771 8443
Email: winesales@tarara.com
Web: www.tarara.com

21. The Williamsburg Winery PAGE 413
5800 Wessex Hundred,
   Williamsburg VA 23185
Ph: 757 229 0999 Fax: 757 229 0911
Email: wine@wmbgwine.com
Web: www.williamsburgwinery.com

22. Unicorn Winery PAGE 283
487 Old Bridge Rd, Amissville VA 20106
Ph: 540 349 5885
Email: bree@unicornwinery.com
Web: www.unicornwinery.com

23. Veramar Vineyard PAGE 290
905 Quarry Rd, Berryville VA 22611
Ph: 540 955 5510 Fax: 540 955 0404
Email: info@veramar.com
Web: www.veramar.com

24. Veritas Vineyard and Winery PAGE 286
145 Saddleback Farm, Afton VA 22920
Ph: 540 456 8000
Email: contact@veritaswines.com
Web: www.veritaswines.com

25. White Rock Vineyards
   & Winery PAGE 465
2117 Bruno Dr, Goodview VA 24095
Ph: 540 890 3359 Fax: 540 890 3359
Email: info@whiterockwines.com
Web: www.whiterockwines.com

26. Willowcroft Farm Vineyards PAGE 361
38906 Mt. Gilead Rd, Leesburg VA 20175
Ph: 703 777 8161 Fax: 703 777 8157
Email: willowine@aol.com
Web: www.willowcroftwine.com

27. Windham Winery PAGE 358
14727 Mountain Rd, Purcellville VA 20132
Ph: 540 668 6464 Fax: 540 668 7679
Email: info@windhamwinery.com
Web: www.windhamwinery.com

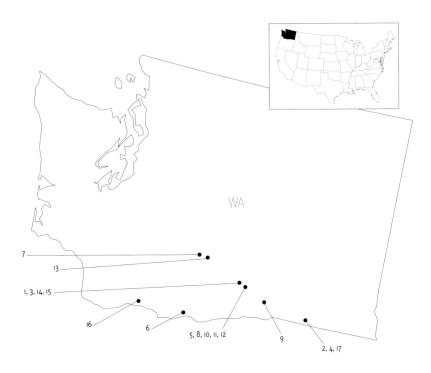

WASHINGTON

1. Alexandria Nicole Cellars PAGE 92
2880 Lee Rd, Prosser WA 99350
Ph: 509 786 3497 Fax: 509 786 3497
Email: info@alexandrianicolecellars.com
Web: www.alexandrianicolecellars.com

2. Beresan Winery PAGE 117
4169 Pepper Bridge Rd,
  Walla Walla WA 99362
Ph: 509 522 2395 Fax: 509 522 9415
Email: info@beresanwines.com
Web: www.beresanwines.com

3. Chinook Wines PAGE 270
Cnr Wine Country Rd & Wittkopf Loop,
  Prosser WA 99350
Ph: 509 786 2725 Fax: 509 786 2777
Email: info@chinookwines.com
Web: www.chinookwines.com

4. Dunham Cellars PAGES 156, 157
150 E. Boeing Ave, Walla Walla WA 99362
Ph: 509 529 4685 Fax: 509 529 0201
Email: info@dunhamcellars.com
Web: www.dunhamcellars.com

5. Hightower Cellars PAGE 146
19418 E. 583 PR NE, Benton City WA 99320
Ph: 509 588 2867 Fax: 509 588 2867
Email: handsorted@hightowercellars.com
Web: www.hightowercellars.com

6. Maryhill Winery PAGE 163
9774 Hwy 14, Goldendale WA 98620
Ph: 509 773 1976 Fax: 509 773 0586
Email: info@maryhillwinery.com
Web: www.maryhillwinery.com

7. Masset Winery PAGE 245
620 East Parker Heights Rd,
   Wapato WA 98951
Ph: 509 877 6675
Email: massetwine@nwinfo.net
Web: www.massetwinery.com

8. Portrait Cellars PAGE 369
27318 E. Ambassador PR NE,
   Benton City WA 99320
Ph: 509 588 4534 Fax: 509 588 8145
Email: eshawvyds@msn.com

**9. Preston Premium Wines/
   Preston Vineyards** PAGE 133
502 E. Vineyard Dr, Pasco WA 99301
Ph: 509 545 1990 Fax: 509 545 1098
Email: info@prestonwines.com
Web: www.prestonwines.com

10. Seth Ryan Winery PAGE 410
35306 Sunset Rd, Benton City WA 99320
Ph: 509 588 6780 Fax: 509 588 6780
Email: grandmajo9@aol.com
Web: www.sethryan.com

11. Tapteil Vineyard Winery PAGE 343
20206 E. 583 PR NE, Benton City WA 99320
Ph: 509 588 4460 Fax: 509 588 4460
Email: winery@tapteil.com
Web: www.tapteil.com

12. Terra Blanca Winery PAGES 124, 125
34715 N. DeMoss Rd, Benton City WA 99320
Ph: 509 588 6082 Fax: 509 588 2634
Email: info@terrablanca.com
Web: www.terrablanca.com

13. Two Mountain Winery PAGE 77
2151 Cheyne Rd, Zillah WA 98953
Ph: 509 829 3900 Fax: 509 829 3904
Email: info@twomountainwinery.com
Web: www.twomountainwinery.com

14. Vineheart Winery PAGE 212
44209 N. McDonald Rd, Prosser WA 99350
Ph: 509 973 2993 Fax: 509 973 2323
Email: wine_duchess@hotmail.com
Web: www.vineheart.com

15. Willow Crest Winery PAGE 284
590 Merlot Dr, Prosser WA 99350
Ph: 509 786 7999 Fax: 509 786 4675
Email: wine@willowcrestwinery.com
Web: www.willowcrestwinery.com

16. Wind River Cellars PAGE 273
196 Spring Creek Rd, Husum WA 98623
Ph: 509 493 2324 Fax: 509 493 2324
Email: info@windrivercellars.com
Web: www.windrivercellars.com

17. Yellow Hawk Cellar PAGE 450
395 Yellowhawk St, Walla Walla WA 99362
Ph: 509 529 1714
Email: info@yellowhawkcellar.com
Web: www.yellowhawkcellar.com

WINE DOGS BREED INDEX

THANK YOU...

Wine Dogs would like to thank the following people who helped us on our journey.

A big thank you to Lisa Kothari, Giant Dog Publishing's first USA employee. Lisa's enthusiasm for our Wine Dogs USA title and her great knowledge of the Washington wine regions was invaluable to our production. Lisa's skill and pursuable nature, like good wine, should be bottled and treasured. Thanks for all your great work, Lisa.

To our great friend and colleague Peter Herring who gave up his time and traveled to Napa with Craig in a February 2006 pre-production trip (Aussies go 'Sideways'). His 'Mr Likeable' nature helped cement some wonderful and hopefully ongoing relationships while we were in California. Thanks to his partner Mary for letting him go!

To our dear friends Martin and Colin for their continued support and enthusiasm. We also have a wonderful network of friends (too many to mention, but you know who you are) whose constant support and help have made this book a lot easier to produce. To our parents, Pat, Norm, Jim and Isobel, for being there whenever we needed them and even when we didn't.

To Tok, Tarka and Stella for the constant laughs.

Along our travels we were helped and encouraged by many wonderful people including Emily and Chris at the Travigne wine bar, Janel Watkins at Darioush, Matthew Branca at Sonoma Wine Hardware, Ryan Moore at Rubicon Estate, the one and only Lisa 'Aussie' Enright at Rubicon Estate, dogless Cindy and Candy at Rubicon Estate, Garret Thomas Murphy and Andy Renda at the Vintners Collective, Napa Valley, Jani Di Carlo and Anton Pestun at Robert Mondavi Winery, Alma Blanton at Domaine Chandon Napa Valley, Ron Schrieve, Gretchen Bender and Carolyn Joy Friedman at Beringer Vineyards, Blakesley and Cyril Chappellet, Alexis Swanson, the wonderful Tina Cao from St Supery, Aaron and Claire Pott at Quintessa, Doug and Lee Nalle at Nalle Winery, Susie Bynum at Davis Bynum, Kristina Dunn and Randy Dunn at Dunn Vineyards, Marie Gilmore from Michigan, Sarah Tracy at Sonoma Valley Visitors Bureau, David and Jan Bruce at David Bruce, Lynn Sakasegawa Stokes at Wines of Carmel, Mike Sanford at Rabbit Ridge, Andrew Weinberger at Sonoma's Readers' Books, Jun Ishimuro at Foto-Grafix Books, Duke Richardson and Anna Lee Knutson at Cabana Cellars, Tanya Roush from Chronicle Books, Sue Horstmann at Willamette Valley Wineries Association, Pat and Robert Parker, Bill Phelps, Fess Parker,

David Lett at The Eyrie Vineyards, Mike Kelley at Kelley Family Vineyards for introducing us to some fine Oregon beers and escorting us out of town afterwards, Adia Wright at Sobel Weber, Cynthia Hiponia from Vineyard Dog in Napa, Peter and Rebecca Work at Ampelos Cellars, Kevin Judd at Cloudy Bay New Zealand, Huon Hooke, Richard Hogan from Zoowines distribution in Australia for his continued support and the fine people at Buffalo Shipping Post in Napa.

And we must draw special attention to the wonderful generosity and hospitality offered to us by Robert and Margrit Mondavi. We really appreciate your support and kindness.

We are extremely grateful to the generous people at Beam Wine Estates for accommodating us during our stay in Sonoma. The Carneros Vineyard House offered to us is located on the Buena Vista's Carneros Estate. The house was wonderful, surrounded by vineyards and coupled with magnificent sunrises and sunsets. It's an experience that we will never forget. Many thanks to Ford Le Strange for making our exhausting travels a little less stressful and Buena Vista's wonderful pinot noir and chardonnay made the visit even more enjoyable. Thanks again.

Our visit to Oregon was highlighted by our stay at Joan Davenport's Wine Country Farm in Dayton. Heralded as one of the 1,000 places in the world you must see before you are pushing up daisies, this inn is sensational and Joan's hospitality seemed like nothing was too much bother. Breathtaking views and Joan's amazing breakfasts made it very difficult to move on. Thanks for looking after us Joan, and we can't wait to come back. Joan's wonder dog, Cobber de Vino, greeted me every morning to check out what dog treats I had in the trunk of the car. Hope he didn't put on too much weight...

Special thanks to all the people who helped us throughout our travels. To all our contributors, Robert Parker, Harvey 'the PR man' Posert, Jack Burton, Bruce Cass, Ralph Steadman, Zar Brooks, Sally Ashton, Dan Berger, Josh Greene, Adam Lechmere, Cole Danehower, Darryl Roberts and the lovely but often evicted Melodie Hilton, for their great work and support. Thanks guys.

Extra thanks also to Harvey Posert for looking after us for a couple of nights in Napa and feeding us what we consider some of the world's best-made popcorn. Wow!